LESS

LESS

Stop Buying So Much Rubbish:
How Having Fewer, Better Things
Can Make Us Happier

Patrick Grant

WILLIAM
COLLINS

William Collins
An imprint of HarperCollins*Publishers*
1 London Bridge Street
London SE1 9GF

WilliamCollinsBooks.com

HarperCollins*Publishers*
Macken House, 39/40 Mayor Street Upper
Dublin 1, D01 C9W8, Ireland

First published in Great Britain in 2024 by William Collins

5

Diagrams drawn by Martin Brown

A catalogue record for this book is
available from the British Library

ISBN 978-0-00-866400-8

Set in Garamond Premier Pro
Printed and bound in the UK using 100%
renewable electricity at CPI Group (UK) Ltd

This book contains FSC™ certified paper and other controlled
sources to ensure responsible forest management.

For more information visit: www.harpercollins.co.uk/green

For Rachael, and for my lovely Mum.

CONTENTS

Part III: WORK

Part IV: LESS

A FEW WORDS ON HAPPINESS

I have a faded plum-coloured 1980s sweatshirt that my granny gave me not long before she died. She found it in the charity shop in which she worked and knew I'd like it, so she bought it for me. Every time I wear it, which I do a lot, I think of her, and it makes me happy.

Simple things make me happy. Time with friends and loved ones, time in nature, doing good deeds, making things, growing flowers and vegetables, and wearing or using good-quality objects with which I feel some personal connection.

My sister gave me a green handmade mug for my fifty-first birthday that she'd bought from a small craft gallery on the Isle of Mull called the Tin Shed Gallery. It is hand thrown and hand glazed, and its well-proportioned handle is ever so slightly on the wonk. It gives me great pleasure every time I use it because of the material from which, and the care and skill with which, it was made; the love and care with which it was chosen, and just the way it feels in my hand. I cherish it. I wash it by hand with the utmost care.

I have always, even as a young man, preferred quality over quantity. I can't pinpoint where this preference came from, but growing up our house was filled with well-made objects. Our furniture was mostly second-hand from the auction houses in Edinburgh: sprung, and stuffed with hair and wool, natural fabrics beautifully faded and worn, the wood richly patinated with age. Our crockery and cutlery were all British made, from Stoke and Sheffield, either hand-me-downs or bought second-hand.

I've also always loved things that have been repaired; perhaps a little peculiarly, the more improvised the repair the better. A knotted rope handle on a weather-worn door, the patchwork of rusted corrugated iron on an old barn roof, a wall with bits painted, and painted again, in never-quite-matching colour. I have a soft spot for a badly taped pair of spectacles. It is the evidence of the intervention of the human hand and mind, the ingenuity, often the thrift, that endears such things to me.

I love hand-sewn or hand-knitted clothes for the same reasons. Their slight imperfections, and the delicacy and deftness of touch that only the human hand can produce, gives them great value. In the porch at my mum's house is a box filled with scarves and mittens knitted by my granny (enthusiastic, but far from an expert, she could never master fingers), which are treasured because they were crafted by her hands, for us, with love. I have a pair of hand-knitted socks that I love so much I very rarely wear them for fear of wearing them out. I bought them from a little shop on the Isle of Lewis around fifteen years ago and have meant for some time to give them to an expert to work out how to knit more. I have hand-knitted sweaters, the tension and loft so different from machine-made sweaters, many bought from the second-hand shops I like to visit wherever I travel.

My everyday wardrobe is just a few simple things. I am a creature of habit and wear the same things most days, which makes getting dressed, or packing for travel, a very simple affair. You will mostly find me wearing one of two types of heavy cotton trousers. The first type I originally designed for E. Tautz and we now make at Community Clothing. They were based on the shape of a 1960s army trouser. I bought two pairs in a second-hand store in Brooklyn and wore both to pieces. I now have five pairs in three colours and they've been a staple since we first designed them in 2015. The second, a more recent design, the 'cameraman pant', is inspired by a workwear pant worn by one of the camera guys on *The Great British Sewing Bee* in 2022. They're heavy canvas, with a wide tapered leg, patch pockets and a drawstring top. I wear them almost always with navy-blue crew-necks: T-shirts in summer, sweatshirts or jumpers when it's colder. Or my faded plum sweatshirt. Nine days out of ten I'm in a navy crew. When it's cold I'll wear a great big hand-knitted jumper (I have a few, in 6-ply and 8-ply wool) over another jumper, because I was brought up to put on a jumper, not the heating. All of these clothes are made well. All of those bought in the last twenty years, and there are not many, were made here in the UK. Some have been repaired. I no longer feel any compulsion to change them. They get better, and I like them more, each time I wear them.

Besides my clothes and my green mug, there are a handful of other possessions that make me happy. A few other old Staffordshire-made china teacups and saucers – Spode, Minton, Wedgwood; a hand-built, hand-painted mug that I bought in Japan. I never tire of my ritual of drinking a cup of tea or coffee from one of these while watching birds in the garden on a Saturday and Sunday morning. I have another mug with a photo on it that I took of Esme Young asleep in our *Sewing Bee* dressing room covered in Frutella wrappers. Sara Pascoe had the mugs made as an end-of-season gift for us all. On it is printed 'Sewing Bee 2021, Sponsored by Frutella'. I've another mug with a picture of a full English breakfast on it from Ste's Place, a greasy spoon in Darwen market, near Blackburn. Both make me smile every time I see them in the cupboard.

I use a Bialetti stove-top espresso which I've had for almost thirty years. Made in Italy from four pieces of high-quality steel and a rubber disc, it is one of the simplest and most perfect pieces of engineering I can think of. I have a Dualit classic toaster, robust and simple; no electronics, just a mechanical lifter and timer, everything replaceable, which I've had since 1995. I have a few good pans, professional quality, made in stainless steel or cast iron, again bought almost thirty years ago. And three good knives. I own a few bikes: a Dawes Super Galaxy, a Dawes Galaxy, a Pashley Classic, a Roy Thame touring bike and a Pete Matthews track bike, all British built, all steel frames. I also have a Trek carbon road bike, now over twenty years old, which my local bike shop deems a 'classic'.

I have a handful of old jugs from various craft potteries, mostly from the UK and France, that I like to fill with flowers and bits from the garden. I have a beautiful Edwardian captain's chair that I inherited from my dad after his death. I remember him sitting in it, reading, for hours when I was a kid. I have his hand-built spice rack too, and the many jars in which he kept his much-used spices. I have some of his wooden-handled gardening tools. When I use them I can feel where his hands have been, my fingers slip naturally into the worn grooves where his fingers sat. These things keep his memory close.

Even the simplest, least expensive objects can have great value if they mean something to us, meaning gained through time and use, by ourselves or by others we love. Only well-made things will last this course. It also stands to reason that the more things we have, the less meaning each one can have to us. Having loads of stuff doesn't interest me. My few cherished, valued objects make me happy.

I also derive a great deal of pleasure from nature. As a kid I spent almost all my waking hours in a wooded valley, now a local nature reserve, called the Hermitage of Braid. We knew every inch of it, every tree root on every path, every rock, crag and cranny, each and every turn of the water in the shallow burn which ran through its centre. We could pass through it almost silently, and could have found our way around it blindfolded and never put a foot out of place. We felt completely part of it. I was a member of a club for kids at Edinburgh

Zoo called the Gannet Club. We'd go and hang out at the zoo in the holidays and get to handle some of the animals. I remember vividly the unexpected dryness of a boa constrictor. I loved the zoo's daily penguin parade, and my class at primary school sponsored a rockhopper, which predictably we called Rocky. I loved Johnny Morris's *Animal Magic*, and all the BBC wildlife programming like *Life on Earth*. If I see a hare or a kestrel, as I do reasonably often, it puts me in the brightest mood. Just hearing an owl hoot in the night makes me smile. Everywhere in Britain we are surrounded by extraordinary wildlife; we just need to slow down, tune in and enjoy it.

Trees and mountains make me happy too. As a kid I had a cherished and much-thumbed copy of the *Ladybird Book of Trees* and I could recognise every native species. I love to be in the outdoors. There are few things that I like more than to sit and enjoy a sandwich and a flask of tea in the sun with my back to a cairn, a tree or a dry-stone wall up a hill with friends, or on my own. To sit above the clouds and see distant peaks laid out before me, to see the sky reach from the farthest reaches of my sight, from left horizon to right, to watch the water make its way from the high ground, gaining power as it collects other fledgling streams, has always filled me with awe and happiness. Reading Nan Shepherd's *The Living Mountain* I saw my own feelings for these places put into words, and it is clear that many people derive great happiness from these wild places in Britain just as I do.

My family have always loved the outdoors. My mum walks up one of Edinburgh's hills, usually the Braids or Blackford, every day. My uncle died whilst walking the 2,200 miles of the Appalachian Trail in his seventies. A few generations back my father's family were hill farmers and shepherds, so I think it might be in the blood. My mum is a passionate gardener, great with flowers. My dad was too, but growing vegetables was his bag. I learned to love the gardening calendar and the structure it provided to the year. I have plant pots and a handful of plants that have been with me since I lived in Liverpool in the late 1990s, moving with me around the country. The gardens I've had have varied in size and scope but now I've got a new garden, a big one, very derelict, with a handful of old stone buildings and a ha-ha. It's a project to begin from scratch, aided by the writings of Gertrude Jekyll and William Robinson.

In 2020 I started a project in Blackburn to grow flax and woad with an old friend and a great big bunch of volunteers from the local community in an attempt to see if it was possible to grow, spin, dye and weave our own textiles completely locally in Lancashire. There's a simple pleasure in clearing and preparing and planting, the magic of germination, the hard but satisfying job of weeding, and at last the well-earned cup of tea and home-made samosa sitting in our field of flax, listening to the birds, watching bees and butterflies flit on the delicate blue blooms on a clear sunny day. I want to live in a way which allows all of nature to thrive, free from our debris and pollution, where the things I use every day – my clothes, my furniture, the vessels I eat and drink from – are made in a way that's harmonious with the natural world, where the materials used to make them can be made or grown in a way that helps not hurts nature, materials which return themselves naturally to the earth when we've finished with them. I tweeted once that nature makes everything better. I think it's true. In any or all of its various forms a connection with nature is great for our souls. The thought that our society is rapidly destroying the natural world motivates me to work harder to make positive change.

The final great source of my happiness is my work. I am good at what I do, I feel valuable, and I know that people respect me for it because they often tell me so. I am proud of what I have achieved and am excited and eager to do more, and better, in the future. It is not just the work. I love the workplaces too. They are unique communities, and I enjoy the interactions I have with my colleagues at work most days. I spent eighteen years working at Norton & Sons on Savile Row. The camaraderie, the gossip, the long-running jokes were a wonderful part of my life. There is a ridiculous game that's played in the workrooms there called 'whistle and bar' which never fails to make me laugh when played well. My former colleagues Nick, Dave, and John Kent had a real talent and passion for it, but there are fewer masters than there once were. The tailors and cutters in Savile Row are so good at what they do that they can work and talk, and it makes for a workplace that is convivial and endlessly social.

I like the odd rituals. When I walk into my factory in Blackburn at the start of each day I shout 'good morning' to the team on the shop floor, and they shout 'good morning' back. I enjoy waving to my colleagues through the funny little windows to the offices in our very 80s-style office suite. The little signs that are dotted about the factory make me happy too. 'Please don't put wet teaspoons in the coffee', 'Please wash your own pots'. Reminders that we all need to find a way to rub along, through the exercise of small acts of common courtesy. I love the factory bell which punctuates my day. I love finding out what Dave my factory manager's mum is cooking for his tea, Dave's absolute joy no matter what it is; just knowing that Dave's mum really loves to cook for her fifty-year-old son makes me smile. Discovering Dave's dinner plans are part of our end-of-day ritual. He pops his head round my office door when he's leaving, he asks if I've got my factory keys, I ask what he's having. Mostly it's steak, a cottage pie, a fry-up or a chicken dinner.

I'm fortunate that I get to work alongside lots of different people. I work with close to a hundred British manufacturing businesses and a long list of fantastic brands (mostly British but some European, Japanese and American). I also work in television and radio, at live events, with several charities, local and national government, and several arts organisations. My work is endlessly varied, occasionally overwhelming, but always stimulating and challenging. Through it I get to work with many brilliant, hilarious, and often idiosyncratic humans of all ages.

The work we do, and the places we do it in, play a very big role in our happiness. We spend more time working than doing anything else in life except sleeping, and some of us do a lot more of the former than the latter. Mixed in with the good parts, there is also a lot of hard or tedious and sometimes emotionally difficult stuff too. Some days it seems my job is only the hard stuff, but even on those days I still feel pride in my work. The work we do should be good for us, physically and mentally, it should allow us to enjoy a healthy life as well as our leisure time. The fun jobs, like running a business, or investment banking, or playing football, are the best rewarded. Many people today work for charities or social enterprises or in health and social care, jobs which are among the hardest, both physically and emotionally, yet are often the worst paid. This doesn't make much sense to me.

The happiest people I know are happy because of what they *do*, not what they *own*. In our clamour to grow the monetary wealth of our nation, most specifically the wealth of the very rich, we have forgotten that millions of people need something meaningful to do and that every single member of society, given the right education, can and should have some role to play. We all want to feel useful, we want to play our part, it's simple human nature. Letting the markets decide, the now-universal mantra of our leaders, has landed millions in this country on the scrapheap. Jobs are important. They give us purpose, they make us feel valued, they can bring us closer to our neighbours and those in our local community; they create bonds, foster tolerance across races, religions and genders.

No matter how we might shape society, not everyone will find happiness, but we would stand a much better chance if we all had the opportunity to find the thing we're good at. And this means having the opportunity to enjoy an education that is fun, and which allows us to discover and develop our niche, whether that's in science, the arts, sport, or making something with our hands. To get the sort of start in life that kids born into wealthy families enjoy. An education that gives all young people the confidence that they can contribute positively to our society, that prepares them for a life in which what they do will be valued. Everyone deserves a fair crack. I was lucky, I was born into a middle-class family who gave me the best start in life I could have asked for. I think almost all of us would feel happier if we thought everyone enjoyed the same fortune.

And we'd stand a better chance of happiness if we knew that waiting for us when we finished our education was a job and a rewarding long-term career, not one hundreds of miles away in a big city where we know few people and can't afford the rent, but one where we grew up, where our friends and family form part of an established and supportive community, where we feel at home.

I count myself very lucky that on the whole I am healthy, happy and contented in life. I have been brought up not to want too much, to live within my means. I need money to pay my rent, and to buy the odd thing that can't be fixed and needs replacing, or to pay for repairs I can't do myself. But I don't need a lot. My job makes me happy and I earn a reasonable amount; my average salary over the past twenty years has been around £50k a year, and I work hard for it. I enjoy the company of my colleagues, work gives me a purpose, and I feel proud of what I do every day because I know that what I'm doing is good, not just for me but for the wider community, and for nature and the planet. And there are the other things that make me happy: hot buttered toast, a board game with friends, growing the odd vegetable, an old chair, a darned jumper, a walk up a hill and a packed lunch and a cup of tea from a flask with a view across the mountaintops on a sunny day. None of these things cost the earth.

INTRODUCTION

For the first 300,000 years of our existence we lived quietly and harmoniously with nature, content to have just the few possessions we needed, a few items to decorate our homes and our persons. Every object we made we made to the very best of our ability, because we understood that only high-quality things would improve our lives. And we all worked – real, meaningful work, the work of finding and preparing food, agricultural work, the work of making. We used our skilled hands and our acquired knowledge together to solve the practical problems posed by the natural materials we made things from, to create objects that earned us the respect of our communities. Those communities were close knit, our families were close knit, we worked together, we endured together, we celebrated each part of the natural cycle together.

Our natural curiosity about how things were made and how things worked allowed great advances in the quality of the everyday objects we surrounded ourselves with. Science and engineering took us forward, we followed it, and it improved our lives. We made things, we traded, we bought things. We owned just a few high-quality objects, made well, made (with the exception of some of the finery of the rich)

locally, máde with pride. The materials used were natural, their processing and forming done in harmony with nature, in a genuinely and
perfectly sustainable manner. We all understood quality, we all cherished as valuable every object we possessed, we maintained and repaired
those objects, every single thing we owned was passed on.

Across all of early history there was a great deal of discussion and
thinking amongst religious and moral philosophers on the subject of
our happiness, both individual and collective. Society was run in ways
which attempted at least to consider our emotional as well as our financial wellbeing. We were taught to live simply, with the fewest things, to
avoid greed and to banish thoughts of envy which would destroy our
satisfaction and contentment.

Populations grew, and technology allowed us to both feed and
clothe ourselves, and provide shelter for our swelling numbers, but still
we lived in balance with nature, guided by its principles and cycles. We
had access to land, and within our families and communities we could
grow and make all that we needed, giving us freedom and self-reliance.

But around three hundred years ago a new way of seeing the world
grew up in the minds of men, a new way of viewing the wealth of individuals and nations. According to capitalism, if we simply made more,
and made people want more, then we could accumulate greater wealth,
and if we were able to keep growing this want, and this production, and
this consumption for ever, to stretch it elastically, then those of us who
had wealth could become infinitely more wealthy. Men and women
ceased to be seen as living, feeling beings, they became simply units of
labour and of consumption, to be utilised to grow the wealth of others.
There were many who warned against it, but their objections were
drowned out by others, many of them smart people who argued that
this deliberately manipulated economic growth would bring great
benefits to our society (and they were partly right), and many others
who saw only their own enrichment.

The process was initially somewhat slow and relatively benign. Some of the local owners and investors who characterised capitalism's earliest form took pains to ensure the health and happiness of their workforce and their wider community, the benefits of the growing wealth flowing back into local economies and raising living standards for many. But as the capitalist economy grew it became impatient and greedy, its empathetic human face replaced by a disconnected, faceless global form whose only concern was the increase of profit and wealth.

Spurred on by the pursuit of money, industry artificially and aggressively stoked our wants and desires, inflaming our envy, finding new and irresistible enticements to make us consume more. And the scientists and engineers were put to work to find ways, not to make things better, but to make them cheaper, and faster, so that want could be further increased, consumption grown. The quality of the everyday items we used began to fall, slowly at first, and then more rapidly, until in recent times thousands of years of knowledge and understanding in the making of good things was completely abandoned, so that everything we buy is now cheap and disposable.

Business, with its great wealth, wielded great power, and its wishes came to take precedence over all others in society, trampling on the rights of those who did the work to enjoy a fair share of the spoils, trampling on our rights to enjoy the place we lived free from pollution and waste, and allowing the earth's natural resources to be destroyed and consumed in the relentless quest for ever-growing profit and wealth. We are already one of the richest nations in the world, yet that wealth has done precisely nothing to increase our happiness. And despite this wealth, many working citizens now face a daily choice between heating their home and feeding their family. Yet still the priority of our political leaders is to keep big business growing, just as it has done for the past half century.

The work of making, once fulfilling, rewarding and a source of personal and community pride, became meaningless and dispiriting. Humans were reduced to servants of the machines they had initially built to serve them. And then, when our machines could no longer make the profits the shareholders desired, they took their machines and their factories and moved them to places where people could be paid less to operate them, and millions of working men and women were thrown on the scrapheap. We meekly accepted that mass production, automation and offshoring was all in the name of economic progress. The proud, skilled, fulfilling work of making and doing that occupied almost all of us, work that shaped and gave purpose to our lives, was taken from us for the further enrichment of a wealthy few. We were told this would be good for us, for such wealth would 'trickle down'. But after half a century most of us are still waiting for our trickle.

———

We have more of everything we might imagine would make us happy than even our relatively recent ancestors could ever have dreamed of. Thanks to modern agriculture we can eat whatever we like, whenever we like. Our supermarkets sell a dizzying array of produce, always fresh, and never out of season. At the tap of a few buttons on our phones we can have food from any country on the planet delivered to us, wherever we might happen to be, in a matter of minutes. We have inside toilets, hot showers, and our homes are warmed in winter. We have turned those homes from basic shelters into places to entertain friends and family, filled with labour-saving devices including machines to wash and dry our clothes and our dishes. Most now have a gigantic screen on which we can watch an almost limitless array of television and films, and with our voices we can instantly call up the entire back catalogue of almost every recorded musician in history. And all of this entertainment can be enjoyed wherever we are in the world, through our phones, so we need never be bored. We decorate and personalise our homes, fill them with great assortments of furniture and domestic objects in an array of colours and patterns, and have soft comfortable beds to sleep in and sofas to sit on, both of which we adorn with additional and needless cushions. Our walls are richly painted or papered, we burn candles for fun, and all of this bounty can be, and often is, changed with ease and relatively little expense according to our whims.

We have more clothing than any generation before us. The wardrobes in our homes are filled to bursting with hundreds and in some cases thousands of garments. For some people a whole new outfit of clothes every week is normal. On average in the UK we have about ten times as many pieces of clothing as we did when I was born just fifty years ago, and I thought I had plenty then. We have so many clothes that we are unable to wear even half of them and we throw away enough each year to have clothed the entire planet just a generation ago. Between just half a dozen of the leading fast fashion brands we are offered a choice of almost ten thousand new things to buy every single day, which we can do with just a couple of taps of our finger. If we buy an item in bed at night it might arrive before we wake up, delivered to our home or workplace personally (in the case of the biggest fast fashion brand on the planet, from the other side of the world). We can wear it, photograph ourselves in it, then send it back. And if we are canny about how we do all of this it might cost us nothing. We have become so blasé about the genuine miracle of science and engineering that is the telephone in our pockets, an object that just forty years ago was something only imagined in science fiction, that we discard them every twelve months for the latest one, the promise of which is virtually unchanged from the one we had before.

We have freedom; personal freedom to live where we wish, to live with whom we wish, to live as whoever we wish. We have the right and the means to express ourselves freely, we can broadcast our thoughts and feelings to the entire world through the phones in our pockets. If we feel injustice we can proclaim it and all can hear it if they choose. We can travel quickly and cheaply to almost anywhere on the planet. We enjoy all the things that in the past only the richest in society would have enjoyed, and more that they could not have imagined.

But has all of this made us happy? Do we feel fulfilled and valued? Have we found lasting contentment? For the very great majority of us the answer is no.

How do we build a healthier, more prosperous society? How do we raise our levels of individual happiness? We're continually told that the answer lies in ever more economic growth, but we've had unparalleled economic growth for the past 50 years and very few of us feel better off, and a good many of us feel considerably worse off now than we did before. Wealth inequality is a global problem and it is getting worse at an alarming rate. The way our economy has been run over the past fifty years has only benefited the wealthiest in society. The average income, adjusted for inflation, of the bottom 90 per cent has been essentially stagnant for the past forty-two years.

The US has the worst inequality, but in the UK, where we copy the US economic model, we're a very close second. We measure inequality through what's called the Gini coefficient, and in most countries it has been increasing steadily for the past thirty or so years. But in some countries, such as France and Norway, it has not. The global economy is the same for all of us, so why are the outcomes in some places different? As Nobel prize -winning economist Joseph Stiglitz puts it, 'inequality is a choice'. Countries that pursued policies designed to reduce inequality have done just that and their overall economies have fared no better or worse than ours by the standard measures. It is perfectly possible to lower inequality and have a thriving economy. The statistics around wealth distribution are staggering. The poorest 50 per cent of the world's population own just 2 per cent of total net wealth. The five richest families in the UK are wealthier than all of the bottom 20 per cent of the UK population combined, almost 13 million people.

If ploughing on in the same old way isn't the answer, then what is? We might start by looking at what actually makes us happy and content. If more and more cheap low-quality things is not the answer then maybe having less but better might be? Fewer things with more meaning, things we feel connected too, things we enjoy and cherish. And we might think again about the world of work. There is a short phrase in The Road to Nab End, William Woodruff's story of growing up in a Lancashire textile town, which comes back to me often. 'Work was everything.' In our clamour for growth and profit, we've forgotten that work is far more important than just the money it brings in. Work was structure, it was community, it was personal fulfilment and personal and civic pride. My grandparents lived in Scotland's textile region, and I have worked in manufacturing all my adult life, I've seen the jobs go and manufacturing towns crumble. It makes me sad and angry to see so much skill, knowledge and endeavour go to waste. We could choose to design an economy whose primary goal is to give every member of society a chance to enjoy a great education, a rewarding job and a decent career. We can all as individuals choose to spend our money in ways that does good for those people and things we most care about. And we can carve up the economic pie differently, give more of the financial benefit to the doers and makers, and less to the takers.

In 2016 I launched a business called Community Clothing, which at its heart attempts to do just that. It supports and creates local jobs by making good clothes, which we sell at affordable prices, and in doing so helps rebuild supportive, integrated communities people can feel proud to belong to. I don't know if it will succeed in the long term, but I'm happy to say that I've proven that our model works in principle.

Every decision we take as a business is geared towards creating the maximum value, both economic and social, for the people living in the communities where our clothes are made. So far we've created well over a third of a million hours of work and we've barely got started.

In 2022, Community Clothing was invited to be part of an exhibition at Harewood House, near Leeds, called Radical Acts. Putting people and good jobs first and doing everything we can to make the highest quality things shouldn't be radical. I hope that what we do might encourage others in our industry, and those in other, similar industries, to think and act differently. Perhaps in the not-too-distant future striving for an economy that works for the benefit and happiness of all might not seem quite like such a radical act.

Part I

WANT

1

How We Went from Needing Very Little to Wanting Everything

As recently as five hundred years ago most of us had nothing. But in a relatively short space of time we've gone from needing very little to wanting lots of everything.

For several centuries now the apparatus of commerce has, in increasingly sophisticated ways, stoked our envy and our greed to make us want more. Once largely content, now we are dissatisfied. To live happily we need to understand the difference between what we want and what we need. What makes individuals happy, what makes happy societies, what even is happiness? These have been the difficult but crucial questions philosophers from Aristotle onwards have wrestled with. They were important questions to the early economists too, following Jeremy Bentham's principle of 'Utility' which said that the success of an economy should be measured by the degree to which it promoted human happiness. But from the early twentieth century the focus of economic thinking shifted away from increasing happiness to increasing output, production and consumption. Humans were reduced to 'factors of production', and the single-minded pursuit of growth dominates economics to this day.

Then, towards the end of the last century, scientists began once again to question the wisdom of this focus on consumption and growth to the exclusion of all else. Academics renewed their interest in our personal happiness, nations began to ask us directly if we were happy, and the results were startling. Most people, after what on paper had been half a century of unprecedented economic 'success' where the amount of money we earned, and of the things we owned, had grown to unprecedented levels, were no happier, and were in many cases less happy, than before.

Those with a vested interest in growth had told us that money equalled happiness, but Richard Easterlin, a pioneer in the study of happiness in the 1970s, discovered that in fact increasing wealth was having no impact on our happiness at all. In the US, over the seventy-year period for which good data is available, people's incomes have tripled but their happiness has actually *diminished*. Ruut Veenhoven, a Dutch sociologist, defines happiness as the degree to which an individual judges the overall quality of his or her life as being favourable. Happiness is a judgement based broadly on four major factors: first, our baseline disposition (how happy we are naturally); second, our circumstances; third, our aspirations; and fourth, most crucially, how we feel we're doing compared with others. Our happiness is relative. When we evaluate our personal happiness we do so against a reference level, which in the case of money and material possessions is the people we interact with daily. Today, thanks to social media, we are endlessly exposed to the lives of luxury and leisure of the most privileged in society. Even if our personal income goes up, if everyone else's goes up by *more* we feel *less* happy.

What we *want* and what we *have* are also crucial to our perception of a good life. As people's incomes grow they tend to *have* a great deal more, but the things they *want* tend to grow by at least the same amount. As incomes go up, happiness fails to increase because the scale of our unfulfilled wants remains the same, or even increases. As Ralph

Waldo Emerson put it, 'WANT is a growing giant whom the coat of HAVE was never large enough to cover.' Or as Samuel Johnson said back in 1751: 'every man is rich or poor according to the proportion between his desires and his enjoyments; any enlargement of wishes is therefore equally as destructive to happiness [as] the diminution of possessions'. Wanting more makes us as unhappy as having less. Karl Marx suggested the same thing: 'A house may be large or small; as long as the neighbouring houses are likewise small it satisfies all social requirement for a residence. But let there arise next to the little house a palace and the little house shrinks to a Hut.'

But if want of things makes us unhappy, what makes us happy? Richard Easterlin says that in fact many of the things that people enjoy most in life are simple, non-material things: socialising with friends and family, playing sport, reading books, taking walks, crafting, listening to music, all of which are largely free. After years of total dedication to his work, Charles Darwin reflected on his loss of interest in literature, music and art: 'the loss of these tastes is a loss of happiness.' What we need is less of the material things and more of life's simple pleasures.

Early History

We know from the DNA of human-dwelling fleas that we've been wearing clothes since the latter part of the Palaeolithic period, between about 100,000 and 30,000 years ago, though no one seems quite sure. At that time humans had begun migrating to the cold and wet north, and some ingenious folks had looked at the pelt they'd just removed from the animal they were planning to eat and thought it might help them to stay warm and fend off the rain. They realised too that if these pieces of pelt could be joined together it would make for a snugger fit, so they whittled a needle out of bone and with a bit of gut or sinew for thread sewed them together. Hey presto, clothes were born.

Several thousand years later, during the Neolithic period, we switched from being hunters and gatherers to an agricultural life, at first nomadic but later dwelling in fixed settlements, building more permanent dwellings and cultivating cereals for food. This permanent settlement saw the emergence in society of the haves and have-nots. Some people accumulated – through skill, cunning, luck or violence – livestock, goods, land and power, and by the end of the Bronze Age these fortunate few had developed laws to safeguard their acquired wealth. Clothes remained a practical necessity for most, but for the elite they became symbols of status and power. The wealthy acquired a taste for the finer things, for goods of a better, or simply different, quality to those available from their local markets, and so a trade in fine, richly coloured textiles and dyestuffs was established between India, Persia, China, Southeast Asia, and the advanced early Europeans in Greece and Rome. We know from tomb finds dating back 6,000 years that the wealthy of northeastern Africa were adorning themselves with semi-precious lapis lazuli from Afghanistan, over 4,000 kilometres away.

Ordinary people had very few physical possessions, but even those with very little cherished some items for purely ornamental or sentimental reasons, like broken pots crudely fixed with leather, kept despite being no longer useful for carrying food or liquid. Little changed in what most people wore, and what they owned, from the end of the Iron Age, around 900 BC, right through to the start of the early modern period in around 1500 AD.

Pre-Industrial Paucity

By the end of the Middle Ages, about five hundred years ago, England's rulers had grown wealthy, mostly from their land, while most ordinary folk owned almost nothing. Over 70 per cent of us in the UK worked the land, and at that time many enjoyed rights over the land they farmed and access to common grazing. Only three things mattered: food, clothing and shelter, and in all of those we had a sufficiency and no more. Those people who were employed by others, either as domestic staff or as field labourers, were fed and housed by their employers, but everyone else lived in impermanent shelters, simple single-storey dwellings mostly made of wood and earth, with no glass windows and no chimney. Homes had few or no comforts and most contained little beyond the practical: a wooden stool, maybe a wooden cot with a straw mat, perhaps with a simple covering, a few items of rudimentary cooking equipment such as an iron pot or skillet (a few homes had a simple bread oven), and some items of 'treen', simple wooden objects such as bowls and spoons. Many people ate what they could grow on their small plots of land, some grains to be eaten mashed, or milled to make flour and bread. Most of us had a cow, some a few sheep or poultry, or if you were doing well, a pig or two. Some households had the luxury of butter- or cheese-making equipment, others had the kit to brew cider or beer. But many people had no means of cooking at home at all and would instead buy cheap meals in the alehouses that existed in even the smallest villages, serving up a pot of beer, a pipe of tobacco, a pennyworth of eggs, some broth or meat, or re-baked bread and wizened cheese that it was commonly suggested would kill a horse.

Within the local economy there was a significant amount of barter in goods and services. Communities would often work together to produce simple goods, especially cloth and basic clothing. What few things we bought came from travelling pedlars or market towns, but trips to market in rural areas often involved long journeys on foot. Most people owned just the clothes on their backs, one set of very rudimentary woollen, linen or hemp garments, and a pair of leather or felt shoes. In the UK around a fifth of households kept sheep, a similar proportion had wheels for spinning either wool or linen (seldom the same ones), and about one in ten families had a weaving loom. The work was spread about. One family might provide the wool, another might spin it, another weave it. A group of neighbours might get together to 'full' or finish the cloth, working it collectively and singing while they did so. Skilled seamstresses or tailors within the local community would transform that woven cloth into clothing. In the quiet periods in the agricultural calendar most people would pick up what other work they could, and for those least well off there was some assistance. 'Poor Laws' required every parish in England to keep a store of wool, hemp and flax that was issued to the unemployed who then spun and wove it, selling it back to the parish in return for money for rent.

Entertainment in daily life was limited; fairs, held to celebrate saints' days, the end of the harvests and other important dates within the community, were the highlight of the social calendar, offering the chance to get together with friends, get stuck into some ale, and wonder at new-fangled foods, clothes and other novel items. Most such events lasted from a few days to a week. People sang, exchanged gossip and were entertained by clowns, jugglers, puppet shows and performing animals. It is hard to know whether people were happy, because no one officially asked. Agricultural life came with certain anxieties – crop failure, the health of livestock – but besides the feelings of jealousy that another man had a tidier barn, or his cow might be a better milker, there was limited cause for envy. None of your immediate neighbours would have had much more or less than you, and the local nobility lived in a way very few genuinely imagined themselves emulating.

In the early sixteenth century, if you had £20 worth of personal wealth, equivalent to about twenty cows, ten dozen sheep or a weaving loom, you were considered well off. Most people, labourers, husbandmen (farmers) and lower paid craftsmen such as shoemakers and weavers, had less than this, and in 1524 around 25 per cent of people owned nothing at all, literally not one single durable item, nor any land. But as the century progressed, improvements in the technology of making and the growth of specialisation allowed the prices of household items to fall, enabling ordinary people to accumulate a few more clothes; and because clothing was now a little finer, lighter and less durable, these items might be replaced a couple of times during their lifetime. Unlike today when our wills only mention the big valuable things like houses, and much of the huge quantity of things we own at our deaths are given to charity shops or simply binned, in the sixteenth century those who left wills carefully detailed every single possession, including food and every article of clothing. Everything was passed on. Almost no one died leaving any money at all.

Most ordinary people bought no new clothes in their entire lifetime. It was common practice for wealthy families to provide clothing not only for family members but for domestic servants and any employed agricultural labourers, who received clothes, whether uniform or not, as part of their pay. All clothing was highly prized and any allowance in clothing was very carefully measured. Most was made new, but employers wasted no opportunity to pass off old clothing and shoes – a good pair of boots, a woollen coat or suit – to their workforce, typically of much better quality than the recipient would be used to. But all payments of this kind were meticulously calculated and monetary values deducted from wages. *The Preindustrial Consumer in England and America* notes that 'Robert Gibson to have £3 wages, and an old hat, or else 3s in money whether he will'. At the time a good suit of wool clothes could cost £4 to £5, as much as a servant's yearly wage – in some cases twice as much – and about the total cost of all the furnishings in a labourer's cottage. There was no ready-to-wear clothing and commissioning the making of new cloth or clothing required down payments for services in advance, or good credit. Whilst it was not unknown for benevolent employers to provide the credit guarantee, for most ordinary citizens new clothes were well beyond their means.

Sourcing clothing was a complicated business requiring considerable specialist knowledge. If the buyer were lucky enough to have good-quality craftspeople nearby they might commission cloth from them. Alternatively, finished cloth might be bought from the linen drapers and mercers that were now popping up in larger market towns, or from the travelling sellers, higglers, regraters and pedlars; many of these were poor women who provided a door-to-door service, with the cloth being made by growing numbers of specialist manufacturers that were becoming well established, notably in the North and Southwest.

Some households might employ domestic servants with sewing skills, but the majority would engage specialist tailors, dressmakers and shoemakers who would live with the family whilst they made or repaired their clothes. Seventeenth-century diarist Nicholas Blundell records, 'Catherine Fazakerley helped my wife to make some head cloths and she lodged here because she is to sew for my wife for some time.' The accounts of a Sir Thomas Haggerston contain entries such as, 'To a spinner woman for eight weeks spinning for my wife', 'to William Bell for 30 yards cloth weaving', 'to Robert Simmons for my wife's cloth dying' and 'to an old Scotch woman for bleaching two webs cloth'. A man called Henry Best wrote a guidebook for his heirs containing among other things detailed advice on buying clothing: 'Such linen cloth as here made in England and commonly called housewife cloth which cost 14D or 15D a yard and which our maid servants usually buy for holiday aprons and neck cloths'. A higher grade priced at two shillings was 'used of gentle folks for shirts'. Linen from Scotland could also be had: 'the worst sort of Scotch cloth is 18d a yard and the best sort of all two shillings 6d and eight groats a yard, it is spun by the lairds wife and much used here for handkerchiefs'. The finest linen however came from Holland, 'spun by the nuns', 'strong cloth and much used by mens bands, gentlewomen's handkerchiefs and half shirts etc'.

The head of the household, whether employer or father, bore the primary responsibility for buying everything for family members, their entire staff and any hired labour. Wives would usually shop for food and some durables but had no legal control over money. Ordinary working people had no sovereignty over their consumption at all, though this began to change during the early seventeenth century, and by the end of that century most people received their wages entirely in cash.

But as well as not having the means to buy things, we were told it was morally and religiously good to content ourselves with few material possessions. The rich didn't go to heaven, earthly possessions were temporary, and just as we came into the world with nothing so we should leave it that way. Greed and envy, they preached, were mortal sins. And if all of that were not enough to discourage people from having much stuff, the authorities enacted laws specifying what different people could and could not buy. Throughout history the wealthy had worn fine clothing to set themselves apart from the common man and their silks, velvets, furs and jewels had always been beyond the means of ordinary folk, but the new merchant class now had the money to afford such finery, and the rich didn't like it. Sumptuary laws (laws of con*sumpt*ion) were passed to stop those of lower rank dressing in the trappings of the nobility. Whilst those in charge of the treasury worried about the negative effects the import of foreign goods would have on our balance of trade, others were more concerned with the blurring of the social order, and some simply thought most people were too stupid to exercise good judgement. They concocted elaborate specifications as to what could and could not be worn at various socioeconomic levels; only the peerage could wear gold, silver, red or blue velvet. If you earned over £200 a year you could wear one thing, over £100 something else. Knights couldn't wear pointy shoes (with a penalty of a 40p fine), wives and daughters couldn't wear veils costing more than 12p, anyone below the gentry had to wear a cap instead of a hat on Sundays. Ninety per cent of the population had restrictions placed on what they could and couldn't wear, but the application of these laws was patchy at best and predictably the only people prosecuted were the very poorest. The laws didn't last long, partly because people were fed up with ridiculous arguments about who should be allowed to wear what hat, but more crucially because many of those making the laws were involved in the trade of such items and didn't want their commercial interests harmed.

As manufacturing became more specialised its organisation and equipment improved, as did the skills involved. Quality increased, and between the late sixteenth century and the early eighteenth the cost of most cloths fell by half or more, and the introduction in the eighteenth century of ready-made garments had a huge impact on both the cost and availability of clothes. Prior to 1700 you could buy ready-made small accessories like stockings, gloves, hankies and not much else, but the production of high volumes of military clothes for soldiers fighting the French wars of the 1690s created a system of ready-made clothing in standardised sizes, and when hostilities ceased the manufacturers of these goods transferred their attention to making civilian clobber.

Unlike in France, where there was an enormous divide in income between peasant and aristocrat, in England thousands of closely spaced layers of society began to manifest themselves. The stratification made social mobility and social emulation possible at all levels of English society, and this would prove to be a significant factor in the huge growth in consumer spending. We started to accumulate a few more things in our homes. Linen tableware, books and clocks began to pop up in our wills, showing a modest growth in consumption, but for the time being this went no further than the newly affluent middle class.

The Emergence of Consumerism

In the 1750s a change to the way we thought about the economy, consumption, work and wealth took place that dramatically, and perhaps catastrophically, altered the course of human society. Until this time the wealthy had seen no financial benefit to themselves in ordinary people buying things. The dominant economic doctrine was 'mercantilism', where all that mattered was the gold in the country's vaults, our 'treasury', and trade was thought of only in terms of the inflow or outflow of gold. Importing goods was bad because our gold flowed out to pay for them, exporting was good because other countries' gold flowed in. Money and wealth were seen as zero-sum: if I gained then someone else lost, and vice versa. But a completely new school of economic thought was developing as people watched the effects of the rise in production and consumption during the early years of the Industrial Revolution. It became clear that money was not fixed but elastic; money could create more money. All of a sudden the wealthy began to think very differently about ordinary people buying stuff. In 1776 Scottish economist and philosopher Adam Smith wrote *An Inquiry into the Nature and Causes of the Wealth of Nations*. It described in detail a new way of thinking about national economies in which the value of the economy was the value of all the goods and services that were traded within it, not the value of the gold in the vaults.

Smith understood there to be two broad categories of people: those with just enough money to make ends meet, and those with money to spare. Smith called the spare money 'Capital'. In the system he described, spare money is invested in materials, tools and labour to produce goods. Those goods are then sold for more than the amount you've paid to make them. You trouser the difference, the profit, and start again. Ordinary people were placed at the heart of the system in the role of consumers. In theory, the more you produced the more profit you could make, as long as people consumed it all, and the more capital you could accumulate. And in theory at least there were no limits. This radical new thinking had many opponents, but it was viewed by many, including Smith himself, as a positive enhancement to society. The thinking was that, whilst the rich would undoubtedly get richer, the rising tide of overall wealth would at the same time raise millions out of poverty.

In the 1690s we had gone mad for cheap, colourful fabrics imported by the East India Company, and it was the fervour with which these cheap Indian calicoes and muslins were consumed that provided the first evidence of the elastic nature of markets. People's basic desire to keep up with a fashion for bright printed cloth encouraged them to spend more. The spending generated money, which flowed back around allowing more spending in a continuously elastic cycle. Envy and vanity provided the stimulus to a complete rethinking of how economics worked. It became clear to those with wealth that here was a way to get wealthier, fast, and so a country that for a thousand years had followed the creed that thrift was the route to happiness, and where the wealthy had done their level best to prevent the lower classes from buying anything at all, suddenly got on board with the idea that buying lots of stuff was good.

The idea was revolutionary. The prevailing moral orthodoxy had heavily disapproved of self-indulgence and vanity, and contemporary commentators discussed at length the social and moral implications that such a fundamental change might bring. Many feared what might be unleashed if the lower social ranks were given the wherewithal, and the moral freedom, to consume. But many saw only positives. Author on trade John Houghton wrote, 'our high living so far from prejudicing the nation, it enriches it'. The idea of *fashion* as a propulsive force for the generation of wealth emerged. Fashion, stated English economist Nicholas Barbon, 'occasions the expense of clothes before the old ones are worn out', a concept completely radical to the subsistence-living seventeenth-century Brit. 'Nature may be satisfied with little,' Barbon wrote, 'but it is the wants of the mind, fashion and the desire for novelties and things scarce that causes trade.' Another economist, Sir Dudley North, saw envy as a positive force: 'if men contented themselves with bare necessaries', he said, 'we should have a poor world'. Envy, he claimed, was a positive goad to industry. The idea of every citizen becoming a consuming cog in a wealth-creating machine presented too many political as well as moral threats to gain immediate widespread acceptance, but by 1776 Adam Smith could state almost without challenge that 'consumption is the sole end and purpose of all production; and the interest of the producer ought to be attended to only so far as it may be necessary for promoting that of the consumer'.

Smith famously described four stages of the evolution of human society: the Age of Hunters, simple subsistence supported by hunting and gathering; the Age of Shepherds, where a nomadic life is supported by animal husbandry, an age where wealth and power first emerge through livestock ownership; the Age of Agriculture, where settled living on cultivated land allows population growth, the stratification of society, and a further rise in property ownership and inequality; and finally the Age of Commerce, where the culture of want is firmly established and where the division between haves and have-nots accelerates rapidly. The change from mercantilist to capitalist thinking was a watershed moment. As those with money realised that by turning all citizens into consumers, they could increase their wealth, so the moral and religious objections to consumption came tumbling down. The wealthy embraced capitalism wholeheartedly, providing the money to invest in production and systems of distribution that would allow people access to new goods all the time. And they invested in the apparatus of selling and marketing, because they quickly understood that an ever-growing quantity of production required an ever-growing demand. People needed to want things they didn't need, so ever more sophisticated ways of making this happen were deployed.

Britain became more urbanised, wages rose as manufacturing work replaced agriculture, and shops became commonplace. By 1759 there was one shop for every forty-two people in England, and the variety, quantity and quality of the goods they sold went up considerably. The customers and the amounts they spent changed too. In the sixteenth century all shoppers were Sirs, Gents and Esquires, and their purchases substantial, but by the late seventeenth century ordinary householders and farmers were shopping and three-quarters of transactions were for less than one shilling, an average day's wage. Shops spread into rural areas, but whilst you could buy everyday necessities in your local shop, market towns were enticing shoppers with ever-growing novelty and choice. What really caused shopping to take off, however, were the peculiarly British fancies: tea, sugar and white bread. When shops only sold things we bought less often, like clothes, there was no need for them to be close by – you could happily make occasional purchases at your nearest market town. But when we got hooked on tea and sugar this changed. Because these goods were expensive, we bought a little but often, and we certainly didn't want to walk a twenty-mile round trip for a spoonful of tea. We needed local shops.

Consumption and Fashion

Even into the early eighteenth century, the wealthy still weren't entirely comfortable with the idea of the self-improvement of the lower and middle classes through spending. Henry Fielding wrote:

> While the nobleman will emulate the grandeur of the Prince
> and the gentleman will aspire to the proper state of a nobleman
> the tradesman stepped from behind his counter into the vacant

place of the gentleman. Nor doth the confusion end there. It reaches the very dregs of the people who aspire still to a degree beyond that which belongs to them.

People were concerned that if things went on that way, there would be 'no common folk at all'.

In 1714, Anglo-Dutch philosopher Bernard Mandeville published a book entitled *The Fable of The Bees: or, Private Vices, Publick Benefits.* Mandeville decried as hypocrites those who preached virtue while profiting from the wealth generated by the stoking of greed and envy throughout society. Incensed moralists denounced him as a champion of vice and luxury, but Mandeville was convinced by the universal social and economic benefits to be had from all the current 'luxury, avarice, prodigality, pride, envy and vanity'. He went so far as to suggest that the economy would collapse if consumption ended, writing that 'mercers, upholsterers, tailors and many others would be starved in half a year's time if pride and luxury were at once to be banished by the nation'. 'What use was a rich man,' he said, 'if he did not lavishly spend his wealth and stimulate the economy through employment and consumption.' He poked fun at the virtuous by stating that even the harlot encouraged trade. The prodigal, he claimed, was a blessing to the whole society, whereas 'frugality was like honesty, a mean starving virtue'. Mandeville recognised the necessity to create work for all, saying, 'it is an idling dreaming virtue that employs no hands and therefore very useless in a trading country where there are vast numbers that one way or other must all be set to work'.

Those who had previously possessed very little bought a little more; those who had ample added new; and those with more than they needed in the first place bought a whole lot more according to the prevailing fashion. Many had for a long time had the money to shop, they just hadn't had the motivating force and the moral freedom to do so. Growing consumption was driven by fashion: clothing, furniture, pottery, cutlery, glassware, and the fashion for drinking tea, the consumption of which went up fifteenfold in the eighteenth century. Everyone was at it. Pehr Kalm wrote of 'Farmers wives dressing like ladies of quality', god forbid. Between 1700 and 1800 overall consumption per head grew 400 per cent, and the sale of some fashionable textiles grew ten times faster than the population.

In England the pursuit of luxury was now seen as socially desirable, new wants stimulating increased consumption and output. London had grown from some 200,000 inhabitants in 1600 to over 900,000 in 1800 and made the country highly susceptible to the dissemination of new fashions. London was home to 11 per cent of the entire population and nearly a fifth of all adults regularly passed through its fashionable orbit. London was a shop window for the whole country, creating a conformity of taste which well suited the standardised production of the new factory system. The large number of women in domestic service rapidly spread the latest styles of their upper- and middle-class employers through all social strata. The English had always been obsessed with fine clothing and fashion. In 1595 Philip Stubbs wrote that 'No other nation take such pride in apparel as England', and 'No peoples of the world are so curious in new fangles', while Robert Burton in his *Anatomy of Melancholy* said similarly, 'he is only fantastical that is *not* in fashion'. And whilst they might not have had the means, the poor certainly did not lack the desire for fine clothes. In 1600 Wiliam Vaughan commented that he'd known various servants who would 'bestow all the money they had in the world on sumptuous garments'.

There is nothing new about the idea of 'fashion'. The Roman poet Ovid wrote in 8 AD, 'I cannot keep track of all the vagaries of fashion, every day, so it seems, brings in a new style.' Almost every contemporary social commentator, at every stage in history, believes that what they are witnessing are changes in fashions at speeds that could never be imagined or exceeded. In fact fashions in England, until Tudor times at least, changed very slowly indeed. In the late sixteenth century people were reported to be wearing the same fashions as they had during the reign of Henry VIII some fifty years before. But the mid-eighteenth century marked a major turning point. The revolution in industrial production needed a parallel revolution in consumption to keep the wheels of industry turning, and in England people started buying. 'The luxury and extravagance of the lower and middling classes had risen to such a pitch as never before seen in the world,' wrote one commentator. Prussian historian Johann von Archenholtz said, 'England surpasses all the other nations of Europe in luxury, and the luxury is increased daily. All classes enjoy the accumulation of riches, luxury and pleasure.' Consumption was led by the rich, who bought superlative furniture from Chippendale and Sheraton, pottery from Worcester and Wedgwood, cutlery from the master smiths of Sheffield. Boring pets were out; the rich assembled menageries of exotic animals like private zoos. For ordinary people, new high-quality brightly coloured clothing suddenly became an affordable reality. By 1860, 80 per cent of the population bought their clothes ready-made. In 1892 Leeds alone had fifty-four factories making ready-to-wear suits. Retailers and department stores sprang up selling new clothes that were by now both easily available, and affordable. And where the rich led, the middle and working classes followed, hypnotised by fashion and excess. Traditional shops grew in number; new and ever more sophisticated sales techniques were deployed to capture the attention of consumers; items were made fashionable through conspicuous placement with well-known society figures and stars of the theatre and music hall, the influencers of the Georgian era.

Fashion designers, that is designers of fashionable clothes, first began to make their mark on the public consciousness in the early eighteenth century. In the 1720s, Françoise Leclerc, dressmaker to the Queen of

France, became widely sought-after by the women of the French aristocracy. The spread of the latest fashion intelligence gained new momentum through novel means. Dolls, before they became popular toys, were fashion marketing tools. Also known as Pandoras, *poupées de mode* or Queen Anne Dolls (Queen Anne was a fan), these beautifully carved and painted wooden, typically half-scale dolls (some, for the most important clients, were life size, perfect replicas of the client's form), with real hair, were dressed in exquisitely executed scale versions of new fashions. They had been used for centuries by dressmakers in Italy and in France to show potential customers their wares, but new, cheaper, more democratic dolls from London now began to emerge, part of a shift from fashion which was exclusive and slow and aristocratic in origin, to fashion which was fast and directly aimed at the masses. Illustrated fashion adverts began appearing regularly in the London and provincial press, and new magazines devoted to nothing but fashion sprang up. By 1800 the process was unmistakable: looking at and lusting after the clothes of our social superiors had become an obsession for middle- and working-class Brits. The growth of the fashion industry did not happen by accident. It was a deliberate, carefully conceived and skilfully executed process of social manipulation.

The Rise of the Brand

We started branding our livestock almost five thousand years ago, but it wasn't until an innovative potter from Stoke stuck his name on the cups and saucers he sold that the idea of the fashion brand emerged. Josiah Wedgwood was an English potter and materials scientist (and therefore a very good egg), and was already well on his way to commercial success when St James's Palace commissioned him to make a creamware tea set for Queen Charlotte. Wedgwood didn't miss a trick and took the opportunity to send samples of his other wares along with his tea set, which happily met with royal approval. The Queen bestowed her name upon Wedgwood's innovative creamware, commanding it to be called Queensware, and honouring him by appointing him Her Majesty's Potter. The royal potter was not slow to capitalise on his growing fame, adding the title to his pamphlets, invoices and orders. Wedgwood was a pioneering marketeer in all sorts of ways: he was the first to do direct mail, money-back guarantees, free delivery, buy-one-get-one-free, and illustrated catalogues.

Thomas Chippendale was the son of a joiner from Otley in North Yorkshire. He trained as a cabinet maker, starting at home with his father, then moving to York, before finally settling in London. In 1754 he set up in partnership with James Rannie, a wealthy Scottish merchant who financed the business. Chippendale's stroke of marketing genius was to publish a book of his designs, called *The Gentleman and Cabinet Maker's Director*. Chippendale's catalogue was a first, allowing customers to browse designs in the comfort of their home before ordering a predesigned piece of furniture. His designs were considered the height of fashion in London and set the standard for his competitors, of which there were many.

George Hepplewhite was another northern cabinet maker. Born in Ryton in County Durham, he set up shop in London and claimed royal patronage, but his great fame did not come until after his death, when his widow Alice published his *Cabinet-Maker and Upholsterer's Guide*, containing nearly three hundred designs for simple, elegant neoclassical furniture. Yet another northern cabinet maker, and another Thomas, this one Sheraton, was born in Stockton-on-Tees, County Durham, and apprenticed locally before also setting up in London. In 1791, following Chippendale and Hepplewhite's lead, he published the four-volume *The Cabinet Maker's and Upholsterer's Drawing Book*. Unlike Chippendale and Hepplewhite, he didn't have his own workshop but was purely a designer, the Sheraton chair being of his design.

His early success was followed with *The Cabinet Dictionary*, and then shortly before his death with *The Cabinet Maker, Upholsterer and General Artist's Encyclopaedia*. These three forward-looking men established English furniture brands as the global luxury standard.

Much later than the emergence of branded pottery and furniture, it was not until 1858 that the first recognisable fashion house was founded, in Paris, by Englishman Charles Frederick Worth. Worth had begun his career selling silk for a prestigious Parisian cloth house, but his talent for dress designing was quickly spotted and his employer offered him the chance to open his own dress-making department within the store. He created prize-winning designs for the Great Exhibition of 1851 in London, and in 1860 a ball dress designed for Princess de Metternich was admired by Empress Eugénie, who asked for the dressmaker's name and demanded he attend her. From that point forward, Worth's salon in Paris attracted royalty from across Europe, and where royalty led monied society followed. Worth invented the idea of designing and showing ever-changing collections of clothes. Before Worth, customers ordered bespoke designs in consultation with their dressmaker or tailor, but Worth held shows of his fashions four times a year, presenting garments for every time of day and occasion. Shows would always finish with a wedding dress, a tradition upheld by some fashion houses to this day. Worth had a great knack for promotion. He was the first designer to sell clothes labelled with his own name and he dressed stars of the theatre and concert stage, making performance costumes and personal wardrobes for leading actresses and singers such as Sarah Bernhardt and Lillie Langtry – a sprinkling of stardust that aroused excitement and desire among his paying clients. It was all a masterstroke, and wealthy women flocked to Paris to purchase their entire wardrobes, some many times per year.

The emergence of seasonal fashion represented a turning point; appealing today, discardable tomorrow. Never before had things been made with planned obsolescence in mind, a fixed shelf life after which the object, beautifully crafted and still perfectly usable, would be replaced. But the public accepted it without question. And why should they not? They were told by all that consumption was good, while the makers of such things, Worth, Wedgwood and Chippendale, were revered household names. The world and its resources seemed vast, limitless, and every discarded item, whether clothing, pottery or furniture, was happily picked up and reused by another.

American Consumerism

For the first six thousand years of making and selling things, people had mostly done it for their own benefit, and had been free to choose how and at what scale they went about it. But with the birth of organised capitalism, business had to focus on creating purely *financial* benefit for investors, and those investors wanted big valuations and more profit. They represented an entirely new force in the world, and no nation embraced the idea with greater zeal than the USA. Whilst eighteenth-century England was going through a consumer revolution, America retained much of its original rural self-reliant character well into the nineteenth century. But it wouldn't hold out for ever. From a slower start, American business, with the help of the huge amounts of capital invested by new banks and insurance companies, and relentless innovations in advertising, marketing and selling, embraced the production and sale of an ever-growing volume of ever-cheaper goods, transforming American society, once pious and ashamed of consumption, into one wholly preoccupied with wanting and buying. American corporations created a cultish zeal for the idea of the new, as Emerson wrote: 'One should seek the new ... for the spiritual rebirth, insight and virtue that might be discovered or encountered there.'

In 1907, Harvard professor Arthur Hadley wrote admiringly that 'the modern industrial corporation was developed as a means of meeting the need for capital by large industries far beyond the power of any one man or any small group of partners to furnish'. By 1900, enlarged through consolidations and mergers, they had been reshaping the economy into a system obsessed with making profits rather than with making goods. The bankers were unconcerned about the value or utility of goods, they simply wanted expansion. Edward Mead wrote, 'Great corporate beings grow continuously and are continuously adding to their equipment in order to increase their profits.' Corporations grew wealthier, and as they did so gained the power to control the very nature of society, work, wealth, goods and happiness. In the words of economist and sociologist Thorstein Veblen, the corporation had by 1900 'come not only to dominate the economic structure but to be the master institution of civilised life'. To drive this relentless growth in consumption, new consumer enticements were created: department stores, advertising, magazines, easy credit. And people were powerless to resist.

From 1880 department stores had begun to appear in Europe and Japan, but only in the capital cities. Gallery: Galeries Lafayette, Printemps and Bon Marché in Paris, Mitsukoshi in Tokyo, and Harrods, Whiteleys and Selfridges in London. But in America great department stores were built everywhere, transforming the way people shopped. Ordinary people could now escape the dullness and drudgery of their everyday lives in beautiful shopping palaces, their interiors overflowing with previously unseen and unimagined delights. In the 1870s the biggest was in New York, A.T. Stewart & Co., owned by Scottish/Irish immigrant Alex Turney Stewart. It had five storeys, selling sumptuous luxuries on four of them and manufacturing the goods on the other. Some condemned Stewart for his ostentation, but the editor of *Harper's Bazaar* was unsurprisingly supportive. 'We all want money and luxury,' they wrote, 'we only decry it when we can't get it.'

Stewart died in 1876 and was buried in a gold casket. New department stores were springing up all over the country, reflecting the great expansion in US manufacturing; in the 1880s most had just fifteen departments, but by 1910 the number had grown to over 125, selling everything you could imagine, including lion and panther cubs. To begin with, some owned mills and factories, but by the 1920s this tendency had all but disappeared, leaving their owners to focus on the business of retail.

Thanks to their ability to secure huge amounts of cash, retailers could carry more goods, in more locations, and sell them to you in the comfort of your own home. Sears Roebuck created the first nationwide US mail order business to serve the still huge rural American market. Woolworths, funded by Lehman Brothers and Goldman Sachs, grew from eighteen stores in 1892 to six hundred in 1912. America's small independent stores couldn't compete, and many sought unsuccessfully to push back against the growing power of the big retailer.

But not everyone was convinced this was progress. Many, including John Wanamaker, the Philadelphia department store magnate and one of America's wealthiest men, publicly voiced their concerns. 'We have had the iron age and the stone age,' Wanamaker wrote, 'and this is the business age, and all over the world men are worshipping the most helpless god of all – MONEY – the dumb god without power to add a handbreadth to a man's life.' Some in American business lost confidence, fearing that the lure of seemingly easy money would lead to overproduction and crisis, precipitating a national debate about the distribution of wealth. Many feared worker exploitation and lobbied for a minimum wage which would ensure that their employees could continue to play their part in keeping the wheels of consumption turning. On the other side it was argued that workers should get what the 'market' decreed, that the market would distribute wealth as it saw fit, and that argument, by and large, prevailed.

But the natural working of a free market was not enough to sell ever-increasing quantities of goods. The wealthy had money and were spending it, but the challenge at the start of the twentieth century was to get everyone in American society buying more. 'We are not concerned with the ability to pay,' wrote advertiser Emily Fogg Mead, 'but with the ability to WANT.' Without wants there would be no demand, so business in America set about creating them.

Billboards plonked on every building, bus and street corner, electric signs, posters painted by leading artists of the day, spectacular window displays – all were part of a strategy to show off their goods day and night, by whatever means possible. On seeing a show window in New York, Theodore Dreiser wrote, 'What a stinging, quivering zest they display, stirring up in onlookers a desire to secure but a part of what they see.' Novelist and playwright Edna Ferber wrote of another in Chicago that 'it is a work of art that window, a breeder of anarchism, a destroyer of contentment, a second feast of Tantalus'. This visual advertising had in the past been looked down upon as the domain of the showman. Newspapers and magazines had little advertising, and what they did have was dull. In 1880 businesses in America spent just $30 million on advertising; by 1910 that figure had grown to more than $600 million, or 4 per cent of the country's gross domestic product. Magazines were launched on the strength of new advertising revenues, some big brands running daily campaigns. 'The time to advertise is all the time,' said Wanamaker. In the 1880s there were only two copywriters in America; by 1915 there were thousands. Everyone, manufacturers, brands and stores, advertised relentlessly in all available media: magazines, direct mail, newspapers, door-to-door demonstrations, free samples, advertising cards and billboards. Image was paramount: 'Pictures are the lesson books of the uneducated,' wrote Wanamaker chillingly. Of a new catalogue, one advertiser wrote, 'A woman can buy almost as satisfactorily from one of these plates as from the counter.'

Artemas Ward, an advertising pioneer, said, 'It creates desire for the goods it displays, it imprints on the buying memory, it speaks the universal picture language', reaching everyone, 'foreigners, children, people in every station of life'.

Outdoor billboards and electric signs appeared on buses, trams and subways. A giant Coca Cola sign blocked the view of Niagara Falls. As Emily Fogg Mead said, 'The successful advert is obtrusive, it continually forces itself upon the attention. It is a subtle, persistent, unavoidable presence that creeps into the reader's inner consciousness.' O. J. Gude, a pioneer in electric signs, advised that they be 'so placed that everybody must read them, and absorb them, and absorb the advertiser's lesson, willingly or unwillingly'. Broadway in New York became well-known for such signs, including a 45ft Heinz pickle. Thousands of tourists flocked to view what was described by Gude as the 'phantasmagoria of the lights and electric signs'. At a time when most homes lacked electric light, the impact was shocking and highly arresting. But they were far from universally admired. Emily Fogg Mead wrote, 'the weary traveller becomes impatient at staring at streetcar ads, and the desecration of rocks and cliffs and beautiful scenery'. Sociologist Edward Ross wrote similarly that 'every accessible spot where the eye may wander frantically proclaims the merits of somebody's pickles or Scotch Whisky ... why should a man be allowed violently to seize and wrench my attention every time I step out of doors, to flash his wares into my brain'. Wealthy neighbourhoods exercised their right not to have signs, but in poorer districts and on roads and highways, the billboard industry forced its announcements onto Americans.

Commercial artists created extraordinary billboards, posters, catalogues and display advertising for newspapers and magazines; the most famous of all was Maxfield Parrish, America's greatest commercial artist and a highly regarded artist in his own right (his paintings now sell for many millions of dollars). Parrish created images for baking powder,

Colgate toothpaste, soap and light bulbs, placing the goods in Renaissance, medieval or classical settings. For seventeen years he created calendars for Edison's Mazda light bulbs. His car adverts were so successful that as one observer put it, 'the public stopped and stared and forgot to notice what the pictures advertised'.

In the world of window displays, L. Frank Baum, author of *The Wizard of Oz*, was the star. Born to a wealthy New York industrial and banking family, Baum's first love was theatre, but having moved to his wife's family home in South Dakota, he first ran a store, then the local newspaper. When recession saw his newspaper fail, he headed for Chicago where he took a job at a crockery and glass wholesaler, emerging as their most gifted salesman. Baum enjoyed the entertainment side of selling and with his experience in the theatre devised an entirely new way of displaying and selling goods, the show window. There was more than a hint of the carnival in these; they featured moving displays, vanishing ladies, mechanical animals, electric lights – anything to get the customer to 'watch the window'. No one was immune to their pull: 'Even the male mind, naturally obtuse on such matters, is forced to marvel at the beauty of the display.' With his dazzling, enticing pieces of theatre, Baum brought 'a peep into Elysium' and huge selling power. Then in 1900 *The Wizard of Oz* was published, and Baum was gone.

Designer fashion created a sense of glamour and luxury no other goods could match. It allowed women to feel special and to play out fantasies of a life beyond their normal humdrum. But it stirred up restlessness and anxiety, especially in a society where all fought for status and wealth, where many feared being scorned for failing to keep up, playing to vanity and envy. It strove to create an addiction to the relentless novelty needed to maintain the fiction of glamour and uniqueness. Thorstein Veblen wrote in 1894, 'nothing can be worn that is out of date ... a new wasteful trinket or garment must constantly supersede the old one'. According to one business editor, 'A demand is created which cannot but result most happily for those in business to cater to it. Where wearing of last year's hat or coat or costume is evidence of inability to buy, an inability which every American hates to admit.' Fashion pressed people to buy, dispose of, and buy again. It dealt not with utility or the craftsmanship and quality of goods, but with their fleeting appeal.

Merchants promoted this volatility by the ritualistic pronouncement of the coming season's fashions, supported by the fashion magazines, which had begun in the middle of the nineteenth century. The retailers understood the power of the press – 'The only type of model that our public would then buy had been thoroughly publicized in the various fashion journals' – and the power of newness: 'Constant change is essential to the prosperity alike of producers and distributors,' wrote one, 'find out what the woman at the counter wants, make it; then promptly drop it and go on to something else to which fickle fashion is turning her attention.' Supporting the merchants was a new textile and clothing production system which sprang up in several cities, growing at least twice as fast as any other US industry. By 1915 clothing was America's third largest industry behind steel and oil, with an output of well over $1 billion. Textile mills sprang up across New England, Pennsylvania and the south. There were over 15,000 womenswear businesses in New York alone, employing 500,000 mainly immigrant women and children on 'dirt-low' wages.

From the early 1900s the Americans began to copy Charles Worth's regular Paris fashion shows, creating huge runways through their stores that seated thousands of guests. Invitations were highly prized, and to be seen at the gala shows was the preserve of the famous or the big spender. The unfashionable majority were permitted their turn afterwards, and hundreds of thousands attended. Designers embraced the cult of celebrity: by 1920 the Parisian shows of designers like Coco Chanel, Vionnet and Schiaparelli were filled with socialites and royalty.

In those early years there were some attempts at discretion, especially with royal patrons in attendance, and it was almost a hundred years after the birth of the fashion show before designers allowed photographers inside. By the 1950s, however, interest in celebrities was growing fast. On the streets of Rome the new paparazzi, armed with SLRs and Vespas, targeted cinema stars like Sophia Loren, Brigitte Bardot and Audrey Hepburn. From the 1960s onwards, stars from music and film flocked to the fashion shows, the exposure working perfectly for star and designer alike.

Credit

In the early days of the artisan seller, and in the world of the small local retailer, service had been an undiscussed but ever-present part of the offer. All business was done on a personal basis, with sellers and customers enjoying relationships that were nurtured over long periods. The retailer knew their customer and tailored the products they sold, the terms of credit, ad-hoc discounts (a few free sweets, an extra apple, a bone for the dog) and other small but welcome perks that were entirely individual. But as the corporations took over these relationships disappeared. Prices and terms became standardised, there was no haggling or barter, and staff turnover meant relationships were brief if they existed at all. But in the corporate retail world, hungry to find new ways to sell more, service became a new lever to pull. All the things that the small retailer had always taken care of – free, no-quibble returns, home delivery (think butchers' bikes), credit – were packaged up as 'service' in the new retail world. Reliable and free home delivery became the norm, with nearly three-quarters of stores offering it by 1913, one offering free delivery to anywhere in the world on any item bought over $5. They offered generous returns policies, which was just as well because in the world of mass-produced goods many were substandard. But in a world where they needed everyone to buy, the biggest thing they could do was offer every customer credit, no matter what their financial situation. In America, not being able to afford something need no longer prevent you from buying it.

In previous eras, Christian Americans had regarded money-lenders with contempt for exploiting the poor, and lending for profit had been an unspeakable act. But now that money-lending oiled the wheels of commerce, moral objections quickly fell away. Small loan businesses began to appear, and by the turn of the century at least two chains had over a hundred offices nationwide. Banks didn't lend money for consumer spending, so stores did it themselves. Most already offered their wealthiest clients charge accounts, but soon stores were offering such privileges to less wealthy shoppers. 'Temptations have been flung broadcast to everyone,' wrote one contemporary observer. 'Charge it,' wrote one credit man, 'is the slogan of the great American consumer.' An ability to pay was no longer either an economic or a moral barrier. Don't worry whether the consumer can repay, just get them to want it. As Wanamaker said, 'Where desire is earnest, means can always be found.' Charge account customers bought more impulsively and spent more, why wouldn't you? Customers were offered inducements to nominate friends, and accounts meant mailing lists, which meant stores could market to you directly.

Retailers began to tailor instalment plans to their less wealthy customers in poor southern Black and northern immigrant communities. Multilingual pedlars sold everything through instalments, usually with a hefty down payment that would cover the cost of the goods. Leon Trotsky, living in New York at the time, furnished his apartment in the Bronx on instalment. Whilst some of these sellers were liked in their communities, many preyed on the poor. Dorothy Day described such plans as 'a plague on the poor ... that dishonesty by which the poor are robbed of their earnings'. Stores committed customers to fun-sound-ing 'instalment clubs'. And what good was endless credit if the stores were closed for more than half the day? As early as 1900, stores built switchboards staffed by hundreds of telephone operators who were available to take customers' orders twenty-four hours a day. Stores built creches, playgrounds and tearooms, ran free concerts – anything to keep people coming to the stores and make sure they stayed there for longer. Service gave their relentless drive for profit a smiley moral face.

The extent of easy credit was reflected in the rising number of cases of bad debt, and it wasn't just the poorest who were living beyond their means. Americans today have on average three or four credit cards, whilst only one in four French or Germans have any at all, and Americans carry more consumer debt than all the other peoples in the world combined.

Cult of the New

In a world where meaningful work was being removed from millions, taking with it much of the fulfilment in their lives, consumption stepped in to fill the void. People found what theologian Joseph Haroutunian called 'being' through 'having', the idea that men and women might become fulfilled human beings not through spiritual good but through the acquisition of goods. Historian William Leach wrote, 'The cardinal features of this culture were acquisition and consumption as the means of achieving happiness; the cult of the new; and money value as the predominant measure of all value in society.'

Critics reported an impoverishment of life in industrial communities. Edmund Wilson wrote: 'Those who receive dividends care little or nothing about those whose labour makes dividends possible. The capitalist system makes it very much easier for people not to realise what they're doing, nor to know about the danger and hardship, the despair and humiliation, that their way of life implies for others.' By the early twentieth century, people were less and less aware of how things were made and who made them. To acknowledge any suffering caused by this consumption would be to arouse one's own guilt and to cause one distress. Consumerism became a whole new way of life in the early twentieth century and Americans devoted themselves to the idea that luxury and comfort were the essential elements of a good life. But consumerism also had some fierce opponents, including journalist Samuel Strauss. His essay, 'Things Are in the Saddle', published in *The Atlantic* in 1924, was a meditation on materialism in which he described the excessive emphasis on consumerism in the 1920s as an 'empire of things', suggesting that the American nation had been overwhelmed by the ethics of 'consumptionism', which he defined as 'the science of compelling men to use more and more things'. In another essay, entitled 'Epicurus and America', he argued that consumerism was a philosophy that committed human beings to endlessly growing production, 'more this year than last year, more next year than this', that the inescapable and manipulative presence of business in our lives compelled us to buy what was not needed: 'American citizens' first importance is no longer that of citizen, but that of consumer ... No more damnable philosophy was ever offered mankind.'

By 1929, a combination of reckless lenders, consumers with no understanding or fear of the consequences, and ever more successful advertising and selling techniques drove consumer credit in the US to a whopping $7 billion, a value greater than twice its GDP. But this first great wave of consumer credit came to a sudden and catastrophic end the same year when economic stagnation led to panic on Wall Street. On 24 October, Black Thursday, the US stock market collapsed, kicking off the longest, deepest and most widespread economic depression of the twentieth century.

When the crash hit some welcomed it, hoping it might break the grip of capitalism and consumption on our society. Edmund Wilson wrote, 'One couldn't help being exhilarated at the sudden unexpected collapse of that stupid gigantic fraud.' The Great Depression brought a temporary cessation to the relentless growth, and some began to question whether such increase in consumption was really such a good idea. The industrialists of the early twentieth century never considered that the world might have limits. But some, including American sociologist Lewis Mumford, urged the rejection of the myth of infinite growth and an acceptance of the idea that the world's resources had limits. Many called for a pause to allow the restoration of more human values within society, the values of family, community, art and culture, and of pleasure in work. According to Joseph Haroutunian, 'good is not in goods, the good is in justice, mercy and peace, it is in consistency and integrity, in living according to truth and right. It is in men and not in things.' There were growing concerns about the social and economic deprivation being wrought on those people who made the ever-growing volume of ever cheaper goods. As Wesley Mitchell wrote, 'business must be held accountable for the miseries and chaos that strike the economy laying waste our days'.

From 1860 to 1920 the US economy had gone through an extraordinary expansion, with output growing twelve times whilst the population grew just three. Ordinary people's working conditions had improved, they were paid more and worked fewer hours than before. Philosopher and economist John Stuart Mill had described how a steady-state economy, capable of meeting the basic needs of all, was absolutely possible, and that such a state was likely to be an improvement on 'the trampling, crushing, elbowing and treading on each other's heels ... the disagreeable symptoms of one of the phases of industrial progress'. It was suggested that it would be feasible to reduce hours of work further and release workers for the spiritual and pleasurable activities of free time with families and communities, and creative or educational pursuits.

In the evolution of societies there is often a point where a conflict arises between the short-term interest of the ruling elite and the long-term interest of society as a whole. A continuation of growth in the economy was good for those whose capital was invested in its apparatus. And on the flip side it was not clear that there was any great threat to the general population, and certainly no thought was given to the impact on the planet – which at this stage, if it was considered at all, was considered boundless. The owners of business saw no incentive to reduce the speed of their expansion. At this crossroads, where US citizens could have chosen a stable, more balanced, more humane society, instead they chose to continue their push for growth.

Businesses chose to believe that success was simply a matter of 'educating' consumers in the ways of acquisition. Whatever was sufficient one year must be insufficient the next. President Hoover's 1929 Committee on Recent Economic Changes reported with delight on the American people's 'almost insatiable appetite for goods and services'. They wrote that there would be 'a boundless field before us ... new wants that make way endlessly for newer wants, as fast as they are satisfied'. Historian Frederick Allen wrote, 'Business had learned as never before the importance of the ultimate consumer'; he must be 'persuaded to buy and buy lavishly' or the whole house of cards would come crashing down. Those involved with the drive to increase want were plain in their speaking. Edward Bernays, the leading figure in public relations, wrote in his 1928 book *Propaganda*, 'Mass production is profitable only if its rhythm can be maintained – that is if it can continue to sell its product in steady or increasing quantity.' Charles Kettering, a director at General Motors, authored an article called 'Keep the Consumer Dissatisfied', in which he wrote that 'there is no place anyone can sit and rest in an industrial situation. It is a question of change, change all the time – and it is always going to be that way because the world only goes along one road, the road of progress.' The trick they pulled was to equate growing consumption with progress. No consumer must be allowed to feel happy with their lot, for in happiness and satisfaction lies the end to consumption.

It was at this time that Joseph Schumpeter developed his theory of capitalism as 'creative destruction'. Schumpeter, an Austrian political economist and ardent pro-capitalist, served as his country's finance minister before moving to America and taking up a professorship at Harvard where he remained until the end of his career. His theory of capitalism was one of continuous renewal, an endless process by which new technologies and products, new methods of production and new forms of distribution, such as mail order – or more recently e-commerce – make old ones obsolete, forcing businesses to adapt or die. Schumpeter saw endless innovation as fundamental to the success of the economy: 'Capitalism, then, is by nature a form or method of economic change and not only never is, but never can be stationary.' This ever-moving desire to chuck out the 'old' and replace it with the new was considered 'progress', a means to perpetuate consumption. The idea that a person could have enough must be discounted.

The Creative Revolution in Advertising and PR

The advertising revolution of the early 1900s, the artful posters and magazine images, the animated billboard and neon signs, had become passé and by the 1950s had been replaced by highly scientific advertising messages, mostly describing the effectiveness or usefulness of the product, carefully scripted, rigorously tested, and then relentlessly driven home via print and radio. It was of course highly effective. Different lines of argument, some truthful, would be tested on consumers until the most promising weak spot had been identified. This would then be broadcast mercilessly, sometimes for years – decades even – until the message was firmly driven home. Responses were tested, sales were tracked, coupons counted. 'Originality,' said Rosser Reeves, the inventor of the USP, the unique selling proposition, 'is the most dangerous word in all of advertising.'

But then along came a whole new generation of creative advertisers, led by the legendary Bill Bernbach and his mavericks at Doyle Dane Bernbach. Bernbach had only one rule and that was that every advert had to contain a fresh idea. Originality was everything. Their ads had wit, personality and style. In 1959 they created a series of adverts for the VW Beetle, including 'Think Small' and 'Lemon', which many, including their great rival David Ogilvie, consider to be the best of all time. Bernbach kicked off a creative revolution in advertising, which according to *Ad Age* gave 'permission to surprise, to defy and to engage the consumer'. 'Let us prove to the world,' wrote Bernbach, 'that good taste, good art, good writing can be good selling.' And good selling it was. They turned their back on the dry, plainly manipulative advertising of the 1940s and 50s, but this was no less of a manipulation – it just had a human face and a dose of wit, and was no less effective for it.

The advent of television put 'a screen in every home', a marketeer's dream, and created another great leap forward in the effectiveness of advertising, allowing for greater creative freedom and more complex storytelling. The best creative minds, and some of the world's great directors (Ridley Scott shot the iconic Hovis 'boy on a bike' advert), conspired to make us believe that everything from cars to cigars to sliced bread was going to make our lives better. They sold us more of everything, and made us smile and feel good while we did it. Happiness, as they said, is a cigar called Hamlet. The great advertising agencies of the second half of the twentieth century were phenomenally successful at keeping every stratum of society in a consuming frenzy.

If by some miracle they were able to resist the allure of advertising, consumers in the late twentieth century also had to contend with the perfidious public relations industry, a world of whisperers, quietly and carefully managing and manipulating consumers' opinions on everything from toothpaste to politicians. Noam Chomsky deemed PR 'some of the most powerful and influential institutions of the contemporary industrial state'. PR was not new to the 1950s, but its influence increased as the century progressed. Edward Bernays had described the role of the PR professional in the 1920s as guiding society imperceptibly in its choices, as benign manipulators: 'The conscious and intelligent manipulation of the organized habits and opinions of the masses is an important element in democratic society,' he wrote. In Bernays' mind the general public could not be trusted to think for themselves, particularly when that came to buying new things. 'Only through the active energy of the intelligent few can the public at large become aware of and act upon new ideas.' The 'intelligent few' of the PR industry were hugely successful in helping giant corporations to sell their products to the public at large, often without that public feeling they had been sold to. And not just products, political ideas were sold too. 'Democracy is administered by the intelligent minority who know how to regiment and guide the masses.'

Paying opinion formers to manipulate our choices is now a century-old selling technique. In the 1950s the PR industry used trusted individuals, often doctors, to convince us that everything from fatty foods to alcohol was good for us. Long after health concerns about cigarettes had been broadly publicised within the scientific community, manufacturers used doctors in cigarette adverts to convince the public of their product's safety. Lucky Strike ran an image of a doctor alongside the line '20,679 physicians say "Luckies are less irritating"', while Camel went with another grinning physician and the line 'More doctors smoke Camels than any other cigarette'.

Warnings

Whilst most observers saw nothing but upside in the era of super-charged consumption, some warnings began to be heard. Philosopher Herbert Marcuse was critical of the way in which, in striving for the satisfaction of ever greater wants, we were making ourselves ever more dependent on the exploitative apparatus of consumption. We worked to acquire, and the more we acquired the more we wanted and so the more we became enslaved. He saw a need for government to act, to rid us of our addiction and to reposition our collective values away from materialism. He also noted the need for 'a restoration of nature after the horrors of capitalist industrialisation have been done away with'. In 1957, American journalist and social critic Vance Packard wrote a book entitled *The Hidden Persuaders* in which he exposed what he saw as the increasingly malignant force of the advertising and PR industry. Alarmed by the sophisticated tools used to persuade people to keep buying, he wrote, 'Many of us are being influenced and manipulated, far more than we realize,' like 'the chilling world of George Orwell and his Big Brother'. Another dissenting voice was that of John Kenneth Galbraith. Galbraith had worked for Roosevelt on the New Deal and later ran the wartime Office of Price Administration, which controlled the rationing and price of many scarce goods during the Second World War. He was a staunch advocate for greater regulation of business and for a larger public sector. In 1958 Galbraith wrote *The Affluent Society*, still described by many economists as the greatest ever insight into contemporary capitalism. Galbraith pointed out that classical capitalism, as described by Adam Smith et al., did not make sense in a world where most of what we bought was based on want, rather than need. He was against the use of GDP as a means of measuring the success of a national economy, pointing out that it was a poor measure of social and personal wellbeing, and he strongly criticised the industry of

'Want Creation' and the cult of consumption. He railed against deliberate wastefulness, and what he believed was the pernicious 'dependence effect' being deliberately created among consumers. He also sounded an early warning against the danger of depleting 'the materials which nature has stocked in the earth's crust and which have been drawn upon more heavily in this century than in all previous time together'.

Much of what Galbraith wrote over sixty-five years ago is as relevant, arguably more so, today than it was then. In the 1960s, alongside the general cautions there emerged more specific warnings detailing the harm that unchecked industrial growth was causing the natural environment. In 1972 the starkest warning of all was published. A group of like-minded global scientists got together under the banner of The Club of Rome and, taking advantage of huge advances in dynamic systems modelling and the enormous computing power at MIT in Boston, modelled the dynamic and deeply interrelated effects of exponentially growing population, food production, industrial output, non-renewable natural resource depletion, and pollution and waste. Their findings, published in a short book called *The Limits to Growth*, were simply stated, easy to understand and extraordinarily bleak. It quickly became a bestseller and a global phenomenon. Whilst many had warned of the potential dangers, no one before had modelled what would happen if the growth in the human system were to be left unchecked. If not artificially restricted, the authors stated, then the growth of the human population, its need for food and its associated industrial activities would lead to the catastrophic exhaustion of one or more of the earth's vital capabilities to support us within a hundred years. The global system would collapse suddenly and uncontrollably.

The following year, another groundbreaking book with far-reaching, radical views on the future of society and the planet was published.

Following a similar train of thought, and echoing and amplifying some of the ideas put forward in *The Limits to Growth*, *Small is Beautiful: A study of economics as if people mattered* by Fritz Schumacher, a German-born British philosopher, became another cautionary bestseller. Extensively discussed among left-leaning and ecologically minded folk in the mid-1970s, it is an extraordinary book, prescient and precise. Schumacher tackled many of the issues currently taxing contemporary academics struggling with the negative outcomes for society and the planet of the unchecked growth in consumption. It was a call to action, but also a practical plan, offering solutions as well as posing questions. 'Our most important task,' wrote Schumacher, 'is to get off our present collision course. Who is to tackle such a task? I think every one of us.' 'To talk about the future,' he said, 'is useful only if it leads to action now.' Fifty years later, we are still waiting for action. Schumacher understood that for many people in the 1970s life had never been so good, so asking them to make radical change was a big ask. But he saw then that the writing was on the wall and called on us to be brave. We were not.

Schumacher's central thesis, written at a time when the worship of what he called giantism among our business and political leaders was rampant, was that bigger was not always preferable, and that in many aspects of the economy small or smaller was better, or best. He asked why, when we had all that we could ever want, we were more isolated, anxious and depressed than ever before. He advocated for a return to more human values: family, health, connection with meaningful work. He argued that greed and envy, deliberately inflamed to make us buy more, caused us to lose sight of what really matters in life. 'A man driven by greed or envy loses the power of seeing things as they really are, of seeing things in their roundedness and wholeness, and his very successes become failures.' He decried our loss of connection with nature, arguing that industrialisation makes it 'impossible to keep man in real touch with living nature; in fact, it supports all the most dangerous modern tendencies of violence, alienation, and environmental destruction'. He asked the very simple question, is GDP growth good or bad, and for whom? In short, are we too busy worrying about growing to enjoy actually living?

Schumacher suggested that 'work' meant far more than just money. In a healthy society, work also needed to offer security, fulfilment, status, solidarity and conviviality, something that was overlooked by politicians. He demanded access to good work for all who are capable of it. He suggested that to achieve these aims we must all be open to the idea of evolving an entirely new lifestyle, with new methods of production and new patterns of consumption, a lifestyle designed for permanence. Permanence was a central idea: any new system must be designed such that it might work in a way which had positive outcomes for all in perpetuity. He pointed out the huge flaw in the argument that other countries should follow the lead of the industrialised economies. Schumacher calculated that citizens of the US, making up just 5.6 per cent of the world population, used 40 per cent of the world's primary resources. Taking this model to the rest of the world clearly doesn't add up. Schumacher suggested areas where radical new thinking was required. In agriculture and horticulture we needed to adopt and perfect farming methods which worked in harmony with nature and improved soil fertility, what today we call regenerative agriculture. In industry we needed to evolve what he called 'small scale technology, non-violent technology, technology with a human face'; methods and systems of production that allowed people to enjoy themselves whilst working, instead of working solely for money to spend trying to enjoy themselves away from work.

Schumacher was alarmed by the acceleration of our depletion of natural resources. He warned that automation and mobile businesses were free to engage labour wherever on the planet it was cheapest, creating a huge threat to work in developed nations like the UK and the US. Like Galbraith, he warned that using GDP or GNP as a measure of success ignored the social and environmental consequences of such success: 'Hence the continuing absurdity of human societies pinning all their hopes on achieving exponential economic growth, of measuring success solely in terms of increased GNP, and of ignoring the social and environmental externalities of contemporary consumerism.' His warnings continued with the assertion written in 1973 that slavish adherence to the economic growth dogma would lead to 'poverty, frustration, alienation, despair, breakdown, crime, escapism, stress, congestion, ugliness, and spiritual death'.

Fifty years later our industrial activity has doubled and doubled again. Do we feel four times better off? Today a majority of us – certainly those I talk to in Blackburn, Bolton, New Tredegar, and the many other post-industrial towns where I work – share every bit of Schumacher's frustration and despair. Why have we worked so hard, for so long, only to see crumbling schools, record NHS waiting lists, millions living in poverty? Twenty-five per cent of all working-age Britons do not have work, that's 9 million people between the ages of sixteen and sixty-four, a number that has risen half a million in the last three years alone. Might it not be time to do as Schumacher suggested and think anew about the priorities of our economy? Some of the contemporary academics I meet, many connected with that oxymoron sustainable fashion, are once again thinking along Schumacher's lines. Kate Fletcher and Mathilda Thiam and their Earth Logic research principle suggest the time has come for a complete paradigmatic shift away from profit and growth at all costs to an earth first view, one in which human happiness and wellbeing is a primary concern. Dilys Williams, of the Centre for Sustainable Fashion at the University of the Arts London, focuses much of her research beyond the idea that technology will solve our problems, as so many in sustainable fashion hope, instead starting with the premise that the whole fashion system

61

(a proxy for any other overconsumption-driven industry you choose) is no longer tenable, and that we need to fundamentally rethink what it means for individuals and business organisations to exist within society, and for society to exist within the natural environment. Many contemporary academics point out how much we might learn from nature, like knowing when to stop. As Schumacher wrote, 'Greater even than the mystery of natural growth is the mystery of the natural cessation of growth.' Nature knows how to self-regulate, it balances, adjusts and repairs.

Politicians on all sides talk about growth, by which they mean growth in GDP, so much and with such total conviction in its righteousness that we never think to ask if it might not be the wrong thing to be aiming for. If what we care about most is our happiness, then maybe that's what we should try to grow? Maybe let's measure that instead. Or is what's really important to us being able to easily meet our cost of living? Measure that. One of the first things you learn when running a business is to set the objectives you want and then measure them. What do we want the economy to do for us? Make us healthy, happy and fulfilled in our work? Well, measure that, report on it, and then people will aim to make it happen. Jason Hickel, author of *Less is More*, claims we are in a crisis caused by capitalism. He takes pains to point out that capitalism is *not* trade, markets or business; these things have been around for thousands of years and are all fine. What Hickel says makes *capitalism*, invented five hundred years ago, different 'is that it is organised around, and dependent, on perpetual growth'. Ever-increasing extraction, production and consumption. 'If it doesn't grow it collapses.' That we believe GDP growth is good for us, Hickel argues, is an ideological coup and he advocates for the turning off or scaling down of the unnecessary parts of the material economy. Less activity, less energy required, making it easier to switch to renewables, echoing what was written in *The Limits to Growth*. And do all of this whilst

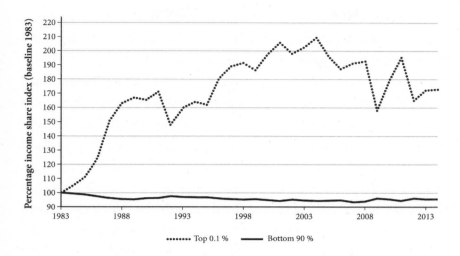

Figure 1

acting to increase human wellbeing. The USA, the richest country in the world, has a GDP per capita of $60,000. Costa Rica's GDP is 80 per cent lower but people there have a greater life expectancy, and higher happiness and wellbeing indicators. They have achieved this by focusing their society and economy on fulfilling human needs.

In 2017 Pope Francis weighed into the debate: 'Labour is not merely a factor in production that, as such, has to adapt to the needs of the production process to increase its efficiency. On the contrary, it is the production process that must be organized in such a way as to enable the human growth of people and harmony between time for family and working life.' Pope Francis says that industry needs to work for us, not the other way round. It needs to provide for us and increase our wellbeing in return for taking our labour. Economist Joseph Stiglitz, much revered by Pope Francis, studies inequality. He has charted the changes in income of different groups in several advanced economies. Since 1972, in both the UK and the US, the richest 1 per cent have got over four times richer, whereas for the great majority of the population, 90 per cent of us in fact, our real wage (what our wage is worth after you factor in how much the stuff we need to pay for has gone up) is the same as it was fifty years ago (see Figure 1).

Stiglitz demonstrates with absolute clarity that 'trickle-down economics', the idea that by making the rich richer the money will find its way down, is an absolute fallacy. If as a country we wish to make the 90 per cent better off, do not attempt to do it by making the 1 per cent richer, do it by giving more money directly to the 90 per cent; increase their wages, reduce their taxes, provide them with better services at lower prices. Let the 1 per cent take their chances with trickle-up.

Online Selling

For a quarter of a century little altered in the way goods were sold to us; there were no great changes to the way in which businesses sought to make us want things. As things got a little cheaper, and we got a little richer, we bought a little more. We shopped in physical shops or through catalogues, we were sold things over the telephone, people came to our houses to try and sell us double-glazed windows. We watched adverts on television, many of which made us laugh. They maybe made us buy a different beer or toothpaste, but they didn't make us buy more of it. Adverts in magazines became more obscure, and radio advertisements changed not one bit.

But then in the 1980s a new technology came along which would, with the help of social media, underpin the latest great acceleration in our consumption. It began, benignly, as an attempt to allow elderly people easier access to basic necessities like breakfast cereal, and eventually facilitated levels of consumption that would, if maintained, literally destroy the planet.

In May 1984 Jane Snowball, a 72-year-old grandmother from Gateshead, sat in an armchair, picked up a special remote control and used it to order cornflakes, eggs and a tub of St Ivel Gold from her local supermarket in what was the world's first online shop.

By the mid-80s, everyone in the UK was familiar with the Ceefax service (so called because you could 'see facts'), the world's first interactive TV system, developed by BBC engineers and launched in 1974. An engineer called Michael Aldrich took the technology used by Ceefax and, using the domestic phone line, connected the TV to three local retailers' computers which were set up to process sales, creating a real-time, multi-user transaction processing system he called Videotex. Videotex was already being used by businesses, but it was a Gateshead council community initiative to help the elderly to shop from home that saw it become the world's first online shopping system. With Videotex connected you could order from three shops: Greggs, Tesco or 'the chemist'. The stores would then process the order, pack it, and a nice man in a van would deliver to the customer's door.

With the exception of buying the odd flight or holiday, teletext shopping didn't really take off, and in the mid-90s if you wanted to shop from the comfort of our own home, you still did it through a catalogue. Tim Berners-Lee had invented the World Wide Web in 1989, but by 1995 fewer than 10 million people worldwide had access to the internet and less than 2 per cent of UK households had a computer. Commercial use of the internet had been prohibited until 1995 (we can choose to restrict new technology if we want to), but in February of that year, US network provider Compuserve linked up with another group of UK retailers including WH Smith, Our Price, PC World, Dixons, Tesco again, and Interflora to launch a service called 'Shopping Centre'. When it went live, the first order was for a copy of *A Suitable Boy* by Vikram Seth which someone bought from WH Smith. Back in 1984 Jane Snowball spent £1.27 on her first order of groceries. Today, almost 30 per cent of purchases here in the UK are done online, amounting to over £80 billion annually, with 60 per cent of that being done through our phones. There's nothing preventing us from shopping everything, anywhere and at any time.

Fast Fashion

Fashion was always about making us buy things we didn't need, about creating a regular cycle of endless new wants to keep the wheels of consumption turning. It was always a luxury. For its first hundred or so years fashion was a fairly benign presence, offering new designs just two or three times a year. But in increasingly rapid steps fashion went from being something small and special, the rarefied world of Saint Laurent, Chanel and Dior, to a gigantic industry, based on ever-growing consumption of harmful, disposable products, made in the cheapest way possible with very little regard to originality or creativity. What we used to think of as the fashion world, the world of designer fashion, sits at the intersection between art and the highest standards of craftsmanship. Garments were originally conceived and painstakingly developed before being hand-made in small quantities from natural materials of exceptional quality – pure wool, pure cotton, pure silk, handmade lace, silk trims, natural horn buttons (made from discarded horn) and naturally tanned leather. It consumed very little, and by and large its practices were ethical. And the clothes sold under its coveted labels were cherished, and often resold or passed on.

Today the designer fashion industry supports an ecosystem of creatives, including clothing designers, textile designers, stylists, photographers, and a network of skilled craftspeople and others including farmers, wool merchants, spinners, weavers, dyers, finishers, printers, embroiderers, knit designers, knitters, linkers, darners, milliners, pattern cutters, seamstresses and tailors. Designer fashion was always about making us buy new things, but at its small scale, it wasn't terrible for the planet, and with the application of new technology in renewable materials it could be reshaped to be fully circular, reducing its carbon emissions to zero. We can repurpose and recycle old materials to make new clothes, as many young designers are doing now. All of this is eminently achievable. Fashion brings much joy to many people, and supports many great jobs. We also happen to be very good at it in the UK.

Until the 1960s the less wealthy would make facsimiles of designer clothes themselves, or commission a local dressmaker or tailor to do so, using high-quality materials sourced from a wide network of haberdashers, themselves stocked with locally made fabrics and trims. But by the end of the decade a new fashion world had begun to emerge, a cheaper, more democratic, more dynamic industry, aimed at younger people, powered by offshore production and new cheap, vibrant synthetic fibres like nylon, polyester and acrylic. This new fashion industry produced low-cost facsimiles of the key trends seen on the designer fashion catwalks and sold them in an environment that encouraged the young to shop for fun. To begin with this new fashion followed in lockstep with its grander, more storied cousin, producing new collections just twice a year, in line with the prevailing retail calendar, but in the early 2000s this began to change. New online-only fashion brands were not tied to the discipline of remerchandising physical stores, their stores were virtual, they could be remerchandised at will and were infinitely expandable. Why should they wait six months to launch a new product when they could launch it whenever it arrived – monthly, weekly, daily? Originally the phrase 'fast fashion' was coined for the speed with which the bigger brands could get a product to market, how quickly they could see a garment on a catwalk or worn by a celebrity, and turn a copy round and have it on sale. It was the *New York Times* that first coined the phrase, in 1989, journalist Anne-Marie Schiro referencing Spanish fast fashion company Zara's boast that it took them a mere fifteen days from first having an idea to getting it into their stores. Now the time taken to get to shops is less relevant, it's the churn which is fast. In 2022 *The Business of Fashion* reported on the number of new styles released by four leading fast fashion brands, and the numbers were staggering. The Chinese fast fashion brand Shein was releasing close to 4,000 new styles every single day. For two decades we thought H&M, Zara and Primark were bad, then ASOS, and later Boohoo, made them all look a little tired, and then Shein came along and made them all look geriatric. They're not. Zara, H&M and others offer thousands of new styles – 2,000 every month. Whatever they might try to claim about the sustainability of their product, that level of newness is designed to do only one thing, and that's to get you to want and to buy more.

What became known as fast fashion began quietly, and was actually not that much faster than anyone else. H&M's forerunner Hennes & Mauritz has been going since the late 1940s, Topshop was founded in 1964, Primark in 1969, and Zara, a relative newcomer, started out in 1975. Topshop began selling clothes by young British designer brands like Mary Quant and Sterling Cooper to teens. Having lost its way in the 1980s it was spectacularly revived in the 90s with a mix of cool, well-designed and affordable clothes. Its 90,000-square-foot Oxford Street flagship, with fast-changing styles, in-house stylists, and DJs became a destination for cool young Londoners. They put on catwalk shows at London Fashion Week and supported the capital's emerging fashion designers, and were an early online player, launching their first online store in 1999. Zara's foundations were a little different: they began by selling low-priced knock-offs of popular designer fashions, spotting trends and quickly copying them. They often beat the original designer products to the stores, making products seem old when the designers released them. They deny copying, and are clever enough to change things just enough, but a quick scroll through Diet Prada, the Instagram-based intellectual property police of the fashion world, reveals countless clear examples. Later Zara began collaborating with big name designers, quite a few of whom were happy to take their money. Zara have been hugely successful. In 2012 founder Amancio Ortega Gaona was the world's third richest man. By 2012 they were making over 840 million pieces of clothing a year, making them the world's biggest fashion retailer, and in 2022 their worldwide sales topped €23 billion.

Hennes & Mauritz began life in Sweden as an ordinary clothes shop, but in 1974 it changed its name, opened in London and began going after the lucrative teen market. It got into mail order in the 1980s by buying a Swedish catalogue company, and was an early e-commerce adopter, launching online in 1998. In 2023 H&M group turned over $22 billion, but it does feel that the wheels are coming off the H&M wagon. Accused repeatedly of greenwashing and poor ethics, they're losing market share and their value is falling.

Another fast fashion brand tarnished by poor ethics is Primark. Founded in 1969 in Ireland as Penneys, it arrived in England in 1974, opening in Derby under its new name. Primark didn't really register on the fast fashion radar until 2005 when they bought Littlewoods, instantly giving them 119 UK stores and making them one of the UK's biggest retailers. Amazingly Primark didn't bother with online sales until the Covid pandemic, nor really with marketing; their model was low cost, no frills. They offered kids' and baby clothes as well as clothing for adults, but their main selling point was that it was all very cheap. Their mostly 100 per cent plastic clothes are made in countries with low wages and poor labour laws. In 2013 a factory in a building in Bangladesh called Rana Plaza collapsed, killing more than 1,100 garment workers who had been packed into the apparently crumbling building making clothes for Primark and several others. It was a tragedy that was waiting to happen somewhere in an industry hellbent on reducing cost by all and any means. Primark paid $9 million in compensation to workers' families. Today they sell over £9 billion worth of clothing through over 430 stores.

But in 2000 a new breed of fast fashion brands appeared which had none of the physical-world baggage of Topshop, Zara and H&M. ASOS was launched as a pure online retailer, originally selling products seen on telly like Jamie Oliver mortars and pestles, under the name 'As Seen On Screen'. With their online-only model they had none of the traditional retail costs of brands like Topshop and H&M – no shop rents, business rates or store staff costs. This huge cost advantage meant that they could spend much more on marketing and still sell for less than the bricks-and-mortar fast fashion brands. By 2018, just eighteen years after its foundation, ASOS was selling $2.4 billion worth of clothing to 18 million customers in 238 countries, and at £9 billion was valued at more than Marks & Spencer.

Where ASOS led others soon followed, but the tone was changing. These weren't brands that truly cared about fashion. They didn't employ designers to make sophisticated fakes of designer clothes; the clothes were somewhat secondary to the lifestyle they promoted, one of vanity and sexualisation, treading a thin line around social irresponsibility, gender stereotyping and objectification. If you had no scruples it was easy to set up an online fast fashion brand. You needed a website, some product from a factory somewhere, a few models, a camera and a bunch of influencers. Boohoo, Pretty Little Things, Nasty Gal, Missguided and various other lookalike ultra-fast fashion brands created a whole new paradigm. Waves of reality TV stars and other influencers were paid eye-watering sums to promote their wares. Influencers, mostly young women, streamed their 'hauls', unpacking orders, trying on clothes and commenting on the experience, garnering millions of views. This is shopping as entertainment and addiction. You watch the show, you watch the counter, you pay a few quid, you get some stuff, you wear it once, you throw it away. The clothes are as disposable as the factories and the people that produce them. Boohoo, founded in 2006 by a team with experience in market trading and Chinese sourcing, sells dresses from £4, claiming they go from design to website in just forty-eight hours, using Leicester garment factories with terrible ethical standards, where workers are reported to be earning less than half the minimum wage. In less than fifteen years Boohoo's sales had grown to over £1.2 billion and the company was valued at £3.5 billion – more than ASOS, or even, amazingly, M&S.

_____

Fast fashion has changed the enjoyment we derive from shopping too. In the late nineteenth century, people took great pleasure in visiting grand and well-appointed stores, light and spacious, filled with beautiful sights and smells of all descriptions, staffed by smiling, friendly and knowledgeable staff who went out of their way to please us. We visited shops as part of our leisure, we would spend whole days shopping with our friends or family. We took time to try things out, to imagine how a thing might fit into our life. Did we need it? Was it good value? Did we really like it?

But today, with shops in our hands all day every day, we buy impulsively, with little or no consideration. Why would we, when the thing we're buying costs so little? In 1970 a dress would have cost about a day's income; today it's less than half an hour's. Many buy things out of habit, as a reflex, while some buy things just to pass the time. The more aggressive fast fashion retailers make their shopping sites and apps highly addictive, with anxiety-inducing countdowns, flash pop-ups, collectible bonuses and game-like incentives. And there is no time and no place where we cannot buy. We shop on the bus, or on our sofas, or in bed at home. If this form of shopping gives us any pleasure at all it is momentary at best.

If fast fashion was bad in the early 2000s it got a whole lot worse in 2015 when Shein was founded. Shein's founders realised that the design in fashion was largely meaningless; with new clothes costing less than half an hour's pay these were purchases made with no consideration or care. Their strategy is simple: show every possible thing that the AI tools can think of, spam the world with a tidal wave of this meaningless product, aggressively marketing via an army of influencers willing to take anyone's money, time-sensitive discounts, ticking countdowns to new drops. Create addiction, normalising almost unthinkable overconsumption. That's the secret.

In November 2023 Reuters reported that in the most recent year H&M had launched an incredible 23,000 new products in the US, whilst Zara launched 40,000. Shein launched 1.5 million. A million and a half new products in 365 days. It is a staggering statistic. They plan to drown every other fast fashion brand in a tidal wave of product. We use our phones on average 3 hours and 15 minutes a day; for every minute we're online, Shein launch twenty-one new products. That's one every three seconds. And it's cheap, unfathomably cheap. On their UK site in January 2024 there were three garments for sale at under £3, and 170 at under £4. Its website at one time had a '99p and under' section. The ethics are shocking. In 2022 a Channel 4 investigation found that workers supplying Shein were paid as little as 3p per garment. To make matters worse, Shein were, until very recently, shipping all of their millions of orders direct from China by air freight, not only giving them an even bigger carbon footprint, but also driving up the cost of freight for everything else we buy from China. Shein sold $23 billion worth of clothes in 2022 and overtook Amazon as the most downloaded app in the US. They have 65 million app users in Europe, and as of December 2023 Shein was the world's biggest fast fashion retailer with 18 per cent, nearly a fifth, of the global fast fashion market, bigger than H&M, Primark, ASOS, Boohoo and Forever 21 put together. Shein established a simple blueprint: make an unfathomable quantity of incredibly low-quality stuff, sell it cheaply, aggressively acquire customers, swamp the competition. In just seven years they've gone from being worth nothing to a valuation of $90 billion. But the problem with that kind of plan is that if they've got enough cash, anyone can make a lot of cheap crap and spend billions marketing it. Enter Temu.

In just six *months*, Temu, the latest of the Chinese online shopping mega-apps, has gone from nothing to nearly half a billion in sales. Temu is arguably the most pernicious driver of consumption ever created. It has no real strategy except to sell stuff cheap, and to gamify the shopping experience by offering big referral incentives to get new app users signed up. And it's working. In less than a year, thanks to its almost unbelievable marketing spend, it is already rapidly catching Shein's app market share. Over a third of its reviews on Trustpilot are the lowest they can be. Temu's quality, even compared to the brands that its customers normally shop from (Amazon, Shein) seems to have plumbed new depths, as summed up in one lovely review: 'even at such low prices this crap isn't worth it'. The Temu bots cheerfully respond to all of the thousands of negative reviews they receive, comments like 'So disappointed with quality' (how much quality were you expecting in a £4 tent?), 'fabric like plastic' (it *is* plastic), 'offers cheap rubbish' (actually, the price isn't cheap for how rubbish it is). Temu is spending close to $2 billion a year on digital advertising and promotion, close to four times its turnover. By both the ratio and the sheer scale it is an extraordinary number. But it is working. A report in June 2023 suggested that 30 per cent of all small packages coming into the US at that time were from Shein and Temu. Temu customers are told to 'shop like billionaires'. Form a queue, Bezos, Musk, Zuckerberg.

If your entire business model is built on churn, low prices, discounts and influencers, there will always be someone who is faster and cheaper than you are, and the influencers who sold your stuff yesterday will happily sell someone else's tomorrow. And if your story is every day something new, everything disposable, then that will apply to your brand just as much as to your product. There is no loyalty. Brands such as these are meaningless constructs. When I was young, fashions lasted for six months and brands lasted centuries. Topshop enjoyed a run which lasted forty-five years, then ASOS killed Topshop. It took Boohoo and Missguided ten years to kill ASOS. Shein killed Boohoo in six. These are fashion houses built on sand. How do the others respond? H&M claim that they still offer their customers 'the best combination of fashion, quality and sustainability, at the best price', but add that they are 'working to bring new collections to the market faster to better compete with … the likes of Shein'. In the face of unprecedented and almost unfathomable fastness their strategy is to try and go faster. Which is unlikely to improve quality, and certainly isn't sustainable.

This is where we are today. As of November 2023, ASOS' value had fallen from £9 billion to just £460 million and Boohoo's from £3.5 billion to £450 million, but we think a six-year-old company which sells the lowest-quality disposable plastic clothes is worth $90 billion. In 2023, 100 billion garments were made worldwide, most by workers paid virtually nothing, 70 per cent of them from plastic textiles made from oil. Thirty per cent of all clothes made are never sold, two-thirds of the clothes we own we never wear, and new clothes are now so cheap they're often thrown away rather than being washed and worn again. Because they're so cheap, it's cheaper to burn them than reprocess them and put them back on sale. The British Fashion Council reported that 23 million returned garments were sent to landfill or incinerated in the UK in 2022 alone. We buy clothes and all sorts of other things with little or no care or consideration. Our consumption is thoughtless and careless. We buy so much, we have so much, and yet we enjoy so little.

Want

In little more than a century we have gone from owning just a few cherished, purposeful objects that lasted a lifetime, the making of which supported satisfying and pleasant work for many, to possessing an overwhelming abundance of valueless, disposable stuff which brings us no more than fleeting enjoyment or satisfaction, and heaps harm on the people who make it and on the planet.

2

How I Used to Love Fashion

I have always loved clothes. And for a good amount of my grown up life I really loved fashion.

I don't know where this came from, but for as long as I can remember I have cared deeply about what I wore and how I wore it. There is a photograph of me on the morning of my first day of school, aged five, beaming in the immaculately put-together uniform of South Morningside Primary School; tie neatly knotted, and perfectly centred in the V of my woollen jumper, grey woollen shorts crisply pressed, woollen socks pulled all the way up, polished leather shoes. I was so keen to make the right impression that I'd given myself a far from successful haircut in the bathroom mirror with my mum's nail scissors.

As a child growing up in the 1970s to middle-class parents (my dad was an accountant, my mum worked as an administrator at the University of Edinburgh), the clothes I wore were a mix of some new and quite a lot of second-hand, or hand-me-downs. I remember lots and lots of jumpers in all manner of colours and patterns, faded and beautifully soft from years of wear. There is a picture of me, aged about five, with a mass of white-blond hair, standing in a field somewhere, probably on a Scottish island, wearing coloured corduroy shorts, yellow wellies and a hand knit. It perfectly encapsulates the joyful hodgepodge of clothes I wore as a kid.

My granny, known to all in the family as GB (my dad always referred to her as Granny Bags), did a bit of knitting. We were all, GB included, comfortable with her lack of skill in this department and enjoyed the fact that because she couldn't knit fingers we only ever wore mittens. But she never let it dampen her enthusiasm. She could manage a passable scarf and a half-decent woolly hat, and the mittens were okay as long as you didn't mind a slightly wonky thumb. The family collection of GB-knitted scarves and mitts are still worn (not always in pairs) for Edinburgh winter walks. They are much cherished because they are filled with her love and care, their slight wonkiness and odd colour choices making them all the more precious.

GB had three jobs in her seventies, one of which was working for a charity shop in Galashiels. One day a consignment of donated clothes came in which included a plum-coloured cotton sweatshirt, with quite an 80s shape, a full sleeve and body, gathered at the cuff and hem. She thought, quite rightly, that I'd like it, so she bought it for me. It was well-aged then, and that was over fifteen years ago. It is probably forty years or so by now, and I love it and wear it often. And every time I do, I think of her.

At school in the 1970s and 1980s we played sport in clothes made from natural fibres. Prep school team sports photos show a grinning me in faded cotton shorts (pretty much everyone else's were pristine navy blue), cotton rugby shirt and slightly shrunken woollen socks. When I was at school, professionals in some sports had started to make the switch to synthetics but rugby players, even at international level, still wore cotton jerseys and shorts. They got wet and heavy, and no one cared one iota. I had a pale blue C&A ski jumper with a rainbow four inches wide right across the chest that I loved. It was 100 per cent acrylic and ended up being eaten by the cat. And I had a selection of beautiful lambswool V-neck sweaters in bottle green, navy, camel, burgundy, grey, and probably other colours too.

The first great grown-up clothes I had were a pair of trousers bought for me by my godfather John as a birthday present. I think I must have been about fourteen, and John took me to the shops on Princes Street. I picked out a beautiful pair of tailored trousers, in a pale grey and charcoal herringbone tweed, pleated, with a deep turnup, very reminiscent of those worn by the magnificent Charles Ryder in the TV version of *Brideshead Revisited*, the costumes from which had a huge impact on my early sense of style. I wore them until, half a dozen years later, I had worn through the cloth.

I was wearing them on my first trip to London (the day I lost my virginity, aged sixteen, in a flat on the Gloucester Road). I can remember the entire outfit, which was a copy of one from the quarterly men's fashion section they'd have in *Elle* in the days before men's fashion magazines. This was 1988 and the smiling male model wore wide-legged pleated tweed trousers, a yellow shirt, a blue tie with white polka dots, a bright red waistcoat and a blue single-breasted jacket. My facsimile of this look had been assembled for a couple of quid through hours diligently scouring the second-hand and charity shops of Edinburgh. The jacket was found at Flip of Hollywood, a supermarket-sized second-hand shop on the bridges. The red waistcoat was from Armstrong's second-hand shop, still there and doing better than ever, and is still in my wardrobe at my mum's house (its significance she may not previously have been aware of). The yellow shirt, with its large 70s collar with rounded points, and the polka-dot tie came from my dad's wardrobe.

It was quite normal for me to tear out the pages of the men's sections of magazines and recreate the outfits from charity shops and the like. I remember a Panama hat I'd accessorised with a Liberty scarf tied around the band. My best friend at the time, Ali, would walk down the street ten paces behind me from the shame.

In the 1980s Edinburgh was an odd mix, style wise. You had the casuals who changed their brands like the rest of us changed our socks; you had middle-class kids dressed like middle-aged men, in their dad's brogues and worn Barbours; and then a tiny coterie of folk who loved fashion, and hung out, looking cool, at the City Café. Working during the summer in the café in Princes Street Gardens with a junior member of the Hibs casuals I got to recognise gear from the continental brands like Chevignon, Chipie, Stone Island, Gallini, Kappa. One of my sister's pals gave me a Sergio Tacchini shell suit, presumably nicked. The casuals in Edinburgh wore Lyle & Scott, Pringle, Aquascutum, Barbour, Burberry, Fred Perry, and whatever they could 'tax' from the tourists. Oddly, for a time, they went around in tweed deerstalkers from Aitken & Niven (where the middle-class kids got their school uniforms).

The small Edinburgh fashion crowd shopped at Corniche, a compact store on Jeffrey Street, just off the Royal Mile, that carried Issy Miyake, Michiko Koshino, Katherine Hamnett and Vivienne Westwood, at least a decade before anyone else in the city sold anything that would be considered fashion. I'd spend hours in there, lovingly examining the clothes, asking endless questions, occasionally trying something on. I couldn't afford Corniche but got lucky one year in the sale and bagged myself my first ever piece of actual fashion, a pair of high-waisted, pirate-style, wide-legged pinstriped Westwood trousers, which I wore right through university and beyond. Because I was tall and quite slim there were occasionally good bits left in my size at the tail end of the sales. I managed to add an Issey Miyake top and one of his famous crinkly jackets, and three pairs of Jean Paul Gaultier trousers. One of my JPG's was an intarsia jean covered with photographs of faces which my friend Dave would occasionally borrow for special nights out.

I went away to boarding school in Barnard Castle, near Newcastle, where I covered the walls of my room in pages torn from *Vogue* and

Elle. The dressers at school wore Farah and Spencers which were having a revival thanks to their adoption on the football terraces, the style of choice in the Northeast being pleated and carrot legged with flecks like a Donegal tweed. I couldn't afford Farahs so I'd taper the legs on my M&S trousers, hand sewing them in our boarding house room.

Giles Deacon, now a celebrated womenswear designer, was two years above me at school. I remember passing Giles on the playing fields in my first term and him giving me the nod and telling me he liked my shoes, heavy mid-tan brogues very like the Trickers I wear now. I'd spend hours during exeat weekends in the clothes shops on High Bridge Street in Newcastle. In the 1960s the street had been dubbed the Carnaby Street of the northeast. There were about half a dozen great little designer clothes stores cheek by jowl along this narrow curving side street, although now just one, Union, remains. They sold the French and Italian brands I'd grown to love during summers spent watching the European tourists parading around Edinburgh. I couldn't afford to buy the clothes, but I loved spending time talking to the staff about clobber.

I remember making a pilgrimage to the Paul Smith store on Floral Street in Covent Garden and buying a pair of socks – knee high, amazing quality, like the best British-made socks still are now – and these were my Friday or Saturday night socks for maybe a decade. Across the road was another fashion store where I bought a Jil Sander suit in the sale.

As a teenager I went through a spell of wearing my dad's clothes. By the age of fourteen I was about the same height and size as he was and so I'd raid the wardrobe for his suits, ties, shirts, collars and collar studs: my dad had beautiful cotton formal shirts, collarless, in plains and stripes, all perfectly pressed, starched and folded by the laundry, and kept in the wardrobe in dense, well-made cardboard boxes. I loved the ritual of dressing. His detachable collars lived in a leather collar box and needed to be attached in a precise order and with some dexterity, using the neat precision-engineered collar studs, themselves housed in their own little leather boxes. His suits were slim cut and modish, robustly constructed by tailors from Edinburgh and around such as Thomson, and crafted from distinctive, durable woollen cloths made just a few miles south of the capital in the historic mills of the Scottish Borders such as Reid & Taylor.

My dad died in 2020 but I still cherish and wear clothes of his. It feels special to wear something that I know he wore often. When I wear his old dinner suit, made (not for him) in 1934, I can imagine my dad as a young man. I remember seeing him wearing it, dressed to perfection, heading off to a dance (he was a brilliant dancer and had been a champion jiver). On occasion, I wear his ties, tied with the same four-in-hand knot that he preferred. Because the woollen linings and the silk itself have moulded themselves through years of use it is only possible to tie it one way, so the knot I tie today always sits in precisely the same spot as it did when he tied it. I can feel the presence of his fingers in the folds of the silk.

As a student on my Erasmus exchange year in Orléans in France I was only an hour from Paris, where I had a friend whose roommate was a photographer. He told me that it was easy to blag your way into the shows, so I came up during fashion week and we gave it a crack. We got into Claude Montana, and outside I passed Helena Christensen (I remember feeling somewhat spellbound). I managed, somehow, to get front-row at Issey Miyake (you could see me on the BBC's *The Clothes Show*, my elbow on the raised catwalk). And we got backstage at the Vivienne Westwood show at the Grand Hotel in Paris. I still have an invitation somewhere, picked up after the show, in which Naomi Campbell famously fell off her huge platform shoes. Front of house, I passed Madonna and Prince, and backstage I did my best to look like I was supposed to be there as Vivienne dressed Naomi, Linda Evangelista,

Christy Turlington and a host of other supermodels. I snapped a few pics on my Minolta instamatic which I still have in a box somewhere. I remember squeezing between Simon and Yasmin Le Bon and being surprised at how tall they both were. Sixteen years later it was Yasmin who annoucned my name when I won Menswear Designer of the Year at the British Fashion Awards, and it was after another Fashion Awards, the night she received a Lifetime Achievement award, shortly before her death, that I shared a cab to the after-party with Vivienne Westwood, Andreas and her crew. She was as brilliant and odd as I'd always hoped she'd be.

I moved to Liverpool in the mid-1990s and spent a large part of most Saturdays at Wade Smith. Robert Wade Smith toured Europe in a van in the 1980s loading it with rare trainers at a time when Liverpool FC were regularly playing across the continent. He rode the wave of the sportswear craze and built a thriving fashion business. By the mid-1990s Wade Smith was the only place in the city to carry the serious designers; Armani, Dolce & Gabbana (when it was good), Prada, and I remember with great excitement when they first began carrying Tom Ford-era Gucci. Most of my wages went into their tills and many of the things I bought then – simple beautiful knits, tailored trousers – I still have to this day. I remember spending three months searching for the perfect shoe for jeans, eventually settling on a pair of all-black lace-up leather Miu Mius with a sole very reminiscent of the current Balenciaga ugly trainers. I have no idea where they've gone.

I loved fashion; the beauty, the designers, the excitement of the shows, the images, the locations. It was all incredibly alluring. I read the monthly magazines, poring over every image. I read biographies of the designers – Christian Dior, Yves Saint Laurent, Paul Poiret – and spent large portions of my life in clothes shops, designer boutiques and second-hand and charity shops. The only aspect of fashion that I didn't consume lots of was the clothing itself. In 1970 the average person owned just twenty-five garments and spent 10 per cent of their income on them. Today we spend just over 3 per cent of what we earn on our clothes and the average Brit has 118 garments in their wardrobe – nearly five times as many, for a third as much money.

But that didn't matter. I don't think anyone in the 1970s or 1980s felt they were bereft of fashion. We didn't have a lot, but what we did buy we bought judiciously, and we wore things for years.

In the 1980s your choice was between designer fashion, sportswear or ordinary clothes. There was no Carnaby Street or Kings Road selling affordable youth fashion in Edinburgh or Newcastle. I can remember almost every piece of clothing I owned, most beautifully made from natural fabrics. I loved how they made me feel and I loved the craftsmanship in every hem, seam and finish. These were clothes which became more beautiful the more they were worn: the wear, and sometimes tear, creating subtle, sometimes startling, changes to the colour and texture of the cloth; sunshine and leaky pens and other mishaps giving them character, increasing their beauty and their value. Clothes have power. They form part of our memory of events in our lives. We become so intimately connected with good-quality clothes over the long years we wear them, and in the not too distant past we believed that some of our soul would pass into them. For this reason people would place an old shoe into a wall or under a floor of a newly built house because they believed that our spirit, held within the shoe, would bring the house good luck. We remember special outfits, graduation suits and wedding frocks – they can take us back to places we have been and help us recall the people we passed our time with.

Today there's still a tiny section of what we call fashion that is special: the bit where art, creativity and craft meet. Where high-quality clothes are still bought with care and become cherished items. But fashion has become an ugly word. Most of what is called fashion today is cheap, disposable, uninspiring, valueless, depressing. I feel sad that many people growing up today may never have worn a good piece of clothing.

3

An Experience Working in High Street Retail

In early 2011 I was approached by the (now defunct) department store Debenhams about putting together a small collection of tailored clothes under my name. At the time, Debenhams sold over 5 per cent of all clothes bought in the UK. They wanted to do an accessibly priced version of the things I was known for on Savile Row, and I went back to them with the idea of relaunching the historic Hammond & Co. brand. I'd bought the Savile Row tailor Norton & Sons in 2005, and the Hammond & Co. name had been part of the Norton family. Hammond, founded in 1776, had been a big name in London in the late eighteenth- and early-nineteenth centuries. They'd clothed four successive British monarchs and had been the sporting tailor of choice amongst the European aristocracy.

The idea was to create simple, well-cut clothing, made in good fabrics and sold at accessible prices. With simple clothes the fit had to be flawless and we spent over a year perfecting the product before its launch in September 2013 as the most premium in-house menswear brand in Debenhams' stable. We sold pure cotton shirts, pure wool jumpers and pure wool suits, in a store that had been following everyone down the path of poly-cotton, wool-nylon and poly-wool blends.

The product was excellent, and excellent value, and from the first week it flew out of the door. From nothing, we grew to a turnover of £27 million in less than five years, and in the process became the most successful Debenhams collaboration ever. We took the collection from twenty stores, to forty, to a hundred and more. We added pants, pyjamas, watches and fragrances. We did Goodyear welted leather shoes for £150, and full leather bags that looked every bit as lux as Tom Ford but cost £160.

I insisted that Hammond have an industry-leading sustainability programme. We started a rolling five-year plan in 2017 in which we followed a simple formula of well-designed pieces that felt like timeless, good investments, and we made sure the fits were great and that they were cut really well. Good cutting costs nothing, so the best way to make high-quality, affordable clothes is to get rid of any extraneous details and concentrate on cutting them well, while making sure you invest in the best cloths and the best manufacturing quality that you can.

A few pieces within the collection would be repeated every season: excellent five-pocket selvedge denim jeans, navy crew-neck lambswool jumpers, navy moleskin trousers, navy raincoats. Essentially lots of navy. But fundamental to Debenhams' model was 'newness' every six months: new styles in store, new colours. We had to redesign perfectly well designed clothes every season simply because they thought they'd sell more. We might have sold 10,000 of our single-breasted blue raincoats, but rather than keeping it as it was we'd change it, sometimes almost imperceptibly: a new undercollar, or an adjustment to the pocket shape, but always new. It made no sense. The smallest change meant a change to the technical packs, re-sourcing trims, resampling the product, re-fitting, formally signing it off, rephotographing it, rewriting the website copy and then loading it as a new product onto the system, both for stores and for the web. Dozens of people across dozens of departments were doing all of this work, with samples flying back and forth, incurring huge cost, for no reason.

To compound the frustration, anyone buying the navy raincoat one season wasn't going to come back and buy another one the following season, or any time soon, because they were good coats and would probably last five years or more even with heavy wear. And when it wore out a lot of men would like to buy exactly the same thing again. Moreover, we'd have to discount any remaining stock at the end of each season to make room for new stock. It was a great big waste of time and money and resources. But this is how the fashion industry works and no one was prepared to do it differently.

It was in the deal that Debenhams would use some British cloths in the collections. We had Mallalieus of Delph and Alfred Moon cloths in the most expensive of our suits and coats, we had Harris tweed in our hats and scarves, made in Scotland. Where we couldn't afford to make things in the UK, we would try to find British suppliers such as Fulton's umbrellas. Wherever I could find a way, I would support local producers, and even a small fragment of the Hammond work meant a lot to some of our suppliers.

The team at Debenhams were superbly professional and they knew their jobs inside out. Their merchandisers were magicians; their ability to forecast and manage their business was incredible. They forecast the season's sales at £14.2 million and we would do £14.3 million. They knew what we would sell each week to within a few hundred quid. It boggled my tiny mind. They knew what pricing would work and what wouldn't. They knew that if you added 5 per cent to a price you might lose 20 per cent of your sales. If you went 10 per cent above the market price you might lose 50 per cent, and if you added 20 per cent you would sell almost nothing at all. However, despite the reliance on science they were prepared to take chances, to admit when they were wrong and back the winners, and our sales were universally fantastic.

There was never a season where we did not beat (even if by only a small amount) our sales targets. I remember vividly the first time we sold over £1 million worth of clothes in a week. I would regularly see people on trains or on the tube wearing our product, or carrying our bags.

The design team's attention to detail was second to none. My design lead, Alastair Waite, had studied at St Martins and cut his teeth at Next. We would go through a hundred small corrections that I wanted across a collection and every one would be actioned just as I asked for it. You might not think this remarkable, but I remember working on comparatively tiny collections for a very well-known premium brand, and there would always be one or two products that turned out nothing like they should have done. The Debenhams team trusted my design instincts. They would sometimes push back, or make suggestions, but always with a view to improving what I suggested. In the end, their experience of working in this way with other external designers (John Rocha, Jasper Conran, etc.) over almost twenty years told. They gave me the space to make the product just that 10 per cent different (or better), and I did. And it worked.

Despite the requirement to follow the wasteful high street fashion model, I learned so much in my eight years working with Debenhams. I learned how to merchandise, I learned about rates of sale, and OTB's and weeks' cover and all the technicalities that you really need to know if you want to make a success of a clothing business. And through selling in over a hundred stores right across the UK, I learned what normal men buy and wear, and crucially, how much they're prepared to pay. I learned so much that would prove to be invaluable when thinking about the idea behind Community Clothing.

Part II

QUALITY

4

How Things Are Made: A Personal Reflection on Quality

As a kid I was always making and building things and was obsessed with making them well. In my early years it was mostly Lego, kept in a shallow wooden box about three foot by two, divided up into a dozen sections in which I segregated my bricks. We didn't have Lego kits then, everything was imagined from scratch. Brick arrangements were never left to chance: I would always precisely arrange the bricks, seeking uniform brick size in any construction, or failing that a gradation or a regular pattern of small and large. The final result was important, but the process of designing, calculating and problem solving was part of the fun. My friends had Meccano, a system of metal strips, wheels, axles, gears, and connecting nuts and bolts which allowed the building of amazing mechanical devices. But we'd also build real things. We built dens in the garden using a few old wooden ladders, rope and bits of old carpet. We built gang huts in the hermitage of quite sophisticated design, camouflaged to avoid detection by Dave Marshall's older gang who'd delight in ransacking them. We built one within dense ground ivy, its entrance a well-concealed tunnel, opening out into a chicken-wire-lined atrium, fully carpeted with moss.

At school I got to make lots of things. We did woodwork and pottery every week. I made a small wooden bookcase, and a pottery biscuit barrel in the shape of a poppy-seed head which now takes pride of place in my mum's kitchen. Quite unusually there was a taxidermy club run by one of our biology teachers on a Friday after school; we stuffed a fox and someone fainted at the smell of its skeleton being boiled. There was fly-tying club with Skiddy Marsh. In physics we built radios, soldering resistors and capacitors onto punched brown circuit boards, until that joyous moment when a crackling tune emerged from the tinny grey cardboard speaker. When I was in sixth form I made miniature caricatures of my friends in Fimo clay; about an inch high, they had tiny fingers and were kitted out with ludicrously fragile accessories.

Even in my early teens I was finickity about the things I bought. I was lucky to grow up surrounded by quality – my dad's wardrobe of well-loved suits, jackets, shirts and jumpers; the second-hand furniture from the sale rooms of Edinburgh; a hand-thrown brown milk jug we used daily; Sheffield cutlery, French glassware, all still in regular use at my mum's house today, almost fifty years later – and I was reluctant to buy anything that didn't feel good.

I won my class science prize at prep school and with my book token I got the *Hamlyn All Colour Encyclopaedia of Science*. It explained the physics and chemistry of the universe and the everyday world around us. I was endlessly fascinated with what things were made from and how they were constructed. Another favourite from childhood, still on my bookshelf, is *How It's Made* by Donald Clarke. As the title suggests, it explained in detail how many of the everyday things that surround us were manufactured. It showed how Dunlop made the Red Flash tennis shoe, not very different from the Green Flash I wore, and I was endlessly fascinated to imagine how the things on my feet had come into being.

Quality

Clarke wrote his book in 1976, before the quality of our everyday things started to take a *really* big nosedive. In his introduction he pointed out that modern mass production had given consumers of the day access to things their grandparents couldn't have dreamed of, but that such abundance was already creating problems. Consumers even then were confronted with a dizzying array of goods at, in Clarke's words, 'any level of quality from excellent to virtually useless'. He pointed out that at every stage of the development and manufacturing process of any given object, from the simplest to the most complicated, decisions are taken on the type and grade of material to be used, and on the method of production, from the painstaking to the slipshod, all of which affect the overall quality of the final item. There is always a trade-off between quality and cost, and the more we as consumers know about how things are made, he said, the less we will be at the mercy of the manufacturer whose only motive is profit. Knowing how to make things arms us in the fight against being flogged low-quality stuff. People from my parents' and grandparents' generations had a greater knowledge of when an object was good or bad. All young women and some men learned to sew, young men were taught to work with metal and wood. Some schools taught car or bike mechanics. Everyone handled tools and materials and gained an appreciation of their properties.

For my own generation this is no longer universally true. I was lucky to go to a school that taught me to make things, and hence taught me how to make quality assessments with my own hands and eyes. How many people today leave school knowing how things are made? How many can tell good quality from bad?

My fascination with how and from what things are made led me to a degree in Materials Science and Engineering. We studied the properties of materials: their strength, toughness, hardness, malleability, elasticity; their ability to conduct light, heat and electrons; the properties which determine a material's suitability for any given application. We learned how to test the properties of a material, and how those properties may be altered through the way we work with and transform that material, how with knowledge and care you can improve the performance of every object we use.

Take iron, which humans have been using for around three thousand years, one of the simplest and most abundant of Earth's natural resources. Pure iron is soft, malleable, ductile and prone to rust. When cast it can become brittle and hard. But if you add carbon to iron it becomes steel which can be stronger, tougher and harder, depending upon the quantity you add. If you add a bit of chromium to the steel you increase its resistance to oxidation, it becomes stainless. Even then, though, the properties of this steel are not fixed. If you heat it up and cool it slowly it will behave differently than if you heat it up and cool it quickly – quench it. If you hold it at a high temperature for longer before cooling it will be different again. If you take that steel and roll or hammer it, it will change once more, and the way it changes depends upon whether you do this when it is hot or cold. The physics and chemistry is complex, but every blacksmith or metal worker knows intuitively how the process by which they make something changes its nature. Humans spent in some cases thousands of years painstakingly refining the manufacture of the things we use, every day, until we had reached the absolute limit of their performance.

Making things well requires the use of high-quality raw materials: the right iron ore with the right percentage of the right types and grades of carbon and chromium. Every deposit, in every mine, right across the planet is different. There is good stainless steel and there is very bad stainless steel. Making a thing well also requires effort and time, which costs money. If the consumer no longer cares about quality, or knows enough to discern good from bad, or even knows that such things exist, then the manufacturer, as Donald Clarke warned, is going to end up selling them an object which is virtually useless. You can produce two objects which look identical, both of which can be made of 'steel', but they can be as different as chalk and cheese.

Care is important. Do the companies which sell us things care about the quality of the things they sell us, or do they simply care about the cost? Do we as consumers care? Roger Ackling, a professor at the London College of Furniture, wrote, 'Craft was really just the application of care.' Some businesses, particularly what we call artisanal ones, whether single craftspeople or larger workshop or factory producers, which sell the objects they make directly to their customers under their own name, tend to care greatly. But the majority of the businesses who sell us things no longer have any hand in their manufacture, and many couldn't care less.

Once a year whilst filming *Sewing Bee* I am put up in a rented corporate flat. I've stayed in several different ones, all built and furnished by developers whose only seeming concern was to equip the place as cheaply as possible. Until staying there I was blissfully unaware of how bad our everyday homewares had become. I last bought things for my kitchen – three pans, two knives, a kettle and a toaster – in 1995 and have had no reason to replace any of them since (although the toaster has had new elements). In the kitchen of one recent rental was a new oven tray. On its first use it went into the oven at 180 degrees and a few minutes later there was a loud clang from inside. I opened the oven door and found the tray had buckled and my chips were littering the oven floor. Now anyone who knows anything about making things with metal will know that metal, if not correctly worked during processing, retains a memory of any earlier form. A small amount of heat had released the tenuous hold my oven tray had held over its form, allowing it to spring back to a shape remembered from its past.

For a century at least we have made oven trays that remain flat when heated in an oven. I have several that are over forty years old and staying flat isn't much to ask; it's really its only job. But now, in our relentless drive for cheapness, they no longer do that one simple thing.

In the kitchen I also found pans with wobbly plastic handles, pans whose coating came off when you cooked with them or took a scourer to them, knives which did not cut, spoons punched out of flat metal, so shallow they held virtually no liquid, their edges and corners still sharp because to smooth them would cost money, leaving them uncomfortable to hold or put in your mouth, forks made of such low-quality steel that they bent in the hand with the merest force. Toilet flushes that did not flush. There were plug sockets so badly manufactured it was only with difficulty that a plug could be pushed into them and light switches where the switch was coming out of its housing. A light switch is a very simple item. There are switches in my house that are still working perfectly after eighty years of use. These are simple things, the making of which we had perfected. But from a peak at some point in the second half of the last century, their quality has, step by small step, got worse and worse, to the point where today they are frankly rubbish. Literally. Stuff that very quickly will end up in the bin.

We buy so many things, with so little consideration to anything except the price. My kettle at home is used most days. It was made by Siemens in Germany. When I bought it in around 1995 I reckon it cost about twice the price of the average kettle. Twenty-nine years later it is still in good working order. In my factory they seem to replace the less expensive kettles they buy almost yearly, thus making cheap kettles about fifteen times more costly than my expensive one.

Until not very long ago we consumed a relatively small quantity of very high-value goods. Anything we buy second-hand that is over about thirty years old is likely to be of significantly higher quality than a new alternative, and will almost certainly last you longer and give you greater pleasure in its use than a new one. And what is more, keeping things for a long time is hugely important environmentally too. Long life in our everyday objects reduces the depletion of non-renewable resources, as well as emissions and pollution. Keeping things for longer is the single best way to reduce environmental harm. In my home are hundreds of objects the age of which I do not know because they were either inherited or bought second-hand. Indeed, very few of the things I use every day were bought new. Beds, chairs, chests, wardrobes and other furniture are eighteenth-, nineteenth- and twentieth-century English, with a few pieces from Denmark; plates, cups, vases and planters are from the wonderful Stoke potteries, or made by mid-twentieth-century craft potters; lamps, rugs, even my bathroom suites and my current kitchen were bought second-hand. I have pieces of furniture as old as my house, which is over three hundred years old. It is a joy to live with an object over a long period, to watch as it develops character and patina over years of use. It's a simple pleasure that the great majority of us never get to enjoy because modern mass-produced objects do not get better with age.

What is Quality?

Quality is the relative degree of excellence of any object or service, relative either to other similar things, or to our own expectations, and it comprises both tangible and intangible components.

Tangible, or objective, quality has two main sides to it:

- *Function*: is it well suited to the job for which it is intended, can it be used simply and pleasurably, will it perform under all required conditions?
- *Durability*: the maintenance of this function over a long period of time. Does it stay waterproof, or warm? Do its buttons stay on?

The second type of quality is intangible, or subjective, quality. This has several components, the chief amongst them being:

- *Beauty*: is it pleasurable to behold, beauty being in the eye of the beholder (the scrappy mutt may be more beautiful than the pedigree hound, or the child-made pinch pot more beautiful than the Doulton bowl)?
- *Provenance*: the story of its creation and its life – the much patched and repaired coat, or the piece of clothing passed on by a loved one. Do the various aspects of the way in which the object came into being make it more valuable to me? Or does the service it has given improve its quality?

Tangible Quality

Tangible or objective quality is relatively simple to understand. Is the object's form well suited to its function, is it simple and pleasurable to use, will it perform its function well under all conditions and circumstances, and will it continue to perform its function to the same level of quality for a long time? Objective quality comes from the quality of the design, the physical characteristics of the materials from which the object has been made, and the process, the skill and the tools or equipment used to produce it. High-quality objects are wonderful to use or to wear, and because of the materials from which they are made their use often becomes more pleasurable with time. Wooden hand tools become more comfortable in the hand, wooden furniture becomes smoother and more beautifully patinated, wool suits and leather shoes become better moulded to the shape of the body that they enclose.

There are ways of making an object which are definably, sometimes measurably, better. I had the great privilege to visit the factory of Firmin & Co., a metalworker in Birmingham. They are Britain's oldest company, founded in 1655 (between the reigns of Charles I and Charles II), and are manufacturers for the military, and other services, of metal buttons and hat badges, cavalry cuirasses, helmets and sword handles, which they make in a manner that has remained largely unchanged for centuries. They use a tool (you might call it a machine) called a drop forge, which allows them to make buttons in a way that cannot be reproduced by button makers using modern tools. A heavy punch drops from a height, striking a metal slug. Because it strikes quickly and bounces back it preserves the fine detail in the mould that a modern hydraulic button press, which squashes with great force, does not. The hydraulic press makes buttons cheaper and faster, but Firmin's drop forge makes them better.

Most tailored clothes are pressed on a flat pressing board, but hand tailors use a tool called a tailor's ham, a firm pad made of hard flat cloth densely filled with horsehair (which will draw excess moisture from the garment during pressing), so called because it is shaped like a joint of ham. It roughly approximates to the shape of the human chest or shoulder, so that when pressed the garment becomes human shaped, not flat. We have a tailor's ham in the workshop of my tailors on Savile Row that might be at least a century old. Balding in places and much patched, it has passed through the hands of several generations of tailors. Pressing flat is fast and relatively simple to learn. Pressing on a ham requires skill and takes time, but is definably better.

The selvedge denim makers of Japan use slow old G3 Toyoda shuttle looms. Donald-John Mackay and other Harris tweed weavers of the Outer Hebridean islands use old foot-treadle or pedal-powered Hattersley looms on which they can weave about 20 metres of cloth a day. A fully automated loom might work at five to ten times that speed, but the beaters or reeds of these older, slower mechanical looms exert more force. They allow you to put more yarn into less cloth, making a more compact, denser and more durable fabric with more character.

And certain materials are objectively better too. Stronger, lighter or harder, less destructive in their means of being grown, extracted or produced. Most modern wood is fast grown industrially; a tree might be felled between ten and twenty years after planting, where an old tree might grow for two to three hundred years. Slow-grown old wood has a much denser ring structure, often three to four times denser, which makes old-grown wood stronger, more stable and more durable, resisting weather, pests and rot. Objects made from old-growth wood are better.

Function

An object needs to do the job for which it was intended. It should do so with the greatest possible ease or facility, and it should give pleasure in so doing. A knife needs to be sharp and easy to hold; a pan needs to hold whatever is put in it, to distribute heat evenly across the cooking surface, to have a handle which remains cool whilst the pan is hot, to be washable. In clothing, function might include fitting well, being comfortable to wear, being warm and water-resistant: in an oven tray it would be retaining the same shape when hot. In order to allow these objects to function they must be well designed, well made and made from the right material. You cannot skimp on any of these and expect the same level of function. It's simple.

Durability

Also within the realm of tangible quality is an object's durability: its ability to keep doing the job it was intended to do, to the same standard, with the same ease, for a very long time. Using the right materials for the job, and using the very best grade of that material, is more expensive, sometimes significantly so, but objects made properly will retain their structural and functional integrity after prolonged use. There might be no noticeable decline in their function over a long time.

By contrast, poor-quality construction, poor-quality materials, objects made with the least possible amount of material – all of this has a significant negative effect on the durability of the object. Low durability leads to increased consumption, so in a business world which seeks to increase consumption the lowest acceptable level of durability is actually a good thing. For the rest of us, and of course for nature and the planet, it is a very bad thing indeed. Once an object starts to fail, it become less pleasurable to use, and of course we will need to replace it, causing an accumulation of waste. In the case of low-quality objects like cheap synthetic clothing, this is often non-recyclable and non-biodegradable. Replacing objects costs us money and causes disruption to our lives. The failure of an object can cause us harm, sometimes fatally.

Ageing

High-quality objects are made from materials that will age in a way which gives great and increasing pleasure to the user. They will develop more character, develop a more beautiful, rich and nuanced patina. A well-crafted object gives pleasure every time we hold it, wear it or use it. And this pleasure only increases with every use. An object made from wood or leather or natural textiles will develop character, it will mould and soften and acquire new form and a new patina with the life you pass to it through its use. Wear may reveal previously hidden detail within a natural material like wood or stone. Natural materials age in ways that are unpredictable and add to their character and value.

Most contemporary objects by contrast are at their best before they are used, their quality decreasing from the moment they are first touched. We might feel a moment of fleeting pleasure when they are new, but poor-quality objects are seldom a joy to use or wear, and their failure and disposal are of no consequence beyond the financial. These are dismal things to which we feel little or no connection, no sense of emotional loss.

Repair

Low-quality objects not only are less likely to be repairable because they are machine assembled, but their low cost means that a small repair, carried out by a skilled person on a UK wage, will often be more costly than replacing the object with a new one. We're caught in a trap of our own creating.

We are by contrast much more likely to repair high-quality objects, for several reasons. First, because of our connection to and love for them; second because they are more often made in such a way that they can readily be repaired; and finally, because the cost of the repair is more likely to be less than the cost of a new replacement. The value of a good object increases further with each repair, the time and human care imbuing even greater character and life. In other cultures, notably in Japan, repaired objects are highly celebrated. There, tattered clothing and textiles are reworked and repaired, often through darning or patching techniques, transforming them into highly valued *Boro*. They also practise Kintsugi, or golden joinery, the art of visibly repairing broken pottery with gold. They do not hide repair, they celebrate it as a reflection of care, frugality and skill. Both practices treat breakage and repair as part of the history of an object, as something to celebrate. On Savile Row we have customers who both understand and value the craftsmanship that goes into every stage of making the clothes we sell, and who value the clothes themselves. Because our clothes are assembled by hand, they can be relatively easily disassembled by the same means to allow for the alterations and repairs which are common on hand-tailored clothes.

Well-made objects, objects which we love to use or with which we feel a connection, are cherished and always where possible repaired. And through their repairs we cherish them more. As Richard Sennett said in *The Culture of the New Capitalism*, 'the Craftsman is proud of what he has made and cherishes it while the consumer discards things that are perfectly serviceable in his restless pursuit of the new'.

Regional Character

Location also imparts both a tangible and an intangible quality to our objects. High-quality goods often have definable local character, from the unique variety of material available in a particular locality, or from the varying techniques employed by individual craftspeople, and often from both. The way in which an object is made may exhibit great variation even over a relatively small area, because most crafts evolved simultaneously in multiple locations before good communications were developed. Such individuality of methods endured until well into the twentieth century and provided colour and narrative to regional products. Similarly in Savile Row, individual makers' methods for each of the garments we produce will vary, sometimes markedly, and whilst all sew by hand to the same level of quality, I know from experience that two pairs of trousers made from the same pattern by two different makers will feel different. In the making of wooden furniture or ceramic bowls, differences between makers and between regions can be read by experts as clearly as any map, and this adds to their quality. Mass-produced objects, made from generic material on standard production machinery, will appear identical, no matter where in the world they are made, representing another loss of quality from our lives.

Raw Materials

In a craft system of manufacture, local, often quite variable materials were turned into product by a series of skilled individuals who had the flexibility of work practice and the knowledge to adapt their process to the materials available to them. The mass manufacturing system that replaced it, worked using completely standard processes which in turn required standardised, homogenous inputs and materials. Adaptable, knowledge-based human manufacturing allows for much greater use of precious materials. Skilled woodworkers can use any shape of tree, adapting the design and making the process fit the material rather than standardising the material to fit the process. The tailors of Savile Row have the skills to sew clothes from almost anything you choose to give them. Whilst some might grumble when the work requires a great deal more than the usual amount of thought, many others relish the challenge of applying their skill to solving a problem. We do on occasions receive requests to make clothes from pieces of heirloom fabric, or from treasured blankets, or to line jackets in old silk scarves. If it can be sewn, our tailors can sew it. My neighbour Davide, a master tailor at Gieves & Hawkes, recently created a quite beautiful tailored jacket from a used coffee sack. Knowledge and skill allows us to make things from all the varied materials we might find around us.

The mass production system in its search for efficiency allows for no flexibility, it needs materials that are standardised and uniform. Man-made materials replaced natural ones, and where natural materials were used they were industrially engineered to conform within the standardised production environment. The mass manufacture of flat-pack furniture, for example, requires perfectly straight trees because machines cannot deal with even small imperfections in the wood. In the UK we are surrounded by beautiful but slightly wonky trees that only a very few of the most highly skilled craftspeople would today be able to utilise. So instead we burn our local wood, and import low-quality furniture made from industrial forests. Food has followed a similar process of industrialisation. Automated packaging systems were unable to deal with vegetables of non-standard shape, so wonky veg was binned.

Intangible Quality

The second side to quality is subjective: the intangible aspects of an object's character, less easy to pin down but of real importance, particularly in a world longing for connections to humanity and nature. How do I feel about this object? What do I know of its character, and its provenance? Where were the materials from which it has been made sourced? How have they been grown and felled and brought together? Who has made the object, and in what workplace? What is the maker's story, from whom did they learn their craft? If it has been made in a factory, what history does this factory have? What particular assets or access to material used in the manufacture of this product makes it unique? What, in short, is its story?

Provenance

The spring from which the spinners at Todd & Duncan draw their water imparts a unique handle to their yarn. The softness of the water is also of great importance in the Scottish Borders where William Lockie and their many neighbours produce knitwear and tweed. The almost black fleece of the Hebridean sheep which live on the Isle of Mull gives unique natural colour to the Ardalanish tweeds. These provide tangible quality, but there is an intangible aspect to their products too, a romance, a connection to these places of great beauty, which I picture in my mind's eye whenever I handle their cloths or their clothes.

It is the same with machines and tools. Alongside the many wonderful and unique tools used at the extraordinary Firmin factory is one called a blacksmith's elm, a small steel anvil mounted on a block of English elm, used for hammering the shape into the backs of helmets. The elm originally provided natural shock absorbency which has long since been lost, but its history, the knowledge that upon this actual tool

368 years' worth of cavalry helmets have been hand formed, helmets that have graced battlefields and paraded every monarch from Charles II to Charles III, imparts an unquantifiably great value. The knowledge that the two men who use it today are the only ones in the world with such skills adds to its quality too. The physical properties of a cloth woven on a Hattersley or Toyoda loom are superior, but more than this the age and history of the particular loom, and in the case of the Hattersley the human energy which powers it, is woven into the story of the cloth.

We might feel a connection to the maker, to their history, or to the lineage of their method. They might be someone known to us, a friend, family member or loved individual, or a famed craftsperson: a hand potter, a furniture maker, a bespoke tailor. Or simply a craftsperson who works in a location to which we have a connection, a place where we or a loved one once lived, somewhere we travelled to; a place whose story has some romance or significance to us. Even the simplest or slightest connection adds meaning, and hence value, to an object. Some places have long and deep histories in a particular craft, like Cremona in Italy where the three greatest violin makers practised their art, or the Outer Hebridean islands where all Harris tweed is made. Every length of tweed woven by Donald-John Mackay in his tin shed overlooking the beautiful Luskentyre beach, where I wild camped during the sunniest week in Hebridean history many years ago, is filled with the spirit of the landscape, and Donald-John's unique charm.

I had the great pleasure to be taught how to turn wood on a pole lathe by the aptly named Robin Wood in his extraordinary stone workshop high up a track on the side of Kinder Scout in the Peak District. I cherish the bowl I made because I made it myself, and in such a unique location. Not only that, but the knowledge that I was taught to do so by the man responsible for resurrecting this ancient craft, and who also, through the foundation of the Heritage Craft Association, has done so much to preserve so many endangered crafts for our nation, almost brings me to tears thinking about it.

We can also feel connected in different ways to the material from which an object is made: wood from a known windblown tree, as several contemporary woodworkers now do, or from a known woodland; steel forged in Sheffield; cloth made from the fleece of sheep from mountains we once walked or visited, like those friendly little Hebrideans at Ardalanish. Objects made by people for whom we care – children, parents, grandparents – can transcend the quality of others. The mittens hand-knitted by my grandmother are amongst the most precious things I own, and I know my mother still treasures the biscuit barrel I made. But any object where the maker, or makers, are known carries greater meaning. All connections create intangible quality.

Objects made by hand allow us to get closer to their creation in ways that machine-made things do not. We can, if we know a little about making, enjoy the questions these objects might pose: how did it come to be this way, how was it formed? We can trace the process of creating a handmade object in our mind because we can understand the steps it may have been through, we can intuit its journey from raw material to finished object. We can see where and how a tool has been applied to a piece of wood to form a wooden stool, or what movement and what pressure of the hand has shaped a lip or spout.

This is not so with the mass-produced objects which make up so much of what we buy today. The route from oil to industrial plastic to injection-moulded object is beyond our understanding and holds no romance or fascination for most. Our lack of connection to such objects, our lack of knowledge of their creation, renders them largely meaningless to us. Faceless, inhuman, remote production systems create objects with no intangible quality.

The ability to reason with an object's creation brings us closer to it. What the hand has made, the hand wishes to touch and to explore;

materials, people and process are intertwined in the object and in our minds, making it more real. Objects can paint pictures of people and places. The story of the creation of the things we live with can and should be meaningful. The objects from which we derive the greatest pleasure are not those of the greatest monetary value, they are the ones to which we have the greatest connection. What would you rush to save from a burning building, the woollen jumper hand-knitted for you by a beloved grandmother, or the expensive cashmere sweater from some ubiquitous luxury brand?

Where Your Money Goes

What do you want your money to do? Where do you want it to go? There is a value to knowing that the money you are spending is doing good. The great irony is that if you buy something of poor quality, the money almost always goes to someone very rich. The owners of H&M are the richest family in Sweden, the owner of Amazon is worth $176 billion and is currently the third richest man on the planet. Yet the people who actually produce the low-quality objects these and others sell are among the poorest on the planet. When we buy cheap things we support a system which places no value on the human labour involved in its production.

By contrast, the great majority of those who make high-quality goods are well rewarded for their skill and work. High-quality objects cost a lot to make, but a much larger proportion, sometimes all of the money ends up in the pockets of the people who make them. The smaller the business, the more equitable the share; in the single-person artisanal business of course the maker takes all. Small businesses tend to spend less on expensive buildings and expensive marketing. My friend Robin Wood now makes axes by hand in a small workshop in Sheffield. They may be the best axes in the world. If you buy one of Robin's axes, where does your money go? A small amount goes to the manufacturer of the steel and the supplier of the wood from which the handles are made, but the rest goes to Robin, in direct payment for the hours of labour he's put into making it, a value forged through the thirty-plus years he has spent honing the skills he needs to produce that axe. We pay Robin well for his labour, which means that in turn Robin has money to pay someone else well for theirs, and so on. Knowing that the people who make the things we buy are valued, both monetarily and emotionally, is an important part of their quality. In both of my businesses a huge proportion, over 90 per cent, of the money you spend on our clothes stays in the local economy, in the case of Community Clothing almost half of it directly as wages. When you buy cheap fashion often as little as 1 per cent of the price goes to the maker. And, moreover, your money circles back around in the local economy doing even more good for the people in those communities.

Brand

Another huge part of the intangible value of a product today is the brand. It used to be the case that the price we paid for an object bore a direct relationship to its quality. Higher price, higher quality. Early branded goods like Wedgwood and Chippendale were expensive because the design, construction processes and materials used produced goods of exceptional quality. And there was a cachet to the brand; everyone knew the name stood for quality and that branded goods had been expensively purchased, imparting social envy. Early branded goods were synonymous with tangible quality. Branded manufacturers developed a good name from having unique designs, and because they made something good, and through the tangible quality of their goods their reputation spread. Most businesses used to make things themselves and a brand's factory would have a specific method of manufacturing the goods they sold, and a specific source of their raw materials. All of this would be reflected in the way their product performed: its function, its durability, its beauty. The brand and the product were intrinsically linked.

But now most of the things we buy – from our clothing to our crockery and cutlery, from furniture to phones – have lost that link to making. They are produced by outsourced manufacturers who in many cases change from year to year. There is an almost total separation of brand from manufacturer. In the world of clothing 99.99 per cent, probably much more, of the clothes sold are made in nameless factories, with unspecified processes and raw materials. The same product is churned for anyone who cares to ask them, while brands move their product from one factory to another in the endless search for lower costs. At the affordable end of the market, and even in many very expensive clothes, there is no longer any connection between brand and tangible product quality.

There are exceptions. In Northampton, where the world's best shoes are made, most factories have a unique way of making. This is why Trickers shoes feel very different from John Lobb or Edward Green. It's why their goods feel special (and why they are all happy to repair them). The same is true of Walsh running shoes, or the US bootmaker Redwing who make their heritage boots (sadly no longer all of their boots) in their own Minnesota factory. The bespoke tailors of Savile Row have unique ways of cutting and sewing, and use unique fabrics. Barbour still produce their classic wax jacket styles in their own factory in South Shields, and for that reason they have a unique and wonderful feel.

Some in the luxury world uphold the tradition of in-house manufacture. Hermès owns some of its manufacturing, including tanneries and the factories which produce its iconic bags, and Chanel is committed to the long-term quality of much of its production and has bought many small ateliers and factories to preserve unique making skills. In my design practice I specify every process and every material, I know every make, and can in many cases trace materials back to single farms.

And everything remains the same, year after year, even if costs rise, because it matters.

Cars are the only big exception to this outsourcing story. Car brands make their own cars, and arguably cars are the one consumer good where the quality has gone up dramatically over the past century. Huge amounts have been spent on research, huge investments made in factories, great care taken over supply chains. Cars today are safer, more fuel efficient, quieter, more comfortable, better equipped than ever.

Utility, in economic terms, refers to the usefulness or direct satisfaction a consumer can gain from a service or an object. In the past, brand and utility were directly linked. Utility is not the same as happiness, though an object can bring us both, usually with the utility coming directly, leading to happiness. In clothing it can be thought of like this: this coat keeps me warm and dry – that is its utility, its usefulness. And from that, on a cold rainy winter's day, flows the feeling of happiness. But today the happiness a consumer feels when buying from a brand is no longer linked to the goods, it is no longer in the utility. Today it is quite simply, in the great majority of cases, in the cachet of the name, a name created through associations with almost everything *but* the object being sold; with luxury, with celebrity, with glamour and beauty (but rarely the beauty of the object itself). Today you find designer brands, new and old, sticking their name, in the largest type they can, on any old piece of clothing – a T-shirt, a hoodie, a jogging bottom. Much designer fashion has simply become merch. But that is enough for many of today's status-obsessed consumers. Quality is of no relevance. They build their persona through the brand they associate with, not the clothing they wear, self-esteem through brand. But this is a dangerous place to be. When quality no longer matters you are exposed. Any brand with enough cash, no matter what they're selling, can pay celebrities and influencers to hype them. They don't check the quality, they count the money.

It is worth thinking about the price we pay for any given object as having two components: first the Object – is it a good object? Does it function well, is it useful, is it beautiful – characteristics determined by the quality of its design and its manufacture, what it's made from and how it is made. And second the Brand – an ephemeral value based on the amount of money a brand spends marketing itself, the images it creates, the celebrities it pays, the money it spends on stores, if it has them – none of which add anything to the tangible quality of any object they sell.

The more they spend on one, the less they have to spend on the other. For a huge number of branded fashion items, designer as well as fast fashion, much if not all of the value is in the latter. By sticking their name in large font on a simple black sweatshirt and using a famous celebrity to promote it, a designer brand may make huge amounts of money (Balenciaga are selling a sweatshirt with a big logo for £950; I reckon it costs about £20 to make), but they have opened the door to other brands doing just the same. The same influencers will take anyone's money. So then what, bar a little history and deeper pockets, makes you different? In fashion and beauty, celebrities endorse, collaborate, and now assume roles as creative directors at major fashion houses. Pharrell has just debuted his first Louis Vuitton collection. Kendall Jenner was recently paid $20 million to put her name to a line of jeans for a British high street brand. All of this is part of the apparatus of continually growing consumption, but it costs huge sums, exponentially more than simply making a good product. Pharrell, Beyoncé and Rihanna might make people buy, but if your brand is built on nothing but celebrity, how do you create lasting value? You can control product quality; you cannot prevent your highly paid Kardashian from doing a line for Boohoo. Or silence Kanye West.

How much is branding worth? Vetements, a hugely successful French fashion brand, made its name in part by putting its name, 'clothes' in French, on its clothes. They released a sock with Reebok, which sold for £75. A similar sock from Reebok itself, already a well-known brand, costs £2. The sock will have cost about 50p, maybe less, to make. That 50p is the value of its physical utility. The difference between your regular Reebok sock and the new one is the word 'Vetements' knitted into the side, which in this case is worth about £74.50 out of £75. In this instance 99.3 per cent of the value is brand. The logo on the Balenciaga sweatshirt makes up about 98 per cent of its value. In the past, brand value was in utility; today it is in image, ego and social standing. Brand does equate to a tangible sense of happiness – print 'Supreme' or 'Off-White' on a plain white cotton T-shirt and the wearer feels happier wearing it – but this happiness is often fragile and impermanent. How do the early Supreme adopters feel about the ubiquity of the brand's products today? We spend a lot of money on things whose value may very easily disappear. And all of this spending on brand ephemera inevitably leads to less spending on items of tangible quality. If product quality conveys just 0.7 per cent of the value to the consumer, why should any brand bother?

Environment

Another important aspect of the quality of an object is how it interacts with the natural world, both when it is made and when it is disposed of. Does it come from a place of harmony or a place of harm? Despite not being directly part of the physical make-up of the object itself, the environmental impact of a product is real and measurable.

When we lived as foragers, hunters and gatherers, we lived in total harmony with nature, but when we adopted an agricultural existence we began to damage the natural environment; we cut down trees and cleared brush, we exposed the soil to the eroding power of the weather. The scale of this damage, and the rate of its advance, was at first very slow. In the UK trees began to grow when the land warmed after the end of the last Ice Age and by about 3000 BC they were growing on all but the highest and windiest or most waterlogged land. And at almost exactly the same time we started to cut them down again, clearing forest to make room for agriculture. During the later Bronze and Iron Ages, clearance accelerated as tools improved and we continued to fell and burn, converting forest to arable land and pasture for hundreds of years. By the time of the Domesday Book in 1086, just 15 per cent of the UK was covered in forest. Thanks to the genuine need for wood for building, and for land on which to grow food for a growing population, as well as a healthy dose of common greed on the part of landowners, by the end of the nineteenth century England's forest and woodland coverage had dwindled to just 5 per cent.

In the early industrial period the depletion of non-renewable natural resources was low. Consumer waste in the pre-plastic era was not greatly different in composition from the waste which humans had been creating for thousands of years: our homewares were ceramic and metal, our furniture of wood, wool or horsehair, our children's toys of wood and metal, and our clothes cotton, linen and wool. All were biodegradable and would return to the soil.

The move from water- and wind-powered industry to coal and now oil power, the change from naturally grown and processed raw materials to materials produced or refined by large-scale industrial chemistry, as well as the move to the widespread use of non-biodegradable materials, has been responsible for the most extraordinary deterioration of our natural environment.

Dirty air and foul rivers were not new to the Industrial Revolution. Hippocrates recorded concerns over corrupted air in 400 BC. He discussed the adverse effects on health of the poisonous emanations from putrefying organic matter and the dust particles of early metal smelting and other industries. The residents of Rome in the first century AD complained about their air quality, the philosopher Seneca describing 'the oppressive atmosphere of the city and that reek of smoking cookers which pour out, along with clouds of ashes, all the poisonous fumes' and by 535 AD the Byzantine emperor Justinian proclaimed that clean air and water should be the birthright of all citizens. In the mid-thirteenth century the total deforestation of London led us to switch to seacoal as a fuel, causing Londoners to complain vociferously about smoke. In 1273 Parliament passed the Smoke Abatement Act, prohibiting the burning of soft coal which it deemed 'prejudicial to health', but only within the city walls. And once London's population had recovered from the Black Death, air pollution from coal, and its grave effects on health, again became a major source of concern in the city. In 1661 John Evelyn published *Fumifugium, or, The Inconveniencie of the Aer and Smoak of London*, one of the earliest known treatises on air pollution and still considered a significant work in the history of the science of air pollution. But the new steam-powered factories of the Industrial Revolution burned quantities of coal never seen before. Railways and ships burned coal, and newly wealthy Britons could afford to burn coal to heat their homes. The impacts on human health began to be more widely studied. In 1775 English surgeon Percivall Pott demonstrated the carcinogenic effects of soot on chimney sweeps.

Then scientists began to suspect a link not just between pollution and human health, but between industrial activity and the environment and climate. In 1820 British chemist Luke Howard, the 'father of meteorology', described a heat island effect which contributed to the accumulation of London's fog. Laws began to be enacted to tackle the growing threat of pollution: the Alkali Act in 1863, then the 1875 Public Health Act which led to the appointment of a Royal Commission on Noxious Vapours to study industrial air pollution. But even whilst they acknowledged that this pollution was caused by ever-expanding industry, they warned against doing anything that might get in the way of economic growth. Today we are acutely aware not just of air pollution and climate change, but of the huge and ever-growing problem of non-biodegradable plastic waste, including microfibres from our clothes, turning our once beautiful coasts into rubbish heaps littered with discarded low-quality plastic items.

By the 1970s serious warnings were being sounded about the limits of the planet to support the growth in the population. As we have seen, the warnings of a group of scientists in the 1972 book *The Limits to Growth* were stark: if not artificially restricted, the exponential growth of population and industry would lead to sudden and uncontrolled collapse of the world system within 100 years. But no sooner had these warnings been sounded, and their implications understood, than we went straight back to the business of encouraging people to want more. We have not slowed our rate of growth since 1972; in fact it has accelerated.

Modern agriculture, a combination of intensive tilling, lack of cover crops, synthetic fertilisers and pesticide use, has left arable land stripped of the nutrients, minerals and microbes that support healthy plant life, destroying our ability to grow our food. At current rates the UN's Food and Agriculture Organisation has calculated that we will have destroyed all of the world's topsoil by 2080. Some scientists put the date as early as 2040. Without topsoil, the earth's ability to filter water, absorb carbon and feed the human race collapses. The rate of reduction in forest cover has accelerated massively. Ten thousand years ago the earth was covered in around 6 billion hectares of forest. By 1900 that number was around 5 billion, today it's about 4 billion. In the last hundred years we have cut down as much forest as we did in the previous 9,900 years.

Human impact on climate change is not a newly discovered phenomenon, but it was marginalised until relatively recent times. As far back as 1860 the physicist John Tyndall recognised the Earth's natural greenhouse effect and suggested that changes in atmospheric composition could lead to changes in climate. The question continued to be researched and debated amongst academics. Advances in the understanding of climate change phenomena were published throughout the twentieth century, but it was not until 1988 that the UN established the Intergovernmental Panel on Climate Change (IPCC) and climate science finally began to be taken seriously.

Population growth, the huge rise in per capita consumption, and the change from natural materials which biodegrade to synthetic materials which do not, have shifted the dynamics dramatically for the worse. Individually today we buy over a hundred times as much clothing as our pre-industrial forebears, and at least ten times what we bought half a century ago. Seventy per cent of the material that goes into our clothing is plastic, but almost every single garment produced on the planet, over 100 billion last year, contains some plastic. Even on 100 per cent cotton clothes the labels and the thread are plastic, and the clothes are folded into plastic bags or delivered on plastic hangers. The toys we buy our children are now all plastic too. The furniture we buy is made predominantly of plastic, our carpets and rugs are plastic (polypropylene), we have vinyl flooring (plastic) in our kitchens and bathrooms instead of natural linoleum (made of linseed and jute), our lampshades are plastic, we fill our homes with plastic trinkets of an infinite variety. And the quality of all this stuff has fallen so far that it has become disposable. We throw it away and replace it continuously. It isn't just clothes: my ex-girlfriend bought an expensive sofa from a well-known, much-advertised furniture company. It was manufactured cheaply in China, and within six months the springs had failed.

It is not just in our own personal consumption that we have seen a move from durable to disposable, from natural to non-biodegradable. Our public procurement, a huge element of our national spending, including items used by our National Health Service, has seen a whole-sale move from locally made reusable items to overseas-made single-use items. I had not given this any thought until during the Covid pandemic I was involved in the UK's attempt to fill the gap left when the factories which supplied those single-use items closed. In the past, surgical gowns and medical face coverings were reusable, and were laundered in large hospital laundries. Today gowns, curtains and face coverings are single use and all are made of plastic – polypropylene – the same stuff as J-cloths. During Covid a few hospitals whose laundries had not been closed switched back to reusable gowns, made locally. I was involved in a project to develop a system for recycling face masks, again all done locally, but as soon as the Chinese factories reopened after the first wave of the pandemic, the government switched straight back to procuring these vital goods at the lowest cost from China – with no value to the UK economy.

5

From Always Striving For Excellence To Making Nothing But Rubbish

O ver the course of three million years, humans' curiosity, ingenuity and determination enabled us to work out how to make the things we needed to the most incredible quality. But then, in the space of less than a hundred years, in the name of economic progress, we discarded pretty much everything science and engineering had ever taught us about making things well, and today the things we make are of lower quality than at arguably any point in history.

What distinguishes us from most other species is our natural inclination to make things. We've been making from the moment we emerged as a species. Even before the emergence of the earliest *Homo* species, other related primates were fashioning tools to help with foraging, hunting, and preparing food. The first made objects to be discovered, simple stone tools for cutting and hammering, date from the pre-human era over 3 million years ago. We also made things from wood, which tends to decompose, but we have found prehistoric wooden spears in Germany that date back 300,000 years.

We have an instinctive desire not just to make things but to make them really well. Making good things gives us great satisfaction. Early humans would go to great lengths to select the perfect material for any job, splitting and carving the right type of stone or the best type of wood. We strove constantly to make tools sharper, harder, tougher, improving our ability to live well through their improved function. We experimented with fire in the processing of our tools; charred digging tools 171,000 years old have been found in Italy, similar to those still used by hunter-gatherers in Australia.

Throughout early prehistory every one of us was intimately connected to the making of things, as well as to their use; to the collecting and sorting of the materials – stone, bone, wood – from which our tools were made, and to the fashioning of them. We needed sharp slicing tools to butcher the animals we killed, we needed digging tools to unearth roots or grubs and mashing tools to make meat or plants easier to swallow and digest. Early humans had an affinity with quality and a natural eye for it. As long ago as the Neolithic period there's evidence of a long-distance Mediterranean trade in obsidian, a black volcanic glassy rock much prized for making the sharpest cutting tool, over distances of up to 500 miles.

We were constantly curious about the world around us. Around 6000–5000 BC, humans living in northeastern Africa spotted green streaks in the rocks and thought it might be something special. Either by accident or design we worked out that when you heated this ore for long enough, and to a high enough temperature, you could transform it into metal, in this case copper. We used it to make strong, sharp, durable tools that if broken could be remelted and made again. We learned how to control fire, using it to smelt and work these metals. We knew from smelting outdoors that a flow of air made the fire burn hotter, so we made bellows to increase and control the temperature of our fires. We learned through experimentation that hammering metal items whilst hot changed their properties. We learned to alloy copper and tin, making harder, more useful bronze. We made moulds of stone or clay to shape molten metal, and we

Jumper repair, William Lockie, Hawick

Tea break at Joshua Ellis, Pudsey

Postcards, William Lockie, Hawick

Knitting socks, J Alex Swift, Hathern

Time cards, ESP Leicester

Linda inspecting
finished jumpers,
William Lockie, Hawick

Observing the knitting process,
William Lockie, Hawick

Luskentyre Harris Tweed, Isle of Harris

Finished trainers, Walsh, Bolton

A proper brew, Century Dyeing, Elland, Leeds

discovered that quenching hot metal made it harder and stronger. We wanted better, more useful, more durable things. We strove constantly for higher quality.

By around four thousand years ago certain makers, in certain regions, had begun to develop specialist skills. Local differences in available raw materials, either mined or grown, and the differences in evolution of the technology of production led to the establishment of clear regional variations in the quality and availability of goods, and demand for the best quality led to the development of local as well as longer-distance trade. All humans understood the need for quality in every tool or object they used, because their lives depended on it.

Through curiosity and experimentation, we discovered that wool fibres from sheep could be felted, and wool and some plant fibres including flax and cotton could be spun, dyed and woven to produce fine, beautiful textiles. Biologists think that cotton plants have grown on earth for over 10 million years. There is evidence that humans spun and wove flax as early as 30,000 years ago. The production of such cloth expanded significantly about 12,000 years ago once humans settled down and began to engage in permanent agriculture and animal husbandry. The domestication, spinning and weaving of cotton to make clothes began about 5,000 years ago, simultaneously in what are today India, Peru and Sudan. Quite highly developed sewing skills produced more comfortable and more beautiful clothing. The Tarkhan dress, an elaborately pleated, fine-woven, striped linen dress found just south of Cairo, is over 4,500 years old (and can be seen in the Petrie Museum in London). We wore simple skirts, dresses, tunics and cloaks, and advances in metalworking allowed the development of fastenings, both simple and elaborately jewelled. Quality was highly prized and textiles were being traded long distances as early as 450 BC, when Greek historian Herodotus remarked on the quality of Indian cotton that 'wild trees bear fleeces for their fruits surpassing those of the sheep in beauty and excellence'. Over thousands of years, cotton and flax plants were selected to improve their yield, to allow them to grow in more varied climates, but also to improve the quality of the fibre, making it stronger and easier to spin. Likewise wool was of great importance and sheep were selected and bred for their long fine fleece, entering mythology in Jason's golden version.

We developed extraordinarily specific tools to enable us to make things well. Such tools required human control, were predominantly powered by human effort, and were mostly designed to do one simple job. As time went by, we developed more complex tools, and began putting multiple parts together to perform more complex functions. We first developed the wooden or ceramic spinning whorl about 7000 BC, allowing us to hand-spin a variety of fibres into high-quality yarn, but it took us another 7,500 years to upgrade to the spinning wheel. It took us around 30,000 years to go from the simplest weaving frame to the mechanical treadle loom, developed in India around 500 BC. Leaving hands free to control the weaving process, these technologies not only allowed much greater output, but crucially much greater control over the quality and consistency of cloth produced.

Pre-Industrial Quality

Until relatively recent times Britain's population was largely rural, the majority of countrymen being either farmers or employed land workers. But amongst them lived and worked some full-time artisan makers, while in addition many who worked the land had skills they put to use between farming's busy periods, making things to top up their income when there was no farm work to do. Those who didn't make things for a living used tools every day and intimately understood and appreciated quality.

We worked out how to make clothing from the things that grew or lived around us locally. We had wool in abundance, and high-quality flax. Hemp and nettle also produced high-quality fibres that could be extracted, spun and woven. We tanned leather naturally using oak bark to make boots, shoes or sandals. We developed our knowledge of how to grow and process flax to give us the highest quality of fibre. Flax farmers knew when to plant, and just what shade of gold the stems should be before the plant was pulled (never cut). They understood for how long, in ever-changing weather conditions, the stems needed to lie on the earth and be turned in order to perfectly ret (or rot) the stem, allowing the fibres to be extracted. We developed tools to break the stalks and remove their outer casing, and others to heckle, or comb out, the fibres. Even in very early times fine high-quality yarn could be spun by hand, and hand weaving produced cloths of exceptionally fine quality. We dyed using woad, madder, walnut shells, lichen and other locally available natural dyestuffs that we had discovered and refined through experimentation, fixing the dyes using natural mordants including ammonia-rich stale urine (which we would collect in a bucket by the back door for the purpose) or alum-rich club moss, both of which we discovered would fix and brighten colours. Dyes were of very variable quality, and also varied regionally dictated by the available local plants and some animal matter. Often woven cloth would contain warp and weft thread spun by different members of the community; it might be dyed by another member of the community, then woven by yet another. Once complete, the lengths of cloth might be 'fulled' or 'waulked' together to finish them. In Harris they sing traditional 'waulking' songs as they knead and pass the 'clo mor', or big cloth, up the table. One cloth might contain the labour of many friends or family members.

Another hugely important and abundant material in early Britain was wood. We used it to make our farm tools, our houses and the furniture within them, and many of the bowls and utensils we used for eating. Dorothy Hartley in her wonderful book *Made in England* describes the process of making things with wood, as still performed in certain parts of England in 1949. 'Wood', she says, 'is not inanimate. A tree standing is a mass of conflicting stresses and strains.' A working country woodman and carpenter begins his knowledge of wood with his knowledge of trees. 'Trees are living organisms, and the wood they produce has life and vitality and character.' Wood is a living material, and how it behaves in its different states, from green to dried, must be understood. The knowledge of how, and over what length of time, these properties change is part of the woodworker's arsenal. Wood has a natural strength and flexibility which, with deep knowledge, can be harnessed to produce objects mirroring these qualities.

Traditionally, high-quality timber was split, cleft or riven following its grain, giving it much greater resistance to further splitting and resistance to rain, its exposed surface being entirely the intact exteriors of the fibres of the tree. Split wood is vastly superior to sawn wood, which is a cheap, poor substitute. Antique furniture made from naturally split timber will significantly outlast even high-quality sawn furniture. A skilled woodworker would use his knowledge to select just the right piece of wood for the job; if a component required a curve or a bend, such a shaped bough or branch might be selected, and the wood split and worked in such a way as to preserve the structural integrity and hence the strength and pliability of the wood when incorporated into the finished piece. All woodworking professionals had such skills. They understood the material as implicitly as they understood their tools and their hands.

The making of even a seemingly simple object like a chair involved an extraordinary array of skills and knowledge, and several different craftsmen. The construction of a Windsor chair is a simple lesson in the lengths to which we once went to achieve great quality. They were typically made in native woods such as oak, elm, fruit-woods or ash, and rarely in yew. The solid seat was frequently made of well-figured native elm, a strongly grained, attractive wood that is resistant to splitting, or sometimes oak. It has hand-turned legs, double back hoops, and outswept, elegantly curved arms on supports which are turned and shaped. Yew was used for the best of these chairs because of its dense texture and superior colour. And the chairs were often made as bespoke items for individual customers' measurements for perfect comfort. The arms and seats on these antique chairs become wonderfully polished through hundreds of years of use and develop a rich patina and character.

The skill in producing a Windsor chair starts with the selection of the right pieces of the right type of wood, then wet-splitting them in the green, unseasoned state. Because it was easier to take the tools to the tree than drag the tree to a workshop, an artisan known as the 'bodger' would often set up camp in the woods close to where a tree had been felled, which was typically done early in the year, before the leaves appeared. The bodger would cut the tops off to preserve the sap in the trunk of the tree, in order to keep the wood green. He would cut the tree into billets, each approximately the length of a chair leg. The green unseasoned billet would be split using a wedge; he would then roughly shape the pieces into chair legs using the side-axe and next, using his drawknife, he would further refine the shape. Finally he would turn the leg with the pole lathe, which he would construct on site. All wood shavings were collected and used for kindling. Nothing was wasted.

Once the leg or the stretchers were finished, being green, they required seasoning. So they would be stored in piles until his quota of work (usually a gross of legs and the requisite stretchers) was complete, which would allow the wood time to season. It was quite normal for the bodger to stay with his tree until it was completely worked. He would deliver the finished work to a chair-making workshop where a benchman would create the seat, using first an adze to roughly carve the form, then a travisher to refine and smooth the hollow, before finally hand-sanding to give the final finish. Arms and bows were steam bent from single pieces, the wood steamed to just the correct degree to give the right amount of suppleness and held for several days after bending to ensure correct drying. Backsticks were turned or tapered using a hand plane. Finally the framer would assemble and finish the chair. Each stage required great skill, knowledge, care and commitment, and an innate eye for the beauty of the forms and the wood being worked.

In the pre-industrial period every object was made using the combined knowledge accumulated and passed on through, in some cases, tens of thousands of years. Every maker had a deep knowledge of and connection with their materials. And there was pride in every object. No corner would be cut in the production of any of the things we owned; every maker strove to make the highest quality thing they could, because people would keep every object that they owned for a lifetime, and pass them on.

Industrial Production – Man and Machine

The first Industrial Revolution brought about many great differences in the way things were made. Items were manufactured in greater volume, for less cost, but also crucially in many cases to the same – and in some instances, such as spun yarn, higher standard. We moved to an even greater specialisation of labour, allowing for even greater skill and control. Larger workshops and factories allowed workspaces and processes to be better optimised. We learned to harness new means of power to reduce the need for backbreaking human effort, and the advances in machines and mechanisation were indeed revolutionary.

People, factories, towns, and in some cases entire regions began to specialise, combining generations of knowledge, the mobility of staff between local firms transferring best practice. Gone were the part-time workers, the hybrid farmer/weavers, the shoemaker/traders. The self-employed artisan was dying out too, replaced by specialist retailers and wholesalers, and specialist manufacturers. With the demise of the artisan retailer a commercial gap developed between retailer and producer, and a larger gap between consumer and producer. In the sixteenth and seventeenth centuries most people, whether agricultural workers or domestic labour, would have had close relations with the makers of most of the things they bought, owned, ate or used daily, but by 1850 society was shifting, and for the first time significant sections of society started to lose those connections. Most people however remained highly practical. Women sewed, knitted, crocheted, spun or wove, keeping them close to the quality of yarn and cloth. Men kept small workshops, weaving, and fixing and building objects in wood and metal. Most people's ability to discern good quality from bad remained acute.

And, crucially, commercial relationships between manufacturer, wholesaler, retailer and customer were by and large long term and stable. Consumers would enjoy lifetime relationships with shopkeepers, whether in buying food or goods for the home. In any given town there might have been just one specialist retailer for many of the things we bought. And relationships between those retailers, and the manufacturers of the goods they sold, whether direct or through wholesale intermediaries, were stable too, such that the quality of goods always mattered. If a product – a door hinge, a skillet or a stool – didn't work properly, or broke before it should have done, everyone along the chain would know exactly where it came from. Consumers knew what to expect from goods and were not afraid to demand satisfaction. Manufacturers knew that they would be held accountable for the goods they produced, and retailers and wholesalers knew they would be held accountable for the goods they sold.

There was a huge leap forward in the technology available to assist in the making process. Simple early machines, mostly wheels, with cogs and axles, sometimes attached to animals or driven by water, had removed a good deal of the requirement for human strength and effort, and allowed greater precision. Eighteenth- and nineteenth-century technology was an even greater aid to humans in their quest to make high-quality objects, but still required their hands and skill in the making process. Man, material and machine worked harmoniously to produce objects of exceptional quality, in greater volume, with less of the backbreaking physical labour that had been required previously.

In clothing and textile production, an industry with a very long history, a certain level of specialisation had been developing, at a slow pace, for in some cases thousands of years, driven by factors including the availability of raw materials (tanneries were established in Northampton because of its local beef trade) and of water power, the settlement of skilled artisans from overseas (such as the Huguenots in East Anglia), and sometimes simply individual skilled craftspeople's technological knowledge, and the development of unique new designs and production processes. As early as the 1720s, Daniel Defoe described the varied and niche specialisations of different towns across the UK. Weaving and spinning had for a long time been segregated between wool, linen and cotton, each of which required significant differences in technology and handling, and between the different grades of cloth, but as industrialisation progressed so specialisation deepened. Where before there were tailors or dressmakers, now there were specialist overcoat, suit, shirt, or dress factories. Knitters specialised not just in socks but specific weights and types. Machinery became more specialised, raw materials were optimised – the right staple length, composition, fineness of fibre, with the right combination of elasticity and strength – to give the greatest comfort and durability in the specific end product. Everything was geared towards increasing quality *as well as* quantity.

All of the innovations, both in technology and in the industrialised factory system, drove a huge demand for more consistent raw materials, especially cotton, which until this point had been imported from India, the Middle East and other old cotton-growing nations. But with raw cotton prices rising rapidly, new plantations sprang up across the Americas, especially in the Caribbean where an unprecedented land grab established new cotton-growing regions, while millions of Africans were enslaved and shipped across the Atlantic to clear and work the land. Mechanical spinning required stronger, longer fibres which were selectively developed by the plant scientists. Their use reduced breakages in the spinning process, producing yarn that was stronger, easier to weave and resulted in more durable, finer, lighter cloth of significantly higher quality. Local wool from native breeds was still in use, but was considered coarse compared to the finer merino wool now being imported in large quantities from the arid regions of Australia. Flax was still grown extensively across the UK and linen production remained a major industry. In flax-producing regions the rivers ran golden yellow with the organic pollutants from retting the flax. Whilst machine-spun yarn may lack the romantic quality and pleasing imperfections of that spun by hand, it was easier to weave: more consistent, stronger, smoother, and causing fewer breakages. All of this innovation and these new sources of raw material radically cut the cost and dramatically improved the quality of everyday cloth, and hence of our clothing.

The early mechanisation of furniture making featured the introduction of powered lathes, the circular saw and bandsaw. Furniture manufacture began to change from purely manual work to a mix of lower-skilled machine processing, taking care of some basic tasks, with elements of highly skilled handcraft. Ceramics had long been a staple and valuable part of the human manufacturing world. We needed pots and jars to carry and store water and food. These were originally made by hand-coiling rods of clay, but in about 5000 BC potters worked out that it was quicker and simpler to build coil pots on a rotating turntable. Later, around 3500 BC, a heavy flywheel was added, first powered by hand and later kicked with the foot, leaving both hands free for shaping the clay.

The technology of throwing pots didn't change much for over five thousand years, until the development of a treadle wheel in the late 1800s. Josiah Wedgwood was the son of a potter, and by the age of nine had proved himself to be skilled in the craft, but a bout of smallpox left him unable to propel the potter's wheel. Instead he threw himself into a study of the science and chemistry of the clays and the mineral glazes used in their finishing. Wedgwood understood the need for precise temperature control; for his invention of the pyrometer, which measured the elevated temperatures needed for firing, he was elected a member of the Royal Society in 1783. Wedgwood developed unique clay bodies, and new glaze colours and techniques. He undertook around five thousand trials to perfect the colour and finish of the highly successful Queensware, a cream-coloured earthenware that was an affordable alternative to porcelain. Wedgwood took the same painstaking approach to the development of the revolutionary stoneware he called Jasperware. The development of clay and glaze chemistry, along with improvements in throwing, and greater control over firing temperatures, enabled pots of exceptional quality to be made. And where Wedgwood led, the competition had to follow, producing ceramics of greater and greater durability, lightness and beauty.

Specialisation led to great advances in design and quality in metal objects too. In 1840 Linus Yale, his family originally from North Wales, set up a lock-making business in New York. Linus Jr joined his father in the business and, following waves of significant innovation, in 1865 patented the Yale cylinder lock which we still use today. In 1848,

German émigré Charles Hager set up shop in St Louis, and over fifty years of dedicated trials eventually created the butt hinge we all think of as a hinge today. Years of dedication to the specialist manufacture of a single product created the conditions where huge leaps forward in both functional and aesthetic quality could occur.

During the Victorian and Edwardian period, everyday objects were produced in such a way as to maximise the quality of the using experience, no matter how marginal it might have seemed. In every aspect of our lives, we were surrounded by objects of astounding quality. On our buildings, in our furniture, in our household objects, everything we possessed was made with skill, care and often considerable aesthetic flourish. Stonemasons carved detail into façades and porticos, on columns, architraves, pilasters and cornicing, on every window surround. Wooden furniture had elegant joints, parts shaped and honed, carved feet, turned handles, beading, marquetry, inlays; mortice and tenon joints were pegged or tusked. Everywhere the natural human desire to express skill and love for the object they were creating was manifested. Blacksmiths and foundries crafted everyday metal objects, adding individual or regional character. From the humble hinge to handles and escutcheons, all told the story of the skill, flair and pride of the maker. There were decorative flourishes even in the modest homes of working-class families, which had the visible hand of the craftsman to elevate them. It is almost impossible to imagine everyday objects today being made with even a small fraction of the care and skill employed then. It is arguable that at that point, in many objects we use every day, we had reached the peak of quality.

Mass Production

In the early period of mechanised production, simple machinery was developed which would aid humans in the making of goods, removing the tedious, time-consuming, physically demanding or low-skilled portion of their labour. Powered looms or wood-turning lathes would free the weaver or woodworker to use both hands without encumbrance, allowing for greater control over the work, and hence greater quality. Techniques of production were not greatly altered, the materials used and the way they were processed were not changed, but the time it took to manufacture each item was shortened, reducing the cost and the selling price without a diminution of quality.

But with mass production this all changed. Where old techniques and methods of making had been built around the infinite flexibility of human hands and bodies, mass production was concerned exclusively with efficiency and flow and required the simplification and standardisation of processes. And it meant, where possible, removing skilled humans and replacing them with the closest facsimile that a machine could offer. All was geared to maximum throughput and minimum cost. Standardisation meant an end to craftsmanship, individual innovation, and personality in products. Uniformity removed all romance. This was production geared up to serve the unprecedented boom in consumption being created by advertising and fashion during the late nineteenth and early twentieth century. In the US, the fastest-growing and most influential economy in the twentieth century, large business corporations had superseded the typical small-scale mid-nineteenth-century firm, and where small-scale private firms had in the past always strived for success through product quality and differentiation, or by manufacturing a single high-quality product, the new corporations wanted high volume, and dominance of mass markets. In this new paradigm, quality became ever less important.

Machines could not replicate human flexibility and dexterity, so to enable mass production the objects themselves were redesigned, simplified – dumbed down – to make them more manufacturable. Any time-consuming assembly methods were removed. And the materials from which objects were made were changed to suit mass processing, minimising the complexity of materials or parts used, simplifying and rationalising supply chains. Mass production sought material efficiency, aiming to use the least amount of material possible to do an acceptable job. Everywhere the amount of material could be reduced it was. Product was now designed in a way to allow for machine manufacturability meaning huge compromises to quality were made.

In furniture production, out went curved, organic shapes and complex high-quality joints. In came squares, straight lines, glued or bolted joints. The use of non-uniform, naturally grown wood, with all of its beautiful subtle variation, required infinite small adaptations to the design and the processes used, which in turn demanded skill, knowledge and an ability to react which machines did not possess. So out went those materials. Machines perform standard operations, they deal in right angles and straight lines; materials must be homogenised, their growth or production industrialised. Out went character and natural material variation.

Circular saws had been invented in the late eighteenth century and were in common use by the mid-nineteenth century. Walter Taylor was the son of a carpenter and apprenticed as a ship's block maker in Southampton. He saw issues in block production and figured out how to improve it, first using horse power, and later with an entirely new steam-driven mill. Where wood had in the past either been split or sawn by hand, it could now be quickly and easily sawn by machine into uniform planks. Band saws, first invented by William Newberry in 1809, allowed for quick cutting of irregular and curved shapes. Iron and steel components were introduced, allowing faster construction by removing the labour required for making complex wooden joints, meaning more changes in design. This was the start of a road that would eventually lead to modern flat-packed, bolted, square-legged, straight-backed chairs. Subtle beauty of material and form was removed, while the standardisation required for mass manufacture saw a significant reduction in quality, both functional and aesthetic. Compare the skill and time entailed in making each Windsor chair with today's flat-pack furniture, industrially produced by machines in seconds.

By 1900, modern business corporations, in alliance with investment bankers, were consolidating and merging into giant entities, preoccupied with making profits rather than with making goods. The bankers cared little what was made, or how. They coughed up their money so that corporations could grow. American economist Thorstein Veblen wrote that this new form of business capital, the philosophy of investment for gain, had begun to supersede any commitment to industry and workmanship, a change in outlook he described, correctly, as 'one of the most significant mutations in man's history'. In Veblen's view quality had become unimportant in this new America. The innovations of the mass manufacturing age were no longer aimed at increasing or even maintaining quality. If an item could be made faster and cheaper to the same standard, that was acceptable, but in a trade-off between volume or cost and quality the latter always lost out.

Before the first Industrial Revolution in Britain, and before the birth of corporate America, the buying of goods and the making of them had been bound together, with buyers and makers living and working closely in local or regional economies. Most people knew where the goods came from because they themselves produced them, they knew their value and understood the costs and efforts required to bring them into being. But in quite a short period of time the two activities became separated. Now it was profit-driven business, not individual moral men and women, which decided upon the character and quality of the goods made. Many corporate businesses made a conscious choice to separate production from selling and by 1910 not a single US retailer was still involved in manufacturing. Volume and profit now trumped quality.

American corporations had once prided themselves on making long-lasting products, but as the twentieth century passed increasing consumption became their primary motivation. Writing in 1955, retail analyst Victor Lebow said, 'Our enormously productive economy demands that we make consumption our way of life. We need things consumed, burned up, replaced and discarded at an ever-accelerating rate.' Vance Packard, in his bestselling book *The Waste Makers*, published in 1960, attacked the corporations and their advertising partners for what he saw as a deliberate strategy to make their goods disposable, detailing ways in which they deliberately designed their products, or the sales strategies that supported them, to ensure that what was bought quickly became obsolete, what he described as 'planned obsolescence'. This was achieved in two ways, each of them arguably equally sinister: first functionally, through reduction in quality such that the product physically deteriorated; and second psychologically – 'designed to become obsolete in the mind of the consumer, even sooner than the components used to make them will fail' because the object was no longer 'the latest'.

It is interesting to compare the philosophy of planned obsolescence in the American car industry, one of the great drivers of the country's economic growth, their vehicles radically redesigned each year to ensure that previous models became recognisably out of date, with the publicly stated aim of Volkswagen and their long-running Beetle. VW's philosophy was that every new Beetle should be technically superior to the previous one, with better brakes, safer seatbelts, greater fuel efficiency, but that it should never be so radically altered cosmetically as to render the previous model undesirable to its owner. The strategy of the American car industry of the 1950s and 60s is analogous to the strategy of Apple and the iPhone today; an endless stream of cosmetically new products with very limited benefit to the user, designed purely to make a previous version undesirable and hence increase consumption.

The 1970s: Synthetics and Offshoring

Two things happened in the 1960s and 1970s which would go on to have a profound effect on the trajectory of product quality. Industrially produced synthetic materials, including textile fibres, became broadly available, and offshoring of manufacture began in earnest.

Synthetic fibres, especially nylon, polyester and acrylic, which had been invented in the late nineteenth and early twentieth century, became fully commercialised, widely available at affordable prices, and in an array of vivid and vibrant colours and patterns made possible by advances in synthetic dyes. Synthetic fabrics meant clothing could be produced more cheaply, and the production of textiles moved away from the long-established, smaller-scale natural textile makers to the giant industrial chemical businesses. ICI, already a leader in the production of synthetic dyestuffs, and Courtaulds (which had seen its future in man-made fibres as early as 1904 when it acquired the patents for viscose) battled to develop and expand production of fibres such as nylon, terylene, crimplene and rayon. Courtaulds became the largest manufacturer of synthetic textiles on the planet and were the fifth largest company in Britain, employing over 100,000 people. This cheap alternative drove many manufacturers of natural fibre fabrics out of business.

As well as using cheaper synthetic materials, retailers began to realise that they could undercut their competition by making clothes in areas where labour was cheap. Sourcing agents and middlemen greased the wheels and made fortunes on the backs of Asian garment and textile workers. Factories in Asia bent over backwards to accommodate, seeing the opportunity for reclaiming the textile industry they had lost to the British during the Industrial Revolution. By making clothes with cheap labour, and using synthetic fabrics, a new wave of lower-cost young fashion brands created a whole new market. Many high street brands chose to take a less aggressive route, moving production to Asia but keeping the quality of their fabrics high. Some stuck to manufacturing in the UK and tried to compete on quality, but in the end they all succumbed, price pressure forcing brands at all levels to move to reduce costs. Natural fabrics were replaced by synthetics, high-quality Asian factories were replaced with lower-quality ones, and a huge number of the remaining UK factories were closed, leaving hundreds of thousands of workers high and dry. A huge race to the bottom on both price and quality had begun.

Long-established clothing retailers whose businesses had always been built on product quality felt forced to reduce costs, their previously well-priced goods now looking expensive by comparison with those of their rivals. Highly skilled technical teams who had overseen the quality of everything from yarn spinning, to dyeing, to sewing, were dispensed with. Many new brands appeared on the scene with no technical knowledge of textiles and clothing at all. Buyers bought on price and nothing else.

The first offshore factories were highly skilled specialists, but as time wore on and costs rose they were replaced by less skilled, less scrupulous manufacturers, prepared to do anything to meet the aggressive cost-reduction targets of the faster and faster fashion industry. Retailers and brands were at the mercy of the sourcing agents and the factories; they no longer had the skills to maintain quality even if they had wanted to. Price was the only consideration; less next season than this season or we go elsewhere was the message. And where manufacturing quality went, design quality soon followed. Why pay expensive UK designers when you can have low-paid Chinese ones? Well-known Western brands had now outsourced everything to do with the product to their Chinese partners.

With each new season the aggressive fast fashion retailers would reduce prices, and even formerly high-quality retailers followed suit. Price and quality began the first of two significant periods of decline.

Sell Cheap, Wear, Dispose, Repeat: A Race to the Bottom

The new wave of online fast fashion brands that hit the scene in the early 2000s took a disregard for quality to new levels. Fabric and fabrication were irrelevant in a world where clothing was disposable, while superficial image was everything. Sell cheap, wear, dispose, repeat was the model. In a little over twenty years, the quality of our clothing has taken such an extraordinary tumble that it's hard to imagine it getting lower. And every downward step in quality the ultra-cheap end of fashion takes, so the rest must follow. High street brands who once put the words 'value' and 'quality' on all their adverts have long since given up on trying to make good clothes; instead they congratulate themselves that their clothes are at least better than the rubbish sold at the very bottom of the market. Now offshore factories are generalists, making anything, in any way they can, for a price. They move, they hire whole new workforces in regions where costs are lower. Skills are secondary, materials are irrelevant. The customer doesn't know. They probably don't care as long as it looks good for a few hours. Quality has become an irrelevance. We have thrown away everything we knew about making good things in our mad scramble to be cheap.

Long-established knowhow and craft skills, alongside twenty-first century science and engineering, offer solutions which can do two things: make things better, and make them cheaper.

For most of our history we listened to those concerned with making things well and did our best to do both of these things. The technological advances of the first Industrial Revolution removed a lot of the physical work, with machines that took away the heavy lifting and a lot of the repetition, but those machines worked alongside human skill and did not entirely replace it. Quality increased, cost decreased. Brilliant. But there were limits, and once those limits had been reached we faced a decision. Improve: improve the quality with no increase in price, or reduce price but only with a commensurate reduction in quality. Today most large businesses who sell manufactured goods are required by the people who own them to continually sell more, and to make ever greater profit. Making things better is hard. The easy way to sell more and make bigger profits is to make things cheaper.

There is nothing clever about what they've done. It's not some efficiency thing, they've made it cheaper by making it worse. Over the past fifty years we have replaced an economy interested in producing and selling high-quality goods with one only interested in making cheap stuff. In clothing, the sort sold by the vast majority of the world's fashion brands, there has been no effort *at all* to improve quality.

The cost of making an object can be broken down into two components: the make, and the materials from which it's made. And each of those two can in turn be broken into two further sub-components. Make cost broadly has two components;

- how long it takes to make
- how much the people who do the making are paid.

Materials cost also has two components:

- how much you use
- how much each unit of material costs.

Here are the things they do to make our clothes more cheaply. First, they make them faster – shirts, for example, were always made with fine handmade French seams, which meant the shirt was more durable, more comfortable and more beautiful. But sewing such seams is time-consuming. Some shirts are made using a machine which does a reasonable representation of the seam, but it's less durable and less refined. The cheapest shirts are simply overlocked together, making them less comfortable and significantly less robust, but much faster to assemble. On jackets and coats time-consuming linings are removed, as are pockets, and in some cases even the fastenings.

Second, they make them somewhere where the makers are paid less. First production moved to Hong Kong, but when labour there agitated for better wages production was moved to mainland China. And then, when the first mainland Chinese workers demanded decent wages, they moved to a cheaper part of China. Then they left China altogether and moved to Bangladesh, or Laos, or Cambodia. Every time you move, you have to train new workers, so quality suffers, but profits go up.

And then you can reduce your material costs, again in two ways. First, use less of the raw materials – make your clothing skinnier, or shorter, or thinner. Second, redesign the object – replace expensive high-quality material with cheaper, lower-quality material, and use the lowest possible grade of this low-quality material. Again, getting rid of linings means less fabric.

The weight of the cloth from which your garment is made contributes significantly to the cost. If one cloth is half the weight of another, it will contain half the raw material of the other, so everything else being equal will cost half as much. Half of a garment's value might be the cost of the cloth, so if that is the case, the garment will be 25 per cent less expensive to make. Winter coats, for example, used to be made from 800g pure wool fabric; now they are typically made of 300g wool/polyester blend. Today many sweatshirts are made of fabric which is less than half the weight of that used in the past. T-shirts are much thinner too. Some brands sell sweatshirts that are the weight of T-shirts in the past. And they've got us wearing leggings instead of jeans or trousers. Many leggings are so thin they're see-through. We're spending far less, but we're getting far less for what we do spend.

They're also using much lower quality materials, like a 50/50 polyester/wool mix instead of pure wool, or a 90/10 mix, or pure polyester – and using bad polyester instead of good polyester, because low-quality polyester is even cheaper. Many people wouldn't imagine there is a difference, while others don't care. So why not just use the cheapest and worst material you can source? Good-quality wool winter coat fabric is *at least* ten times the price of polyester.

The manufacturers have another trick to deploy to make clothes cheaper: making them shorter and skinnier. Overcoats today are the length that jackets were twenty-five years ago. I fought against this trend every winter when I worked with Debenhams. A winter coat used to come to below the knee, have some shape to it and have a broad sleeve. It would use between 3m and 3.5m of fabric to make. Now they are short and slim and use around 2.5m. That alone equates to a 28 per cent reduction in fabric cost. Skinny jeans or trousers use around 35 per cent less material than regular-width ones.

Taking all of this together, an average coat in 1970 contained 2.8kg of wool, an average coat now contains just 375g of wool. Your modern overcoat contains just 13 per cent of the wool of a coat from fifty years ago (many now contain no wool at all), and the cost of the cloth in a modern coat is less than 10 per cent of what it was then.

Clothes haven't got cheaper, they've just got thinner, shorter, skinnier, more synthetic and less well made. Since about 1970, when clothing brands started to compete seriously on price, they have, season after season, iteration after iteration, reduced price by reducing quality, twice a year for fifty years – a hundred small cuts, each time producing a poorer-quality copy of what went before. It looks a bit like the thing you started with, but it has none of the quality or integrity of the original object. Every six months the same conversation with suppliers: can you make it cheaper? And if the answer is no, there'll always be another supplier desperate to make a dollar who will find a way.

Because fewer people are buying high-quality goods, the volume of such goods being produced has fallen, which has caused their prices to rise. So the poor-quality cheap goods have become cheaper and cheaper, and worse and worse in quality, and the high-quality goods have become comparatively much more expensive, so that today only the wealthy can afford them (or believe they can afford them). If you earn even an average salary, the chances are that you can only afford, or feel that you can afford, low-quality goods. But because high-quality goods are much better made, not only will the wealthy gain far greater enjoyment from their use, but because of the goods' great durability the wealthy will need to buy fewer of them and therefore they will cost much less in the long run. Terry Pratchett described it as the Boots theory of socioeconomic unfairness. To paraphrase: 'A really good pair of leather boots cost fifty dollars. But an affordable pair of boots, which were sort of OK for a season or two, cost about ten dollars. The good boots lasted for years and years. A man who could afford fifty dollars had a pair of boots that would still be keeping his feet dry in ten years' time, while the poor man who could only afford cheap boots would have spent a hundred dollars on boots in the same time and would still have wet feet.'

Jumpers should last a thousand wears but they last a hundred, socks should last a hundred wears but they last ten. We should only make clothes that last. I have a jumper that I wear regularly that I bought eighteen years ago. It was made in Scotland from English-spun lambswool, and I worked out that I have worn it at least a thousand times. It has never pilled, and has retained its shape even after going through the washing machine several times. I often write that our clothes are affordable, and almost every time someone responds to say that I am being ridiculous, and that normal people can't afford £70 jumpers. Of course for many people this is true, but the sad thing is they *really* can't afford ten £20 jumpers.

Why Cheap Stuff Costs Us More

I have a massive bee in my bonnet about pans. I did a talk on stage with Keith Brymer Jones from *The Great Pottery Throw Down* at Blackburn Cathedral in 2023 and spent a large chunk of our allotted time ranting about cookware. Good pans are heavy and made of metal, stainless steel or cast iron. All professional kitchens use such pans for good reason; they'll take all the abuse that you can throw at them and they will never fail. I have pans in my kitchen that are thirty years old and are as good today as the day they were bought. They are made in such a way, and from materials of such quality, that I can see no reason why they will *ever* fail. My pans will last me my entire lifetime. The pans I bought are made from 4kg of easily recyclable high-quality stainless steel and the same one today would cost you £169.

Contrast this to the pans I am obliged to use from time to time in my rental flat. You can buy such pans on a leading supermarket website for £8, made from around 300g of low-grade aluminium, with about 50g of plastic in the handle, and a few grams of low-quality PTFE for the non-stick surface. Lightweight, flimsy, their dangerously wobbly plastic handle attached loosely with a screw, they warp when heated and their non-stick coatings flake off. Because of the coating on the aluminium and the absence of any information about the handle, none of this pan is recyclable. Exploring the customer comments about this pan online gives some idea about its durability. One five-star review from November 2023 said, 'Brilliant in all ways – non-stick, price, handy weight – can't fault it, bought eight before they discontinue.' Eight? The earliest review for this product was November 2019, so assuming the product had been on sale for four years, this customer replaced this five-star pan every six months. Another from March 2023, awarding two stars, says, 'I have a ceramic hob and this pan does not like it. It warped from the middle on first cook. In bin.' A third, also giving two stars, from February 2021 says, 'Left some light scratches after first use, I guess you get what you pay for, but I didn't think it would be this abysmal.'

So how much more do cheap pans cost me? If I have two pans, then a lifetime of good pans will cost me £340, while buying cheap pans would cost me £700. That's £360 *more*. On top of that, there's the indirect cost of going to the shops 140 times, or of having 140 pans delivered, plus the cost we pay in council tax for the waste, collectively about 55 million kg of waste pans a year. Scaling this up to the 28 million UK households, we collectively waste over £200 million a year buying cheap pans. Enough to build nearly five thousand new affordable homes.

And what about other costs? Today there is just one pan maker in the UK that I know of, Samuel Groves, who employ around forty people. We could make all the good pans we need here in the UK. A quick calculation suggests about a thousand skilled makers might be sufficient (though this is a rough estimate), so by not doing so we're costing the UK economy about £25 million worth of wages a year too.

If we imagine the same scenario played out across every similar sector that would be a lot of jobs created, and the planet would be spared a huge amount of waste.

Overcomplication

Good design should produce objects which perform their function well, and do so for a very long time. One of the best ways to increase the durability of an object is to simplify it. The fewest materials, the fewest joins, no features which are unnecessary to its function. This is my philosophy when designing clothes: the fewest pockets, the fewest seams, no unnecessary features. More bells and whistles equals more things to go wrong.

But in an attempt to make us want more new stuff, many of our everyday objects are designed in ways that pay no heed to this basic principle. Many are designed to be unnecessarily complex, this complication creating unnecessary ways in which the product can and does fail. Toilet flushes used to be the simplest mechanisms, a lever and a rigid float; if they failed, which because of their simplicity they seldom did, they could be rapidly repaired with something as simple as a bit of string or a coat hanger. Today press-button flushes are assembled with complex and flimsy bladder systems which work poorly and fail quickly. A toilet used to work for a century. Now they fail after six months, and to repair them the entire system needs to be thrown away and replaced. Kitchen cupboard doors used to just close. Now our cupboard doors are built with complex soft-close mechanisms, cheaply manufactured from low-quality, mostly plastic materials. They fail long before the hinges or the door would fail and must be thrown away and replaced. Why do we need cupboards which close softly? How has this improved our life? There are nearly 25 million kitchens in the UK; if on average they have a dozen cupboards or drawers, and every one were to have soft-close doors, that's 300 million pieces of plastic that we absolutely do not need, and that's before they fail and we have to replace them. Just because we can do something does not mean that we should.

Discerning Quality

Most brands no longer sell quality, and we no longer recognise it. Our ability to discern quality in the objects we buy is at an all-time low. In the 1990s, both in the US and the UK, schools began to remove practical lessons from the syllabus: woodwork, metalwork, 'shop class' in the US; anything that connected us to real objects and tools was quietly phased out. School-age kids no longer made things at school, they no longer handled tools, or wood, metal or clay. They learned about materials from books but no longer understood the properties of or differences between physical materials in any practical sense.

I made a documentary for the BBC about uniforms for the King's coronation, during the filming of which I was talking with an officer in the British Army about clothes. He told me about one of his recent young recruits who had been shocked when he pulled on his army boots for the first time. He had never worn a leather shoe before in his life. He said many had a similar reaction to the weight of their uniform. Many people will never have worn leather, or wool, or cotton. Their entire life may have been spent wearing plastic clothes, walking on plastic carpets, sitting on plastic sofas. They may never have eaten with a well-made knife and fork. Many people simply have no idea what good quality feels like. If we don't educate people, then how can we expect them to make good choices about the things they buy? How can we prevent them from being parted from their hard-earned money for terrible-quality things?

Not Cheaper, Just Worse

The quality and price of our everyday objects has over the course of the past fifty years declined steadily, by small degrees such that most of us, certainly those of us who are buying and discarding things all the time, barely notice the difference. Like the parable of the frog in hot water, each small reduction is barely discernible. But compare a contemporary object with the equivalent from fifty years ago and the difference will be remarkable.

The fall in tandem of price and quality have corresponded with an exponential rise in the quantity of things we buy, because we no longer need to consider the cost of their purchase. In 1500 a dress would have cost over a month's pay; by 1880, at the end of the first Industrial Revolution, about a week's. In 1970, once the effects of offshoring and synthetics kicked in, it might have cost a day's pay, and by the turn of the millennium we could get a dress for about four hours' wages. Today, with the rise of ultra-fast fashion, we can buy a dress for less than half an hour's pay, less than we'd pay for a cup of coffee. And we wonder why people buy so much.

And quality, which increased steadily for over 3 million years, right through to the start of the mass production era, has over the past century declined significantly, and over the last twenty years has

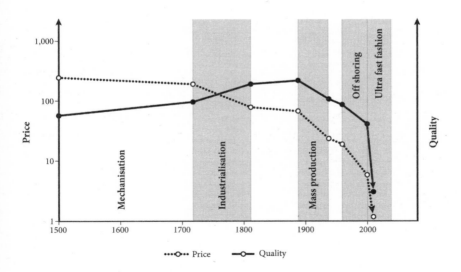

Figure 2

dropped off a cliff. But we seem largely unconcerned that the things we buy are rubbish, and that we spend our lives throwing things away and replacing them.

The tangible quality, the usefulness, the fitness for purpose, as well as the durability of our possessions has declined to a small fraction of what it was at its peak, which for different objects was at different periods in our manufacturing history. But the intangible quality has declined markedly too. We have no connection to the things we buy: there is no story, no history.

The things we buy might cost very little, but they are worth even less.

6

Savile Row Quality

S avile Row is special and unique. The street itself is infinitely more
famous than any of the centuries-old tailoring houses that call it
home. On this quiet Mayfair thoroughfare and its tributaries, cheek-
by-jowl with some of the most expensive addresses on the Monopoly
board, reside a collection of small craft-based clothiers and a community of craftsmen and women, and their ecosystem of very particular
suppliers. There are few other communities like it anywhere on earth.

The art of hand tailoring in London can trace its history back to the
thirteenth century when a new style of creating garments emerged,
taking its name from the French 'tailler', to cut. These clothes were
unlike anything made before, fine fabric cut and shaped by hand, with
a canvas substructure carefully worked using steam and heat to give
human form to flat pieces of cloth, clothes fitted close to the body. The
Fraternity of St John the Baptist of Tailors and Linen-Armourers, the
first company of tailors, was recognised by royal charter in 1327. With
the exception of the lockstitch sewing machine, which is used to sew
seams only, no technology has infringed on the hand-making technique employed by the tailors of Savile Row in seven hundred years.
The materials used, both the main cloth and the various canvases and

other fabrics used inside to give the garments their structure, have not changed in centuries, and the quality of the clothes produced in the small workrooms, located behind hushed showrooms, in basements, or tucked away in creaky garrets, is unrivalled.

Bespoke tailoring is an art, taught, master to apprentice, over years of tireless and repetitive practice. A Savile Row tailor must have patience for learning, great manual dexterity and fine motor skills, a refined eye for line and form, and an unstinting dedication to quality. It is the learned skill and acquired knowledge, along with the freedom to take all pains necessary in the creation of the garment, which gives a suit its physical quality. But the quality of a Savile Row suit extends far beyond the precision of its hand-basted foreparts, or the deft sculpting of canvases in the chest or collar, or the prick-stitched edges so precisely tensioned that no hint of puckering on lapel or pocket flaps mars the perfection of line. It is the intangible quality of the stories of the ancient houses themselves, their associations with powerful, famous, notorious, elegant men; a connection to the lineage of craftsmanship, stretching back over seven hundred years; the story of the craftsman who is sewing your clothes. My longest serving trouser maker has worked on Savile Row since the 1960's and had has personally sewn the trousers in which our current king, several Rolling Stones, David Bowie, Burt Lancaster, Jack Nicholson and countless others he has forgotten have gone about their business. Every garment cut and sewn on that street is imbued with these collected stories.

––––––––––––

In April 2005 I was studying for an MBA at New College, Oxford. Walking to the dining hall one afternoon I was due to have lunch with a good friend, but he cancelled, so I had lunch on my own, grabbing the only paper left, a copy of the *Financial Times*, which despite being a business student I seldom read. Leafing through its dusky pink pages I came to a section entitled 'Businesses for Sale', a section I'd never seen before, let alone read. On that day, and that day only, the owner of Norton & Sons, a bespoke tailor almost two centuries old, had placed a notice advertising it for sale, advising interested parties to write to him at no. 16 Savile Row.

If you were to draw a Venn diagram of all the things I liked most – handmade objects, well-cut clothes, businesses with story and heritage – then the tailoring houses of Savile Row would be in the centre. So I wrote, visited the shop, spoke with the team, and discussed the terms of a deal which we signed in the December of that year. I sold my house, car and everything else I owned, took investment from several friends and my granny, and whilst my fellow MBA grads were heading for hedge funds and management consultants, I took over a 184-year-old, slightly down-at-heel tailoring business.

There was an incredible amount right about Norton & Sons: the tradition and continuity of handcraftsmanship, its long history and untarnished heritage, and it is a business which has arguably the best sustainability credentials of any on the planet. We only make what is needed, largely by hand, using only the very best, sustainably produced, natural, biodegradable materials (wool, linen, cotton, horsehair), so we've a tiny carbon footprint and virtually no waste. If there was a power cut our team could keep on making. We alter and repair the clothes we make for life, which is regularly fifty years or more, ensuring they last as long as possible; it's not uncommon to see a piece back in the workshop for repair or alteration which is close to a hundred years old, and many of my neighbours will say the same thing.

The big challenge, on a street full of the best tailors in the world, is how to stand out. Norton & Sons wasn't the oldest (that was Davies); not the best known (Gieves); not the most expensive (Huntsman); not connected with a particular branch of the armed forces (Dege & Skinner, or Welsh & Jeffries); and not the biggest (Anderson &

Sheppard). I decided that Norton & Sons should celebrate two things: its smallness, and the unique stable of British weavers from which I would source our cloths. I got to know those suppliers intimately, so that I could tell their stories to the people who might be bespeaking of their cloth for a suit, as part of a level of personal service that we think was the equal of that offered anywhere.

I worked in the shop and workshop during the day, then did the accounts, admin, marketing and everything else in the evening and on the slow Saturdays. I did every dirty job, including mopping up the shop when the drains backed up. I learned to live on a £1 lunch budget, and did so for about seven years. In August 2006 only one customer walked through the front door in the entire month. We ran out of cash, and to keep the business alive I had to beg my mother for a small loan from her savings, and the bank for an extension to our overdraft. We were never, in the first five years, more than a few weeks away from running out of money, but something would always come along and save us – a customer would unexpectedly turn up and pay a bill, or someone would walk in unannounced and place a chunky order, the deposit for which would keep the lights on for another month.

In 2006 we had two big bits of luck. The first was the BBC commissioning a documentary about Savile Row, the first ever warts-and-all look behind the scenes at the workings of this unique community. The documentary, filmed and directed by BAFTA winner Ian Denyer, gave a look behind the curtain at what had for many years been a closed world. No one had been allowed such privileged access to the people and businesses of the street before. Ian and I got on well (and still do); he liked that I was the youngest guv'nor on the street, and Nortons was given a far greater share of the limelight than our relative size merited.

Ian came with me to Harris where I was sourcing tweeds, and while we were there it was announced that William Haggas, a textile manufacturer from Yorkshire, had acquired the largest mill on the island. His plan was to industrialise Harris tweed, reduce its production to just four fabrics, and grant his own brand a worldwide exclusive. Haggas had been successful in the textile industry through a focus on efficiency and had for many years been a supplier to M&S, but Harris tweed is more cottage than industry and the island was in an uproar.

Savile Row was the most watched programme on BBC Four that year. It was repeated on the same channel, then shown on BBC Two, then repeated again on both. It made its way to the British Airways inflight entertainment system. Overnight it changed our business. The morning after the first episode aired, four new customers walked in and ordered where previously we'd been taking about one order a week. People began walking into the shop to ask what the latest news was about Harris tweed, while I received dozens of phone calls and letters. I suggested to the BBC that we should make a follow-up series, which happily they agreed to do. The show also brought tailoring as a job to the attention of millions. From about one person a month prior to the series, at least a couple of young people a week came into the shop to ask about apprenticeships and other training opportunities.

The second bit of luck came through my good friend Martin Cole, a hugely talented creative director in advertising, who was making a documentary for Channel 4 called *The Search for Cool*. In it he explored the idea of who and what made things cool, when things became cool and when they stopped being cool. One of the cool-makers interviewed for the show was a young designer, a grad from St Martins, called Kim Jones. When Martin told Kim about Nortons he came to see me, hanging out for hours in the workshop and promising to be in touch.

Six months later he called and asked if we had time to help him with some unusual tailored pieces for his forthcoming collection, since he was struggling to find anyone with the cutting and sewing skills to make them. I made some feeble pretence at checking to see if we could fit him in, before we worked on his Autumn-Winter 2007 show in

New York in January, and on his Spring-Summer 2008 show in London. And through working with Kim we met and worked with or for an amazing line-up of designers, including Alexander McQueen, Christian Louboutin, Christopher Kane, Henry Holland, Giles Deacon, Rag & Bone, The Kooples, Erdem, Louise Gray, Meedham Kirchoff, Richard Nicoll and Jenny Packham, amongst many others. We became known as the Savile Row house that young designers worked with. And thanks to our rising profile we worked with some of the smartest brands on the planet: Cartier, Rolls Royce (we still make the purple lab coats that visitors to the Rolls Royce factory have to wear to prevent scratches to the paintwork), Mercedes (I produced a custom interior for a beautiful vintage Merc for London Fashion Week), Lotus (we created drivers' jackets), Barbour, Trickers, John Lobb, Samsung, LG and lots more. Norton & Sons became a place where contemporary design and traditional craftsmanship intersected.

I had started the business with a few thousand pounds in the bank. After three years of working seventy-plus hours most weeks for almost no pay (I paid myself an average of £7,000 a year for the first three years), we had nearly tripled the size of the business. It was stable and making a small steady profit, and crafting a product of exceptional quality for a bunch of fascinating, and mostly very nice, clients.

Savile Row manages to tread a fine line between being staunchly traditional and yet welcoming and modern in outlook. Whilst the shops (most of them, anyway) have an informal, convivial air, the bespoke tailoring process is still shrouded in an awe and mystery, its language arcane, the roles of the men and women engaged in the craft unique to this small community. The word bespoke, which comes originally from Savile Row, means something very specific there; clear rules set out within the articles of the Savile Row Bespoke Association govern what can and can't be called bespoke. The methods used are those passed down through generations of master tailors, and the rules are important. There are cheaper and quicker ways to make tailored clothes, but in the expert opinion of those who work on Savile Row there are no better ways. You can buy more expensive suits but you cannot buy better ones.

Savile Row, both the clothes it makes and the service it delivers, is for the most part unstintingly understated in a world of luxury that increasingly is about overstatement. Until very recently, suits bought from Savile Row did not even carry a visible brand label. Instead, tucked within the pocket of the coat (what we call a jacket) and sewn into the seat seam of the trousers is a label called a buggy label, which states the customer's name, the date of creation, the cloth number, and the initials of the cutter who cut it. It is incredibly discreet. But Savile Row is far more luxurious than the branded luxury available in every major shopping street and airport, a luxury that is mass produced in overseas factories and worn or carried by millions. It is scarce. The volume of handmade bespoke suits made on Savile Row each year is around about 10,000. The industry largely exists in just a few small workshops. What you pay for is skilled craftsmanship, not marketing, or expensive retail spaces, or unnecessary frills.

Savile Row supports an extended ecosystem, which given how few things it sells is of huge economic value. The tailoring houses are supplied by cloth houses, who design and hold the cloth collections from which the customer selects their fabric. They in turn are supplied by the weavers they commission to weave the cloth, who are in turn supplied by yarn spinners, and they are supplied by sheep farmers. In addition there are trimmings, canvases woven from cotton, linen or horsehair, sourced predominantly from within the UK. Buttons, hooks and bars, zips, thread, all are needed. The tailoring houses have their shops and workshops, while many of the sewing tailors rent their own workshops nearby, separate from those of the houses. All pay rent, business rates and other taxes. Most pop out for coffees and support local sandwich shops and cafés and pubs. The money you spend on Savile Row flows into the pockets of thousands of working people right across the UK, and they spend it locally, so it flows once more, creating more value as it goes.

Savile Row suggests a different way of thinking about jobs and consumption and economic value. People who buy on Savile Row take a great deal of care in the choosing of their clothes. They think very carefully about where and when the clothes will be worn, because to spend such a sum necessitates such care. Nothing is bought on a whim. Only very few Savile Row bespoke tailors produce and show collections. Like dressmakers before Charles Worth, everything made is an individual bespoke commission, a selection made in conversation between customer and tailor. They foist on their customers no incentives to buy, they don't desire new because the tailor has decided that fashions should change. Most buy clothes more from need than from want. There are no sales, no discounts. And there is absolutely no built-in obsolescence on Savile Row. In fact the opposite is true. Savile Row actively seeks to prolong the life of the clothes it makes. The fabrics used are not only wonderful to wear, they are durable. The cloths available to the Savile Row customer include many which are two, or even three times heavier than any cloth available to buy on the high street (we offer cloths up to 32oz in weight), and two or three times longer lasting. Conversation with customers at the point of ordering will almost always include a discussion of durability. Why would it not when they are spending upwards of £5,000 on a suit of clothes? And every tailor on Savile Row will alter and repair the clothes they made in perpetuity.

Importantly, customers on Savile Row *value* these clothes, often more than any others in their wardrobe. The clothes are cherished, hung with care on good hangers, aired, brushed, pressed. Partly because the customer chose them with care, and was involved in the selection of fabric and the choice of detail. But also, crucially, because they have met the men and women who have cut and sewn them. They have stood in the workroom where the clothes are made, and understand the provenance of the fabrics from which they are sewn, in some cases right back to the sheep and the hillsides on which they graze. The clothes gain in value the more they are worn, partly because they become increasingly comfortable – thanks to wear and perspiration and heat they have become a closer match to their owner's form – but also because the wearer has also developed a relationship with them. There is something uniquely satisfying about having the clothes repaired or altered, in extending their life. The owner may even pass them on to a child or grandchild, at which point they become more valuable still.

The scale and ownership of the Savile Row businesses is important too. The great majority of the owners are families, or individuals, or small groups of private individuals. Many work in their business, managing the business from day to day. Importantly, for the most part, those owners are content with the size of their business. Savile Row demonstrates clearly that businesses, and by extension economies, do not need to grow to survive and thrive. They exist at a scale and in a structure in which all actors are happy with the outcome. The tailors are well paid, the weavers and spinners are well paid, the farmers are well paid, those who run the shops are well paid. The owners of the businesses are satisfied with the economic surplus they produce, which is usually quite modest, happy that it provides enough of a buffer for hard times, and enough to invest to keep the business well adapted to the modern age. Customers are always happy with the clothes and the service they receive and are satisfied that they receive good value. The rents and rates get paid, and taxes are paid all the way up and down the supply chain. The whole ecosystem works in a wonderful equilibrium at just the size it is. With few small exceptions it feels no need to grow. And that is a great lesson.

And, perhaps most important of all, everyone involved feels great pride in what they do. There is monetary sufficiency, but also there is a surfeit of satisfaction in the work. It is a happy place. Everyone has a role to play, and all feel valued.

7

The Great British Sewing Bee

*T*he *Great British Sewing Bee* is one of the warmest, kindest, gentlest, jolliest, most collaborative shows on TV, but the message it delivers – quietly, unobtrusively – is deadly serious. We need to think about our clothes differently. Every piece of clothing is precious, every yard of painstakingly crafted textile is too, and these things should be cherished and cared for, altered, repaired, and when their first life is over, their useful material recovered and remade into something new. It says sewing is important, how we make clothes is important; that by knowing how to sew we know about clothes, we know well sewn from cheaply thrown together, we know the difference between natural fabrics and those made from oil, and that this knowledge of quality and how things are made, allows us to make informed choices about the thing that, after food, most of us buy more of in our lives than anything else.

Uniquely *Sewing Bee* has always included a challenge, the second of the three our contestants face each week, where they are asked to make something new out of something old. Originally the alteration challenge, it is now the transformation, during which the contestants regularly demonstrate that extraordinary, beautiful and unique clothes (and, very occasionally, hilariously odd ones) can, with skill and imagination, be made in a very short space of time from what otherwise might have sat unused in a cupboard or wardrobe, or worse, ended up in landfill or burnt. This idea of reuse, commonplace in every home until the advent of cheap clothing in the 1970s, was so important that for series five I suggested we should do a whole week, Reduce Reuse Recycle week (a phrase that has since come into common usage in the world of earth-friendly practice), where every challenge started with old stuff, otherwise unwanted garments or textiles. The participants have made raincoats from old shower curtains and beach tops from old deckchairs; they've turned parachutes into ball gowns and discarded festival tents into dog coats. Some of the most wonderful things to have appeared on the show have been made from old stuff. In the tenth and most recent series of the show, which may or may not have aired by the time this book is published, our contestants, by far our youngest cohort to date, take the reuse of old fabrics to a completely new level, regularly choosing to reclaim and rework something old rather than start with virgin fabric, turning old duvet covers, curtains and tablecloths into dresses in their own makes, dyeing and overprinting and reworking once unloved textiles. This normalisation of remaking by cool, fun people is hugely important.

Sewing Bee came about by happy chance. At the beginning of March 2012, my colleague at Norton & Sons took a phone call from Catherine Lewenden, a producer at Love Productions, the creators of *The Great British Bake Off*. She said that they were at the beginning stages of making a sewing competition for BBC Two, which was to transmit in the autumn (it didn't quite). The idea was to test contestants' skills in making and altering clothes and other objects for their homes (that got dropped quite quickly) and they were looking to find two judges. The commissioning editor of the BBC Four *Savile Row* and *Harris Tweed* documentaries, both of which I'd played a small part in, had seen me on TV. I knew from the *Savile Row* documentary that telly could enact big positive change, encouraging hundreds of young people to take up careers as bespoke tailors and cutters. I hoped that *Sewing Bee* might do the same for home and professional sewing. It also seemed likely to be a lot of fun, and we could all do with more of that in our working lives.

I was screen tested with four potential female judges and one male; one was a fashion lecturer I knew quite well, another a household name in printed textiles. In July I was called back again for another go, this time with a cheerful, kind sewing teacher from the Women's Institute called May Martin. A month later May and I had been cast, as had the befringed televisual brilliance that is Claudia Winkleman. *Bake Off* was already one of the most watched shows on TV; *Sewing Bee* followed a very similar basic format, and was largely made by the same team. We were joined in a creaky old chapel on Balls Pond Road in Dalston by eight charming contestants who were more interested in helping one another than treating it as a competition. There was Jane, a photographer from Kent; Michelle, a charity manager from London; the wonderful Sandra Lavender, a cleaner from Wolverhampton; Stuart Hilliard, now a household name in quilts; Tilly, whose 'Tilly and the Buttons' blog has become a huge success; HGV mechanic Mark, who got into sewing through his love of steampunk; the lovely and very talented Lauren, who now runs the brilliant Guthrie & Ghani haberdashery in Birmingham; and the extraordinary 82-year-old Ann Rowley. Our first recording day ran to about nineteen hours, much of the show's format and tone being worked out on the fly by our producers, Anna, Richard (both of *Bake Off* fame), Susanne and Catherine.

One of the many wonderful things for me about making TV is being thrown together with a team of folk who do things you don't quite understand and who are generally very good at them: directing, producing, the camera, sound, lighting and set folk, the people on snacks, Claire-Louise, our challenge guru, Mitch, who between sharing stories of his love life would tame Winkleman's fringe, and Debbie,

Claudia's long-suffering make-up maestro, who in a previous life had been right-hand woman to first Elton John and then Morrissey, possessor of an inexhaustible trove of unrepeatable stories. We'd play highly competitive Boggle during every spare minute (Claudia is a top Boggler, annoyingly), and we would laugh on set all day long.

Series one of *The Great British Sewing Bee* came on air, complete with jingly-jangly music and slow-mo super-close-up haberdashery action, at 8 p.m. on BBC Two in April 2013. It was charming, warm, encouraging and celebratory, and people loved it. The BBC had hoped to get a million viewers and we got more than twice that. A week later we were the most watched show on the channel and nobody could quite believe it. Our first winner, octogenarian Ann Rowley, was extraordinary, by some way the oldest winner of a TV reality show at that time. Just one contestant, Asmaa Al-Allak, winner of series nine, has matched Ann for pure dressmaking skill, and no one has been the equal of Ann's tailoring technique. She had never been a professional seamstress or tailor; she had simply, like most people born in the 1930s, learned to sew properly at school and at home.

Throughout the series we have been fortunate to have the nicest, funniest and most generous contestants. All of our winners, indeed all of our finalists, have been gifted makers, and even those with limited sewing experience have created extraordinary things. And almost without exception they have had a life-changing, happy and positive experience on the show, which you can see when you watch it.

Our contestants came to sewing for all sorts of different reasons. Some learned from their mothers or grandmothers at an early age, enjoying the simple pleasure of sharing a pastime with a loved family member. Some because they couldn't find clothes from regular clothing brands that matched their taste or suited their bodies. Several came to it simply to switch off and escape the pressure of work, some for reasons of mental health. Sewing, especially hand sewing, can be a very meditative, mindful activity. Some make things simply as an outlet for their natural creativity.

A disproportionately high number of *Sewing Bee* contestants come from caring or teaching professions; we've had a paramedic, several doctors, a surgeon, a nurse, a psychotherapist, several teachers and teaching assistants, and a vet. It's no accident. Craftsmanship is an exercise in caring. We've had lots of high achievers in all fields, and a good handful of scientists and engineers. Does being academic help people to be good at making? Or does making help people to become better in an academic setting? It is almost certainly a little of both. Giving everyone the chance to use their hands as well as their minds at school will undoubtedly help to unlock more people's real potential. Making, crafting, of any kind can unlock much more of our creative faculty. The greatest inventors and business builders of the Industrial Revolution were practical makers. And *Sewing Bee* demonstrates clearly that everyone, and anyone, no matter what their background or upbringing, can find great happiness and contentment in making.

The show now regularly gets five million viewers, and they've made versions of it in eight countries. Our version goes out in Australia, New Zealand and Japan (where I'm dubbed into super-gravelly Japanese). We've been hosted by Claudia, Joe Lycett, Sara Pascoe, and most recently Kiell Smyth Bynoe, the essential glue that holds the show, sometimes the contestants, and even on some occasions their makes, together. Their humour, daftness and kindness with the contestants is what brings the whole show alive. My sidekick since series four has been the no-punches-pulled Rosa Klebb of fashion, Miss Esme Young. She is a one of a kind, a force of nature. It has been an absolute pleasure and privilege to work with all of them.

A good number of the contestants I've remained friends with too, and many have gone on to do amazing things. Esme and I are proud to have played a part in allowing their talents to shine. The show has transformed the world of sewing in the UK. Sewing machine sales shot up something like 400 per cent. Singer, John Lewis, Hobbycraft et al. were cock-a-hoop. Sewing schools popped up all across the country and classes (including a male-only sewing class in Glasgow) sold out. I received a letter from the owner of a small family-run haberdashery in Essex who got in touch to say the show had saved their business, and that rather than closing their doors for good after two generations of dedicated stewardship they were expanding and taking a lease on the shop next door. Sewing had become cool(ish).

Knowing how to make, mend and recycle clothes and textiles is important. Getting people back into even something as simple as fixing clothes rather than binning them, was a big step in the right direction, and teaching people what clothes are made from, and the impact that their manufacture has on the planet, grows more vital as each year passes. *Sewing Bee* has always been quietly pushing in the right direction. Each year we'd mention some astonishing fact about clothing and its impact on the planet, and the responses would be incredible. I was told by a researcher at Royal Holloway that he'd calculated there was enough clothing on the planet at that point to clothe the next six generations of the human race, even allowing for huge population expansion. My own quick calculation suggested it might be like seven. When I said it on *Sewing Bee* the response was extraordinary.

The show's quiet activism has gained it a lot of plaudits. We were nominated for a BAFTA in 2022 and during the ceremony a film was shown about TV's positive influence in fighting climate change, including a clip of me on *Sewing Bee* telling Joe Lycett one of my fascinating clothing industry stats. Our commissioner at the BBC tells us that they now use our show as an example of how to deliver big and difficult truths in a positive and non-preachy way.

Thanks to *Sewing Bee*, my own voice and influence has increased greatly. I appear fairly regularly on radio and TV talking about our industry and its broader impact, both positive and negative, I gave a TED talk about Community Clothing, I've made a documentary for BBC Radio 4 about sustainability in fashion, and one about the Coronation uniforms for BBC One. All have expanded my knowledge and thinking about the world of clothing, manufacturing and work, and none would have happened without the success of *Sewing Bee*.

Once a year the team which make *The Great British Sewing Bee* assemble. Many of the crew have worked on the show for many years, and a couple of us have worked on them all. A few of us are in regular contact throughout the year, working to promote the series just made and to prepare for the series to come, but the great majority come together – now in a century-old textile mill in Leeds – for about two months from the end of August. It takes about five minutes to slip back into familiar routines. Everyone takes enormous pride in being good at their jobs and in making a fantastic bit of telly, but they also all enjoy each other's company because the work would be too hard without the fun.

The set is alive with in-jokes, silly notes stuck to bits of kit, googly eyes stuck on cameras, sweets hidden in viewfinders. I enjoy a silly whisper that only the sound team hear. I love (and hate) the snack table. We laugh a great deal. I love being part of this great big fun, talented crew. It is challenging, it can be physically demanding, but it is hugely rewarding, and it is only as good as it is through the collective talent, commitment and hard work of every person involved. This is how work should be.

Part III

WORK

8

We Love To Make Things, So Why Do So Few Of Us Make Things For A Living?

We have always worked. For most of human existence every member in society had a role to play in sustaining the healthy and happy functioning of their family, community or nation.

For the first 300,000 years or so of our existence, work was a matter of life and death. Finding, preparing and protecting our food, constructing and repairing our shelters, and keeping ourselves warm occupied almost all of our waking lives. From the earliest times we naturally selected the work for which we were best suited. Whilst most early humans would have known how to make basic stone tools, the finest tools were made by a few highly skilled members of the community, their skills making them valued within their society. Everyone had a role and it bound them to their community and allowed all in that community to flourish. Those who worked hardest, or had the greatest skills, lived the best life.

When we settled agriculturally, men and women worked the land and the livestock, and in quieter periods made things – spun, wove, made clothes or furniture – to supplement the family income. If we weren't farming we were making, and every citizen was practical and useful. We worked collectively with family and neighbours as part of a supportive, sustaining community. Our work followed the ebb and flow of nature's cycles, we were bound to the earth by the season and the weather, it was connected work. And we were the masters of our own destiny, self-reliant, free to work at the pace we wished. We understood that hard work and good work led to plenty and that idleness led to poverty, but if we chose to work through the night so that we might enjoy a moment sitting quietly in the sun, that was a choice we were empowered to make. For several thousand years specialist craftsmen produced the objects we needed. In ancient Greece the blacksmith Hephaestus was the god of master craftsmen, famed and revered for his skill and hard work. The Hymn for Hephaestus, one of the Homeric hymns to the gods, celebrates him as the great civilising influence on previously barbaric man, and as the bringer of peace: 'men who before used to dwell in caves in the mountains like wild beasts, now that they have learned crafts ... easily they live a peaceful life'.

When we were an industrialised nation, millions of men and women worked making things; skilled, rewarding work which occupied hands and minds. We made things of great quality that improved people's lives and we could look upon our work and see it as only good. Many did the necessary work of the home, caring for children, preparing food, cleaning, maintaining and repairing the family's valued possessions. Others did work needed by society, caring for the sick, educating our children. Our work was useful and benefited us all.

As a species we innovated endlessly, from the first tools and the early potter's wheel to the advanced machinery of mass production. This innovation at first made our work easier, allowing us to do more, and better, but then slowly the machinery began to replace us. Our nineteenth-century selves did not take this lying down; inspired by the mythical figure of Ned Ludd we responded with violence and sabotage. But the power of money prevailed and technology marched on. Millions had their working lives stripped away or changed beyond recognition. Whatever state planning was done to create alternative work for those displaced was ineffective, poor plans badly managed and underfunded by a political class more interested in the wealth of a few than the wellbeing and happiness of the many. And when the machines failed to produce enough profit to swell the coffers of the wealthy, they took their machines and put them where people could be paid much less. Millions of people lost their work, and the fabric of the nation began to unravel. This time we took it meekly, with Orwellian acceptance. In the UK today millions of people have no work, because the work that was previously available to them has been taken away, replaced by machine or moved offshore. And many of us are left doing work that is meaningless, unfulfilling, emotionally dumbing, and are often paid so little we cannot live at even the lowest acceptable standard.

There are currently almost 9 million 'economically inactive' people in the UK, people of working age who are not in work, a categorisation dreamed up when the coal mines were closed to disguise the number of people without jobs. Some of these are students, some are people with long-term health issues which prevent them from working, but many are simply people for whom the current education system and economy is failing to find a purpose. This lack of work creates huge social problems and growing health, welfare and policing costs. Those without work are pilloried by the same politicians whose failure has created the problem. The economically inactive are a *collective* failure. A failure of our system of educating, training and preparing people for the jobs which exist within our society. There are currently about a million unfilled jobs, including 112,000 in the NHS, 165,000 in social care and 140,000 in construction. We're getting things badly wrong and to mask these failings we pull the only lever we have available to us, that of immigration. Then we make those immigrants scapegoats for our failure, and in doing so we have split our country in two.

The politics of much of the past half century has failed to see work in anything more than purely economic terms. Work is more than money, it is a vital part of our happiness and wellbeing. Work defines us, fulfils us and enriches our lives. It gives structure to our days, a framework to live by, allowing us to plan and shape the path we wish to take through our years. It gives us purpose and binds us to our community, and it allows us to feel that we are useful, that we contribute to the success and the happy functioning of our nation.

The millions without work are the result of a gross failure to plan our society and economy in such a way that all citizens have something useful to do. But we need to see this as a spur to change the way we think about work entirely. In the coming decade the UK government's own report predicts that a further 25 per cent of all jobs will be lost to AI and advanced automation. We need a plan for work, not simply as a means to enrich some people but as the foundation of a well-functioning, happy society. Find everyone a job, ideally one they enjoy, and are good at. And for the essential jobs that are hard, emotionally and physically tough, that few people want to do, reward those people well.

What is work for? Who is work for? We need to answer these questions before we can know how best to proceed. Is the function of work to make a few in society rich, or is it to make all of society healthy and happy? Educate everyone, employ everyone and our society and economy will thrive.

Do We Like Our Work?

According to a 2022 survey only 17 per cent of British workers love their job, and over a quarter of us think we'd be happier doing something else. I am lucky to be amongst the 17 per cent, and many of the people I work with seem to like their jobs a lot, mostly people whose work is making or doing, who do skilled work with their hands and minds. Their work is straightforwardly useful, what they do is almost universally good, and they are rightly proud of the skill they have taken great pains to acquire. Many amongst the community of bespoke tailors with whom I have worked for the past twenty years enjoy their work so much that retirement is unthinkable; some stay at their boards until well into their seventies, or even later. One of my finest tailors, a gentle and charming Hungarian coat maker called Charles, worked for us until his mid-eighties. My best trouser-maker, Chris, is seventy-six and tells me he cannot imagine ever not coming to his small upstairs workshop. Their skill is valued and they work in a way that allows them full expression of that skill in every piece of work they do. It is a recipe for great happiness and satisfaction. My beloved granny held three jobs into her late seventies, working for the Citizens Advice Bureau, at a charity shop, and doing tours of a local stately home. She gained great pleasure and satisfaction from all of them, she did lots of good for others, and she had many friends at work. Her jobs fulfilled and enriched her life.

In the US they have a national holiday called Labor Day. It celebrates the contributions work has made to the development and achievements of the USA. Americans are proud of the way they work and hold the ideal as a part of their personal and national identity. As President Nixon said on Labor Day in 1971, 'The "work ethic" holds that labor is good in itself; that a man or woman becomes a better person by virtue of the act of working. America's competitive spirit, the "work ethic" of this people is alive and well.' Yet just fifty years later it seems this ideal is dying. The loss of meaningful work feels like a loss of identity and is keenly felt. Donald Trump's Make America Great Again reflects the loss felt by many in formerly blue-collar communities. In the UK too, work was a big part of personal and collective identity for many communities. The town of Blackburn where my business is based has the motto *Arte et Labore*, meaning *By Skill and Hard Work*. The bee, the great symbol of industry, adorns the badges of many northern towns and cities. The loss of what many would describe as real work, physical work that engages the hand and mind, has stripped away the soul of once-proud communities. For so many people work has become a source of anxiety, often tedium, monotony, sometimes shame. Nothing but a means to earn the money to pay for the other things we hope will give our lives meaning and provide us with pleasure.

After health and our family life, work is the greatest contributor to our personal happiness. Having or not having work, the type of work we do, the fear of not having a job, are much stronger contributors to our happiness or unhappiness than money. The work we do defines our sense of self, it fulfils our basic need to be useful within our community and society. Through the exhibition of our skill and willingness to work hard for the benefit of all we earn the respect and admiration of those we care about.

Early Work

Until about six thousand years ago early humans led a largely nomadic life, moving from place to place in search of food.

For millions of years humans had roamed the land in small groups seeking out prey, foraging for edible plants. Our bodies were fit and lean and nimble and our ears and eyes were by necessity fine-tuned to nature. We hunted, fished, foraged edible plants and made our own tools from stone and wood to help us do this. Communities worked collectively and collaboratively, with tasks divided according to ability. Some emerged naturally as more adept at tool making, possessing finer hand–eye coordination, greater deftness of touch, a more complete knowledge of which material to use.

We began to live in permanent agricultural settlements about six thousand years ago. A growing scarcity of food brought about by population growth predicated the move to an agricultural society. It has been estimated that the earth could support no more than about 4 million humans living in hunter/gatherer societies, but the technology of agriculture solved this impending crisis for early humans. It was not however without significant drawbacks. The life of an agricultural peasant involved a good deal of drudgery, often entailing tedious and physically demanding work. Whilst, overall, food was significantly more plentiful, individual diets were less varied and of lower quality than those of the hunter/gatherers. Thanks to the risk from weather and changes in climate to the success of single crops, people often starved. In addition, crowded living quarters made them susceptible to the spread of infectious diseases, often caught from domesticated animals. The dawn of the agricultural age also saw the beginning of property, of land ownership and the ownership of livestock and tools, and thus the beginning of a stratified society, of wealth and social inequality. From the perspective of individual happiness, American scientist and author Jared Diamond describes the agricultural revolution as 'the worst mistake in the history of the human race'.

Whilst most people were engaged in the raising of livestock and the growing of crops for food, those with the greatest skills began to specialise in the manufacture of the tools and vessels we needed to grow, prepare and store food and water. Amongst the first were what today we call blacksmiths, from the Proto-Germanic *smithaz* meaning 'skilled worker'. Highly skilled metalworkers, woodworkers and potters emerged as demand grew for better-quality objects. They developed specialist tools in permanent home-based workspaces, and sold or traded the goods they made directly. This pattern of small-scale rural manufacturing with goods traded within the local agricultural community continued for thousands of years.

After food production, textile making employed more people than anything else, and as the demand for textiles for the slowly expanding trade networks grew, manufacturing work took its first steps out of the home and into the factory. As early as the ninth century, small-scale manufacturing began to expand. Across the more developed civilisations of the Middle East, Asia and Africa, tens of thousands of people left the countryside for work in permanent workshops, producing textiles for sale in newly enlarged trade networks. The nature of work changed alongside the technology of making and the expansion of trade. We became more specialised in our making, a process driven in part by the need to acquire more specialist equipment like the treadle loom. The new class of manufacturing professionals were no longer making for themselves, they were making for trade, financed by a new merchant class. Output grew slowly but significantly, but crucially did so without destroying the existing structure and fabric of society.

Pre-Industrial Britain

In 1500 over 70 per cent of Britain's population worked the land, but most had a secondary job that they would pick up during quiet periods in the agricultural calendar. One in five spun yarn, one in ten wove, some made shoes or boots – everyday necessities either for their family or to sell or trade locally. Hand spinning and weaving could be done as and when they had spare time, and could be set aside and left for long periods, so it could easily be done alongside other household work like cooking and childcare. Spinning was almost entirely done by women, but many men wove. Repair work was important too, with everyone engaged periodically in fixing things both at work and in their homes.

Working out of doors had direct rewards: a connection to the beauty of the natural world, a pace and structure to life provided by the ebb and flow of the seasons, the sense of purpose entailed in the continual demands of the agricultural year. Whilst some people were employed as waged labourers, many held rights to the land they farmed, and had access to common grazing land. Throughout much of the medieval period the common field system had given ordinary people rights over the arable and grazing land they farmed. Within communities across England there was almost total self-sufficiency and self-reliance.

But in the sixteenth century the enclosure movement saw those long-held rights begin to be removed. The growing wealthy class resented the imposition on what they saw as their right to profit from the land, so they physically built walls, hedges or fences, removing ancient rights to pasture for cattle, horses or sheep, pannage for pigs, and rights to collect wood. Those who stood to gain argued that enclosure allowed for development or improvement of the land; as reformer and writer John Hales put it, 'that which is possessed of manie in common is neglected by all'. But common land had been well cared for. English farmers met regularly to plan for the coming season, discussing the condition of their lands and sanctioning those who abused the privilege by overstocking. And through communal working the common field systems created the economies of scale that those in favour of enclosure used to justify their actions. The idea that a single man could possess all rights to land to the exclusion of everybody else is a recent one and would have been incomprehensible to most peoples of the past.

Many older farmers tried to resist these changes to their way of life, but younger people saw only the great difficulties of the traditional pastoral existence and were enticed by a new and different way of life in towns and cities. They traded a life which was hard, but self-reliant and free, for the life of the proletariat, tied to a system of waged labour. Between 1520 and 1800 nearly 40 per cent of the rural population left agriculture, work that had been the mainstay of human existence for close to six thousand years.

Many younger people migrated to London, which increased in size from 2 per cent of the English population in 1520 to almost 12 per cent in 1700, and many of those who stayed put moved into new specialised manufacturing trades. In both rural and urban areas a growing proportion of the male population were described as craftsmen, butchers, stonemasons, carpenters, potters, thatchers, blacksmiths, weavers, tailors and shoemakers. Across Britain, specialist trades were becoming established in numerous industrial villages, many of them thanks to the influx of skills brought by immigrants from Europe. Some trades, such as spinning and weaving, shoemaking and certain kinds of woodwork, required little capital outlay, so those doing such work were almost always poor. In the 1500s these makers had still mostly been independent artisans who made and sold their own products directly, but a new class of merchant middleman emerged, organising and financing production, in some cases directly hiring craftsmen for their own workshops, sourcing raw materials and managing trade. Regional specialisations began to emerge as small groups of skilled artisans became larger clusters of knowledge and expertise. In his 1727 book *A Tour Through the Whole Island of Great Britain*, Daniel Defoe describes the outfit of a middle-class country grocer's wife: 'Gown of silk woven in Spitalfields, petticoat from Norwich, quilting cotton from Manchester, lace and edgings from Stratford, linen from Holland, lambskin gloves from Northumberland, riding hood from London and finally ribbons from Coventry.' The map of Britain was a map of its different textile trades.

Wool and woollen textiles were a huge part of the UK economy. In parts of Yorkshire, Lancashire, Cheshire and Devon, wool weaving was carried out in a quarter of all homes. Small workshops with multiple looms began to spring up, while many of these weavers spun too, and in some Yorkshire towns they became expert in the complex art of finishing or 'fulling' the woollen cloth. In 1600 Flemish refugees arrived in England from Europe bringing a knowledge of cotton weaving with them and as early as 1601 a Mr George Arnould of Bolton, Lancashire appears in the records as a cotton weaver, the first of what would become arguably the world's most successful regional industrial economy.

In the early seventeenth century the British East India Company saw the huge moneymaking potential in Indian textiles and quickly set about establishing control. India had become the centre of a global cotton trading network covering half the globe; as one Ottoman official complained, 'so much cash treasury goes for Indian merchandise that the world's wealth accumulates in India'. The East India Company established 'factories' (originally the word described a warehouse with an office) in the key Indian textile-producing areas, sourcing calicoes, chintzes, muslins and silks which they brought back to England. Cheaper, brighter and more comfortable to wear, they were a big hit with the British public and as early as 1621 London wool merchants began to protest, claiming Indian imports were 'injurious to the national interests'. British consumers were blamed, accused of killing their own domestic industry by choosing imported cotton. A pamphlet issued by the woollen trade in 1678 complained that their trade was being 'very much hindered by our own people who do wear many foreign commodities instead of our own'. In 1708 *Defoe's Review* printed a bitter editorial that described 'the real decay of our manufacturers' at the hands of increasing cheap imports, describing 'the bread taken out of [British workers'] mouths'.

Having been the source of much of the nation's earlier wealth the textile owners had clout, and their interests, and those of their workers, were taken seriously. Measures were introduced to protect British business interests under the guise of protecting British jobs. Duties and trade restrictions were imposed, and eventually Indian calico was outlawed altogether. None of this did much for the wool industry, but it was the most incredible boon for the fledgling British cotton textile industry which by then was growing rapidly. Between 1614 and 1700

British cotton exports grew from 12,000 pieces to over 870,000, a seventy-fold increase in under a hundred years.

At the same time trade in Indian cotton increased dramatically. Hundreds of thousands of Indian spinners and weavers produced cloth for export to Europe in quantities which grew from 30 million yards in 1727 to over 80 million yards by the 1790s. European capitalists used armed force, espionage, prohibition and restrictive trade regulations, forcibly removing millions of indigenous inhabitants and conducting a state-supported global land grab. In 1793 the East India Company crowed that thanks to them an 'astonishing mass of wealth has flowed into the lap of Great Britain'. European merchant capitalists caused misery and dislocation on a global scale, destroying long-established social and economic systems, but cemented their wealth and power forever, creating the capital, and the protected trading networks, that were a necessary precondition of the Industrial Revolution.

Industrial Britain

By the middle of the eighteenth century three dramatic and connected changes to society were reshaping the world of work in Britain: our formerly agricultural society had become industrialised; the rapid emergence of new technology had changed the nature of work from manual, to semi-mechanical, and later fully automated; and the emergence of capitalism as the pre-eminent economic doctrine put profit ahead of people.

In the first wave of technological advance, machinery removed many of the purely physical, mundane aspects of work, allowing men and women to do more productive jobs. Later advances began to replace skilled humans altogether. Production moved from small remote workshops to urbanised factories, driven by new forms of power, first steam and later electricity – power which could be provided in any location, at any time, without interruption. Innovation was happening right across the spectrum of British manufacturing, but in no industry was all of this change more apparent than in textiles. The factory system brought large numbers of craftspeople together under one roof and there began a segmentation of the manufacturing process into smaller, more specialised roles. No longer did a craftsman make a product from beginning to end; now a team worked together, each doing the tasks they were best at, improving quality and increasing output.

The small-scale artisan makers who had sold their goods directly to consumers were slowly replaced by retailers and wholesalers, selling goods made by large-scale industrialised manufactories. Many consumers began to lose their connection to the people who made the goods in their lives and the places where they were made, beginning the slow process of devaluing the things we own. The rise of 'fashion' meant we no longer bought based purely on function, with the expectation of using an item in perpetuity. We bought for vanity, spurred on by envy, objects predestined for rapid obsolescence. No longer valued and integrated members of largely homogenous rural communities, makers were now separate members of a stratified urban society.

Rise of the Machines

Since the early eighteenth century, textile manufacturers had been desperately seeking ways to meet the rapidly growing demand for high-quality cloth. The technological progress achieved in just a few short decades was extraordinary, the advances leading to reduced cost and the hugely increased availability of cloth. But it also meant significant changes in the nature of work for tens of thousands of British families for whom the skilled handwork of spinning and weaving had been an essential part of their livelihood. In 1733 the first momentous invention came from John Kay, the son of a woollen manufacturer from Bury. Kay had worked in his father's mill and was an unrelenting improver. At the time, the shuttle of a loom was thrown, or passed, through the warp threads by hand, with two weavers required to weave wide fabrics. Kay's 'Flying Shuttle' had wheels and was propelled from side to side along a track, allowing a single weaver to do the work of two, and significantly faster. His invention also meant that a single weaver now needed four spinners to keep him fed with yarn, spurring on developments in spinning and crucially opening the door for the later development of powered automatic looms which would completely transform weaving.

Another Lancashire native, James Hargreaves, was an uneducated spinner living near Blackburn. One day his daughter Jenny overturned a spinning wheel and Hargreaves observed that the spindle continued to turn in its upright position. He was inspired to design a machine in which the operator turned a handle rotating several spindles within a frame, whilst with the other hand using a bar to draw the thread and then wind it. First eight and later sixteen spindles could be operated at once, tripling the speed at which a single spinner could spin. Despite some limitations it was a remarkable breakthrough and within a few years twenty thousand such machines were in use in homes across Britain. Hargreaves named his machine the Spinning Jenny.

Richard Arkwright, yet another Lancastrian, had been born in 1732 to a poor family in nearby Preston and enjoyed a successful early career as a wig-maker in Bolton before turning his ingenuity to cotton spinning. In 1767, the same year that Hargreaves had demonstrated his Spinning Jenny, Arkwright teamed up with another John Kay (this one a clockmaker from Warrington), who had the technical skills needed to build a prototype of a spinning machine Arkwright had envisaged. Arkwright overcame certain deficiencies in Hargreaves' earlier design, allowing for continuous spinning and making it possible to spin stronger yarn, and significantly faster. But Arkwright's larger machine also required considerable power; he and his partners built a factory on the River Derwent in Derbyshire with huge water wheels to power his spinning machines, which became known as water frames. Arkwright continued to innovate. His Miller Street spinning mill in Manchester was the first to be powered by steam, an innovation meaning that spinning mills could now be built anywhere and run continuously. Arkwright built mills right across the North of England and Scotland; in doing so he demonstrated that it was possible to build, equip, power and staff a brand-new factory and make a profit, encouraging countless others to follow suit.

A decade later a fourth Lancastrian, Samuel Crompton, capped this period of extraordinary technological development, combining elements of the water frame with those of the Jenny. Crompton had as a young man spun cotton on the Jenny and had learned its deficiencies at first hand. His much-improved spinning machine, named the Mule, allowed a single operator to work several hundred, and eventually over a thousand spindles simultaneously, spinning both fine and coarse yarn, later models being powered by James Watt's new steam engine. The bottleneck in production swung back to weaving once more, and as tens of thousands of home-based weavers collectively spent millions of hours at their shuttle looms Edmund Cartwright developed the first powered loom. This catalysed a fifty-year period of innovation during which over twenty individual inventors, all working in a small area of Pennine Lancashire no more than 40 miles across, redesigned and refined weaving machines, until in Blackburn in 1834 James Bullough and William Kenworthy released the first completely automatic weaving loom. Just two years later James Northrop released an even better one, which automatically replenished empty shuttles.

All these innovators, bar John Kay of flying shuttle renown, had come from humble working-class families. Many were self-educated, all were highly practical, their insights into the machines they invented coming from their direct relationship with the skills and tools of their craft, their ingenuity and creativity making an eloquent case for an education that is a mix of both the academic and the practical. And, sadly, all bar Arkwright ended their lives with little more than they started with. Kay and Hargreaves were so despised by the hand-weaving and hand-spinning communities they had consigned to the scrapheap that they were forced to flee their native county.

In the eighteenth century, spinning 100lb of raw cotton had taken around 50,000 hours. By 1825 the spinners of Lancashire, with their automated mules, could spin the same amount in just 135 hours, a 370-fold increase in productivity. The fears of the Luddites were well founded – they did lose their work in hand spinning and hand weaving – but thanks to the huge advantage the technology afforded the British textile manufacturers they were able to find new, though less pleasant and less self-reliant, work on the automated looms and spindles of the booming new factory economy. Supported by well-established global trade networks, British textile manufacturers were able to sell their cloth to the rest of the world, meaning that rather than reduce employment they simply increased output, putting hundreds of thousands of textile workers in other countries out of work instead.

In 1788 there were around 50,000 of Crompton's mule spindles, but by 1821 the number had grown to over 7 million and these hungry machines needed feeding with raw cotton. Cotton doesn't much like the climate of Britain, or anywhere else in Europe for that matter; instead it came mostly from the Ottoman Empire, the Caribbean, India and West Africa. We soon outgrew these traditional cotton-growing regions but with expertise in colonialism, land expropriation and slave trading, Britain was well placed to assist in the development of large swathes of South, Central and North America, displacing indigenous populations from their ancestral lands and forcefully expatriating millions of predominantly West African slaves to clear and farm the land. As commodity prices rose, more land was put to cotton. French-controlled Saint-Domingue imported a quarter of a million slaves between 1784 and 1791 to clear land and farm cotton. Sea Island cotton, brought from the Bahamas, was planted along the coasts of South Carolina and Georgia and it flourished. Exports grew from 10,000lb in 1790 to over 6 million in 1800. But Sea Island cotton didn't enjoy the inland climate, so new varieties were needed. These new 'upland' varieties had shorter fibres, more tenaciously attached to their seeds, which existing machinery struggled to remove. Then, in 1793, Yale graduate Eli Whitney moved to Savannah in Georgia and quickly developed a new cotton gin which could rapidly deseed upland cotton, revolutionising its production. Another huge bottleneck in the production of cotton was removed; as extraction costs fell, incomes rose dramatically and cotton farming spread like wildfire, reigniting the slave trade along with it.

Britain was consuming 56 million pounds of raw cotton a year, an amount which needed over 400,000 acres to grow it on. We bought around 5 million pounds from the Ottoman Empire, 8 million from Brazil and 12 million from the West Indies. By 1830 a million people (almost one in thirteen Americans) grew cotton, most of them slaves. Industrialised cotton growing brought great riches to many, but in the process destroyed the livelihoods of smaller-scale, long-established cotton farmers across the globe.

Prior to the Industrial Revolution 65 per cent of Britons had worked on the land, but by 1850 there had been an extraordinary exodus and this number had fallen to just 15 per cent, a little over 2 million people, three-quarters of whom were now paid employees rather than working their own land. Rural workers, dumped off their lands by enclosure, continued to head for the growing towns and cities. Many with existing weaving and spinning skills found ready employment in the newly expanding factories. Domestic service still employed around 2 million of us, a further million were professional retailers, wholesalers and merchants (the 'nation of shopkeepers' was never quite true). A further half a million worked in public and professional services, the same number in construction, and the same spread across transport, mining and quarrying. But work in industrial Britain was by no means all mechanised. More men worked with horse-drawn transport than on steam-powered railways, and the coal which powered British industry was still dug using muscle and pick.

In newly industrialised Britain manufacturing was the biggest employer, providing work for 3.25 million people, over a fifth of the working population. Cotton mills sprang up across Lancashire and soon came to dominate the landscape, cotton providing over half of all jobs in some towns, especially amongst women. In some mill towns over 75 per cent of women were employed in textiles. Weaving and spinning remained highly skilled occupations employing millions, although the skills required had changed significantly. No longer was it the quiet manual work previously done in 30 per cent of British homes. Textile manufacturing was now a full-time specialist profession carried out in expensively equipped factories or workshops, and the seasonal side hustle agricultural workers had enjoyed during quiet times was no longer an economic possibility.

But British manufacturing was by no means all conducted on the same scale. Small-scale production was still very much alive and there were more full-time craftspeople working from home or in small workshops than in large factories. At the 1851 census there were more than half a million tailors and a quarter of a million shoemakers, far more than worked in clothing factories, and there were more blacksmiths than workers in the large iron foundries.

There were several broad types of business within the textile industry. First there were small manufacturers of all descriptions, of which there were hundreds, often with just a few staff, in many cases sharing larger workshops with other small makers. Second were the medium and larger firms, most controlled by a single family; Elkanah Armitage started as a spinner's helper and built a firm employing 1,650 workers, while Samuel Greg employed 2,084 staff across five mills including the celebrated Quarry Bank in Cheshire, and Samuel Oldknow had an impressive twenty-nine mills under his control. But despite these significant outliers, firms with over two hundred staff made up less than 20 per cent of the industry.

Third were the merchants, supplying raw materials and distributing finished goods. Principally located in Manchester, they held significant power and energetically championed a radical new politics. Industrialised Britain provided significant scope for personal advancement and many smart and enterprising men rose through the factory ranks despite having little or no formal education. The entrepreneurs who built the textile industry were merchants, farmers, weavers and spinners, and some from very humble backgrounds rose to make vast riches.

The new wealth and power, especially amongst the mill owners, gave a whole new class of people influence and control over the affairs of the nation. Those in the cotton industry were primarily local men. In the mid-nineteenth century, some 80 per cent of Lancashire mill owners were born in the county. One contemporary survey revealed that just 3 per cent of partners in Lancashire mills lived away from their business. Whilst there were many successes, there were few super-rich amongst the mill owners. Most remained permanently attached to the communities of their birth and were deeply connected to enhancing local prosperity. The money that individuals earned from this work was spent locally on goods that came from within their own community or other similar communities nearby, supporting not just their own jobs but those of others in towns like theirs. The clothes people wore, the crockery they ate off, the pans they cooked with, the chairs they sat on;

all of it was made where they lived, supporting local jobs in a self-sustaining cycle.

Crucially, in this period, all of the profits stayed in the community too. The sometimes substantial profits from the textile industry (it was not uncommon for firms to deliver to capital owners an annual return of between 10 and 20 per cent) meant that much of the industry was self-financed, allowing mill owners significant control over their decision making. And they could choose where to spend their profit, much of which found its way directly into the local community, building schools, hospitals, technical colleges, art galleries and museums, parks and grand civic buildings. The money improved the lives of all citizens, not just those of the wealthy. The broad civic value of the excess profits of textile production, and all manufacturing, was extraordinary, and its loss in our society is a very significant factor in the overall feeling of decline in many of the former manufacturing regions.

By 1831 cotton was Britain's biggest industry, accounting for 22.4 per cent of GDP and employing 16 per cent of the population; at its peak Britain produced over 65 per cent of the world's cotton textiles. Adding wool and linen, the textile industry made up over 37 per cent of the UK economy. But where Britain boomed other nations foundered. In India the weaving and spinning industry collapsed. Many highly skilled workers were forced to leave their homes, taking up alternative employment as farm labourers, and a great number died of famine, a fact that Gandhi was not slow to remind the Lancashire weavers of when he visited in 1931.

Living Standards

Industrialisation and urbanisation led to big changes in society. Population boomed, driven by soaring marriage rates, and as rising employment provided reliable work for husbands, wives and children, the fear of being unable to provide for the family diminished, causing a sharp rise in birth rates. Factory workers earned more than agricultural workers, power loom weavers more than hand weavers, locomotive drivers more than bargemen, and with a fall in the proportion of lower-paid jobs average wages rose and the prices for many goods, especially manufactured ones, fell. But in many industries real wage rises were modest. Those of a builder rose just 20 per cent between 1750 and 1850. And wages of course are not everything. 'Standard of Living' is an economic concept which only catches the quantifiable, monetary aspects of life. So much of what is important in life escapes its grasp. Thousands of manual craftsmen and women made redundant by mechanisation lost their self-reliance. Foul-smelling smoke-filled living quarters and rampant disease do not appear on economists' graphs, and purely monetary evaluations do not come close to painting a true picture of life. Towns could not cope with their growing populations, death rates rose as densely packed accommodation enabled the spread of infectious diseases, and sanitation was dire – raw sewage flowed into rivers, leading to a series of cholera epidemics. In working-class areas, the human environment was deteriorating markedly. During a period of conscription in Germany only 16 per cent of spinners and 18 per cent of weavers were deemed fit enough to fight.

Working hours increased, with the standard being twelve hours per day. Even after new legislation was introduced in the middle of the nineteenth century, many trades worked sixty to sixty-five hours a week. Ten hours a day operating heavy machinery in noisy, unpleasant conditions would have placed much greater strain on the individual than much longer hours under pre-industrial workshop conditions, or in agricultural work, where hours were dictated by the seasons, the weather and the hours of daylight. Whole families often worked together, with parents taking responsibility for their children's welfare, absolving factory owners of any duty of care.

With the greater intensity of industrial work came greater stress and anxiety. And when legislation limited daily working hours, employees were forced to work at ever greater speeds. Whereas in pre-industrial times work had been done at one's own pace, it now had to be done at the pace dictated by the factory owner. To make their machines pay they exercised ever greater control over workers' output. Attendance registers recorded presence in the workshop at multiple times throughout the day, while some employers resorted to fines, beatings and sackings to gain control over workers. Suicide rates rose as the century wore on. As John Stuart Mill wrote in 1848, 'Hitherto it is questionable if all the mechanical inventions yet made have lightened the day's toil of any human being.'

Many observers, including Engels and Marx, and pioneer social historians John and Barbara Hammond, argued that whilst large-scale manufacturing brought affluence to some it caused an overall deterioration in the living conditions of the working-class population. When work failed there was little safety net for the urban poor. Many would find work searching the rivers, sewers and gutters for anything of value. Removed from their land and the support of a close-knit community, families' only protection against hardship and distress was the weekly wage packet. Whereas in the rural agricultural economy food and lodging may have been included as payment in kind within the terms of their employment, or bartered for labour or other goods, workers now relied on real money for rent, food, clothing and many other important aspects of living. Rent made an increasing claim on people's income, and urban landlords were less tolerant of late payment than rural landlords with whom tenants had enjoyed long relationships. In the growing industrial towns and cities, few workers had gardens on which to grow food. And more cash in the pocket each week meant greater temptation to squander it on drink. Alcoholism rose, as well as the cruelty and degradation that went with it; rents went unpaid, leaving many destitute. Long-held cultural values were rapidly eroded. Rural life had been socially rich, connected to nature and tradition. Urban life was culturally impoverished. The Hammonds wrote:

Everything turned to profit. The Towns had their profitable dirt, their profitable slums, their profitable smoke, their profitable disorder, their profitable ignorance and their profitable despair ... For the new town was not a place where man could find beauty, happiness, leisure, learning ... but a bare and desolate place, without colour, air or laughter, where man, woman and child, worked, ate and slept.

Many travelled to Britain to witness, with a mix of awe and horror, the transformation of British society. French political scientist Alexis de Tocqueville wrote of Manchester, 'a sort of black smoke covers the city. Under this half daylight 300,000 human beings are ceaselessly at work. A thousand noises disturb this damp, dark labyrinth ... but from this foul drain the greatest stream of human industry flows out ... from this filthy sewer pure gold flows. Here civilised man is turned back almost into savages.'

Work for Whose Benefit?

The Industrial Revolution was fuelled by the emergence of a radical new way of thinking about work, money and the economy. It had its opponents, but most economists, including Adam Smith, imagined capitalism being a positive enhancement to society. Whilst the rich undoubtedly got richer, the theory was that the rising tide of overall wealth would raise millions out of poverty, giving them security in work and life. Smith did not see wealth in purely economic terms. He was not a proponent of wealth creation for its own sake; rather he believed it would increase the wealth of happiness we all enjoyed. He imagined a predominantly local system where profit drove local reinvestment and the creation of more jobs, with the surplus profits staying in the local economy for the benefit of those whose consumption and labour had generated them in the first place. Smith could not have imagined that the eventual conclusion of his much-admired system would be one in which no jobs were supported in the local economy and no benefit was felt locally, where the surplus profits, the dividends, of all of this production, distribution and consumption were extracted by a small number of globally nomadic, super-rich individuals.

The great flaw as far as ordinary working people are concerned is the inherent inequity of the system. As designed, capitalism directly sets the wages of labour against profits. For profits to continue to grow, which needs to happen if the system is to work, then wages must continuously decline as a proportion of the price charged for goods. Thus outcomes are skewed in favour of those who for whatever reason begin with capital, allocating them the vast proportion of the financial reward, whilst those who do the work get the minimum they can be forced to accept. For 250 years we've accepted that capitalism is the right way, but we do have choices, not just between capitalism and something else, but between the different forms of capitalism we might follow: the US and UK version, or the more equitable versions practised by places such as Germany, France and the Scandinavian countries. It's simply a question of personal belief. Do we believe that those who do the work deserve an equal share of the financial reward, or not? This was Marx's point. In order for the system to work, the person who makes the goods *has* to be paid less than the full value of their work, with the capital owner extracting the difference and accumulating it.

Division of Labour

One of the fundamental aspects of factory production versus craft making is that in the factory the tasks are divided. Where one craftsperson might make an object from start to finish, in a factory each maker will be allocated just one or a few of the required tasks, but never all.

The division of labour is nothing new. Plato considered it in his *Republic* in 375 BC. 'Well then, how will our state supply these needs? It will need a farmer, a builder, and a weaver, and also, I think, a shoemaker and one or two others to provide for our bodily needs.' The philosopher Xenophon discussed the idea further in *Cyropaedia* in 370 BC:

> In small towns, the same man makes couches, doors, ploughs and tables, and often he even builds houses, and still, he is thankful if only he can find enough work to support himself. And it is impossible for a man of many trades to do all of them well. In large cities, however, because many make demands on each trade, one alone is enough to support a man, and often less than one: for instance one man makes shoes for men, another for women, there are places even where one man earns a living just by mending shoes, another by cutting them out, another just by sewing the uppers together, while there is another who performs none of these operations but assembles the parts. Of necessity, he who pursues a very specialised task will do it best.

Adam Smith begins *The Wealth of Nations* with a description of the manufacture of pins in a factory system:

> One man draws out the wire, another straightens it, a third cuts it, a fourth points it, a fifth grinds it at the top for receiving the head; to make the head requires two or three distinct

operations; to put it on, is a peculiar business, to whiten the pins is another; it is even a trade by itself to put them into the paper; and the important business of making a pin is, in this manner, divided into about eighteen distinct operations, which, in some manufactories, are all performed by distinct hands.

Smith's description of the pin factory is probably the most famous depiction of an industrial process in the history of economic thought. Whilst his account of the division of tasks in pin making is not hugely accurate, the sentiment is correct; by dividing tasks and allocating those tasks to specific workers, overall speed and efficiency, and typically also quality, can be dramatically increased.

However Smith's contemporary, the philosopher Adam Ferguson, warned that such methods of production would also have the effect of diminishing the human satisfaction involved in manufacturing. 'Many parts', he wrote, 'in the practice of every art, and in the detail of every department, require no abilities, or actually tend to contract and to limit the views of the mind.' The division of labour and increased automation in factories, he reasoned, meant makers might increasingly have little idea how their work fitted into the creation of the final product. Divided tasks could become meaningless, isolating, lacking in enjoyable variety, and with no scope to use the mind as well as the hands the work might become tiring and unsatisfying.

Dividing jobs into smaller specialist roles for production makes good sense, and if well structured can provide scope for rewarding work and innovation. If I am tasked with making a single object, I will start at the beginning and work through each stage of production to the end. But task me with making a hundred of that same thing and very quickly I will realise that I do a quicker and better job by breaking the process into discrete tasks, doing the first task a hundred times, then doing the second a hundred times, and so on. Put two or more people in a room and task them to make multiple versions of that same object and almost certainly within a short space of time they'll divide up the tasks between them, quickly becoming specialists in an assembly line which should increase speed, accuracy and output, and improve quality.

Specialist assembly-line jobs require less individual training, allowing a person to move more quickly and simply into a paid job. As early as 5 AD Augustine of Hippo noted:

> the only reason why the combined skill of many workmen was thought necessary, was, that it is better that each part of an art should be learned by a special workman, which can be done speedily and easily, than that they should all be compelled to be perfect in one art throughout all its parts, which they could only attain slowly and with difficulty.

The theory behind the assembly line is simple: separate the production of an object into all its constituent operations, standardise and refine those operations, train operators to do one or two of them, and equip them with the perfect tools for the job. Give operators a workspace which is ergonomically optimised and move the object being assembled to the operator, not vice versa. Balance operations carefully, so that the flow of the line is continuous; if a single operation takes twice as long as others, have two people doing it, and build the line in such a way that the assembled object travels the shortest possible physical distance. How the assembled object moves is important too. If it can move itself, by gravity or by moving conveyor, all the better.

In around 1800 Oliver Evans built the innovative Portsmouth Block Mills, which broke down the production of rigging blocks used by the Royal Navy into twenty-two stages and used bucket elevators driven by a leather belt and canvas belt conveyors to move material through the mill, a set-up which was so successful that it remained in operation until the 1960s. Henry Ford famously introduced assembly-line production techniques that led to significant reduction in the assembly time of a car. Ford also pioneered financial incentives for increasing productivity, but workers complained of the physical and mental stress which resulted from demands for constant increases in line speeds and efficiency.

Into the Twentieth Century

Mass Production

An assembly line does not necessarily mean the end of human skill in the workplace, but in a world where continuously growing profit is the primary motive, each improvement in production efficiency must be followed by another. As the twentieth century progressed the drive for ever greater profits led us into yet another new phase of industrialisation, the age of automated mass production.

Huge leaps forward in mechanical and electrical engineering created sophisticated machines which further reduced, and in more recent years almost completely removed, the human role in manufacturing. In the first half of the twentieth century mass production reduced many human manufacturers to button pushers, relegated to the role of servants of the machine. New roles designing and controlling the machines were created, but these were much less numerous, and required taught academic knowledge that previous making jobs did not. Advances in machine technology allowed an almost total deskilling of jobs in some industries. US oral historian Studs Terkel's excellent *Working* details the thoughts of many Americans in different jobs and for many the overriding feeling was that work had become dull, unstimulating and monotonous, as one put it, 'a monkey could do what I do'. For greatest efficiency, assembly lines require absolute standardisation not only of raw materials, tasks and tools, but of timing of operation and task performance. In fact they perform best when humans cease to be human and become robotic. They are undoubtedly efficient. But in their ultimate form they remove from the workplace any task which a human would ordinarily enjoy.

Corporations

Another huge change to the world of work came about as a result of the way in which businesses were organised. Mergers and consolidations, which had become common in the USA in the early twentieth century, backed by institutional capital, spread to the UK. Small-scale locally owned businesses were replaced by large-scale global corporations. Industrialised local manufacture gave way to globalised mass production. Smaller local textile and clothing businesses who cared about making good products, and about the people they employed and the communities in which they were located, gave way to remote global textile and fashion businesses driven exclusively by share price and profit, with no attachment either to employees, communities or the quality of the product they made. Larger businesses were able to exercise great power over their workforce, and over those who made and enforced the labour laws. Hard-won improvements to working conditions made earlier in the century – shorter hours, more pleasant workplaces – were, with the support of the state, reversed, violently where necessary. Corporate business lost its human face. It was profit driven and indifferent to the needs of employees.

Offshoring

The process of separating manufacturing from selling had begun all the way back in the seventeenth century with the demise of the artisan manufacturer and the rise of the retailer, a separation accelerated in the industrial era. But in the early twentieth century there were still many brands who maintained their own high-quality production, in some if not all of their products. Many of these brands, particularly in advanced countries like the UK, set a gold standard for manufacturing, their brand names being intimately linked with quality. They were large and important employers, and customers for many other manufacturers who supplied them locally. They had the scale to train staff in large numbers, and the money to invest in improvement to their manufacturing, and their well-known and often much-revered name above a factory door gave additional cachet to the jobs they provided. In the UK, clothing brands like Aquascutum, Austin Reed, Barbour, Belstaff, Burberry, Hunter, Lyle & Scott, Mackintosh, Pringle, and many other household names owned UK factories in which they produced the highest-quality items. But as competition increased many brands chose to sacrifice quality and provenance so that they could spend more money on advertising, marketing and driving up consumer want. Some sold off their factories, occasionally to employees, on the understanding that production would remain there. Then they'd squeezed those suppliers, demanding wave after wave of cost reductions, and when they could squeeze no more they dropped them for manufacturers overseas, consigning millions of very skilled, highly efficient workers and factories to the scrapheap. Some skipped the selling-off stage and kept hold of their factories for longer, but almost all in the end succumbed to the lure of the greater profit to be made from moving their factories abroad. They closed their UK factories in some cases, reportedly, to save just a few tens of pence on the production of a garment.

Some kept a certain amount of outsourced UK production, but most severed almost all ties with UK manufacturing. Pringle's Chinese owners closed their Scottish factory in 2008 and moved their production to China, at the same time changing their name to 'Pringle of Scotland'. Their factory had at one time been the largest in the border knitwear town of Hawick, the almost 2,000 people 'Pringle' employed in a town of 14,000 representing about a quarter of all jobs. 'Pringle of Scotland' employ none. Aquascutum, Belstaff, Burberry, Hunter, Lyle & Scott and Mackintosh all closed UK factories; two of these once hugely successful British brands have since gone bust. Burberry have at least kept two of their factories, both in Yorkshire: Castleford where they make their classic trench coat, and the Keighley mill which weaves the gaberdine fabric they're made from. Mackintosh still have a factory in Nelson, Lancashire but their iconic Cumbernauld plant has gone. Between all of these brands, once the backbone of British clothing manufacturing, fewer than a thousand manufacturing jobs remain.

There is only one reason why you would do such a thing, and that is to increase profit. But what good does that increase in profit do any of us? Since 1970 offshoring has caused 5 million of the roughly 8 million men and women who worked in manufacturing to lose their jobs. The evolution of our current version of capitalism emerged in the early 1970s and really took flight with Margaret Thatcher and Ronald Reagan. Capitalism as a system had never been hugely concerned with people, only inasmuch as in the early days it needed them to produce its profits, but many of those who administered it, local owners with deep roots in their communities, were inclined to consider the personal and human effects of their actions, and indeed some of the environmental ones. But the neoliberal version of capitalism currently enjoying an unprecedented fifty-year stranglehold on US and UK economics can be accused of having no such concerns. Neoliberalism roughly translates as 'let business do whatever it wishes, let the nebulous concept of the "market" be the arbitrator of all'. By reducing workers' rights and suppressing the power of the trade unions, and by selling off our public utilities – which previously provided around a third of all public sector jobs – neoliberalism has changed the nature of work in Britain, and facilitated a huge redistribution of wealth and income from ordinary Brits to the very rich.

In other nations, particularly those in Europe, where the form of capitalism is less blindly profit focused than in the US and the UK, and where political leaders are less in the thrall of business corporations, people and the environment are central to decision making. In some countries, notably Germany and Italy, more private ownership prevails. The broader community has a voice in business affairs and it is noticeable that manufacturing in those countries has remained vibrant and profitable. Many European economies, despite a less purely profit-focused business landscape, are faring just as well, if not better than our own, and a realisation is dawning on many that we've been duped. The current form of our economy has not enriched us, monetarily or otherwise. In the UK millions no longer have a route to meaningful work, and what's more we are drowning in a sea of terrible-quality stuff.

Almost a century ago, in response to the Great Depression, President Roosevelt enacted interventionist policies including widespread public works, which led the US economy into the greatest period of economic prosperity in history, and did so whilst reducing wealth inequality. In response to the financial crisis and recession of 2008 the UK government gave public money to bail out the businesses whose profiteering had sparked the crisis in the first place, whilst enacting a decade-long policy of austerity, cutting spending on everything from our health service to schools, heaping misery on millions, and reducing the UK, one of the wealthiest nations on earth, to a country where millions live in poverty and even those in work rely on food banks to feed their families. If our forebears had known then what we know now I would hope that many would have lobbied for a different evolutionary path.

Knowledge Work

In the 1990s in the UK and the US there was a concerted shift in education policy away from anything that had its roots in blue-collar work, the making and doing they had all decided was now to be consigned to our past. No more woodwork, no more metalwork, no more bricklaying. Both Conservative and Labour governments told us that our future was as 'knowledge workers', as if the centuries of technical innovation which had built Britain's great wealth and international standing had somehow been founded on ignorance. Machines would take care of the boring job of making things, increasing efficiency, productivity and of course profit, freeing us, the people, to do the valuable knowledge work instead. Thirty years have now passed since this shift in policy, and artificial intelligence is the new machine. We are told AI will take care of all that boring, tedious knowledge work, and according to the *Harvard Business Review* this will lead to efficiency and productivity gains for knowledge-intensive businesses, freeing us, the people, 'to do more meaningful work'. But what exactly is this 'more meaningful work'?

The *Harvard Business Review* defines knowledge work thus: 'Knowledge work primarily involves cognitive processing of information to generate value-added outputs. It differs from manual labor in the materials used and the types of conversion processes involved.' But much manual work involves all sorts of cognitive processing, and a great deal of knowledge. Most craft work involves making thousands of cognitive decisions daily. In Mike Rose's book *The Mind at Work* he dismantles the idea that blue-collar work is undertaken in ignorance, that such workers are part of a less intelligent class. Rose describes the complex spatial mathematics undertaken by carpenters and the diagnostic acuity of the plumber or the electrician. How often do we think about how much knowledge is required when undertaking such tasks? Is it any less, is it perhaps more, than the work of a legal clerk or a payroll manager? And the practically acquired knowledge of the bricklayer, carpenter or plumber is every bit as valuable to our society as the book-learned knowledge of the legal clerk, payroll manager or bookkeeper. Why is working in an office more meaningful than building a house? The shift towards 'more meaningful work' in the late twentieth century, the abandonment of traditional industry, the dismantling of our technical education systems, has left millions in the UK without work, and left a million jobs, many of them essential to the functioning of society, unfilled. The next shift, the AI revolution, is predicted to cast another 25 per cent of the UK population on the scrapheap before the middle of the next decade. And another thirty years from now? What then? Will any of us have anything meaningful to do?

Online

It may seem trivial but the way in which we buy things has incredibly far-reaching consequences for work and jobs in our society. Fifty years ago the things we bought supported millions of different types of jobs, for all sorts of different types of people, distributed right across the country, and created tax for the UK coffers: VAT, income tax and National Insurance from employees right the way down the supply chain, business rates from shops and factories, and suppliers to those factories, and corporation tax on the profits. But the way we shop today is radically different, and the types of companies we buy from are radically different too. We spend 27 per cent of our money online, and that percentage is rising fast. And we buy from corporations, many of them foreign domiciled, many of whom employ no one here but warehouse staff and delivery drivers, jobs that will be made redundant when they can build smart enough robots. Many pay virtually no UK tax.

Online retailers grew because they offered cheap goods, limitless choice and extreme convenience. Amazon are the largest online retailer in the UK by a very significant margin. At £30 billion sales in 2022 they're almost three times bigger than Sainsbury (number two, £10 billion), and six times the size of Tesco (third, £5 billion). They have a 36 per cent share and are growing faster than anyone else. How do they do it? Well, partly by employing half as many people. Amazon's ratio of turnover per staff member is almost exactly double that of Tesco, and Tesco are pretty efficient. Put another way, for every one job Amazon creates we lose two from somewhere else in the economy. Which is worth remembering when you hear politicians heaping praise on these online companies for creating jobs. Another reason the new online-only retailers win is their capacity for finding ways to avoid paying tax. On a turnover of 23 billion in the UK, Amazon said it paid £648 million in 'direct taxes' in the UK in 2021, less than 3 per cent. Traditionally UK retailers paid three times this much.

To simplify the outcome of our recent change in shopping habits: half as many jobs, a third as much tax to pay for things like the NHS. That doesn't seem like progress.

Amazon are not investing billions in robotics and drone technology for fun. They process 5 billion packages a year, over 13 million a day. They're estimated to have over 2,000 warehouses, fulfilment, processing and delivery centres, with more on the way. In their words they are investing in robotics to 'spur supply chain, fulfilment, and logistics innovation' – in other words, work out how to get rid of humans from warehouses and delivery roles. Their third-generation Sparrow warehouse robots can now identify 65 per cent of all stock items. It will not be long before they can identify them all.

Amazon deliver over 2 million items a day in the UK, and thanks to our love for online shopping we now take delivery of over 5 billion parcels each year. Delivering all of these goods, to warehouses and homes, now employs 1.6 million people in the UK, most of them men. And as well as removing humans from warehouse roles Amazon will get rid of them from the delivery side too. They're already delivering by drone in the US in two locations, and have announced that from 2024 they will begin delivery of parcels by drone in the UK, promising a one-hour service. Amazon have no intention of having humans pick, pack or deliver their parcels. It is perfectly imaginable that in the future a small remote team of humans will manage the AI which will manage the e-commerce activity, generate the images and write the copy, making Amazon even cheaper and more convenient. But at least we won't have to worry about the inhumane working conditions in those warehouses. Which is quite convenient too.

But other online-only brands are even worse. Shein, the Chinese fashion company that sells ultra-cheap synthetic clothes, have grown at an astronomical rate. Globally they turn over $20 billion. In 2022 Shein sold over £1 billion worth of their fashions in the UK with just fourteen UK staff. This is a ratio of sales per employee of £80 million. For comparison, M&S in the 1970s had a ratio of £18,000. So on a like-for-like basis Shein employ 1/4,000th of the number of people. When we buy from these empty online brands we are destroying economic value and jobs here in the UK.

Today online retail accounts for 27 per cent of retail sales. What will happen when that number reaches 50 per cent, then 75 per cent, then 100 per cent? Extrapolate the online-only model to the entire retail economy and there will be no more UK manufacturing, retail or delivery jobs, there will be no income tax, no NI, virtually no business rates, no corporation tax. There will simply be VAT, if they haven't successfully lobbied for its removal. What good is our economic activity if it puts no tax in the UK public purse and creates no jobs in the UK? That's the direction we're heading in.

Work and Happiness

The US government has been collecting happiness data since the early 1970s. In 1973, 34 per cent of those interviewed described themselves as 'very happy'; by the late 1990s the figure was 30 per cent. Despite this being a time of extraordinary economic growth, people in the US have actually become less happy.

The UK government also asks citizens about their happiness, even if they seem uninterested in increasing it. Over the same fifty-year period, people in the UK were no happier at the end than at the beginning despite this being a period of record economic growth and prosperity. One of the questions asked by the UK's Office of National Statistics is, 'Do you feel that the things you do in your life are worthwhile?' Four in ten UK adults are unsatisfied with how they spend their time in a typical week. Thirty per cent of UK adults are unsatisfied with their main job, 25 per cent of people feel anxious and depressed. What do we spend much of our typical week doing? Well, the luckier ones amongst us spend it working.

In her book *Made in England*, Dorothy Hartley notes that 'A normal healthy man desires to work. The interest in his work is the growing point in a man's life, and once this growing point is broken his driving power but presses against a blunted faculty.' Over a quarter of us think we'd be happier in a different job. A quarter of us believe our work has a negative effect on both our mental and our physical health. So what type of work do we want? What work makes people healthiest and happiest?

Well, we know people like to work with their hands and minds, so why not find a way to return to more of that? As long ago as 1683 Joseph Moxon wrote *Mechanick Exercises*, a forerunner to modern DIY manuals. It gives instructions on blacksmithery, casting metal, joinery, engraving, book printing, map making. Moxon wrote, 'many Gentlemen in this Nation of good Rank and high Quality are conversant in Handy-Works ... How pleasant and healthy this their Diversion is, their Minds and Bodyes find.' Dorothy Hartley suggests that craft work, with its close and sympathetic relationship to the natural world, is a vital part of a fulfilling human existence, and many who engage in it 'put it first in his life's interest'. It has been argued that mass production allowed the worker more leisure, but what good is this if his or her creative faculties are stunted, their initiative suppressed? The craft worker was continually called upon to think for him or herself, to solve numberless small issues that arise from working with natural materials. No amount of leisure can compensate for the monotony of dull work, or worse, of no work at all.

Work During My Lifetime

I was born in 1972. At that time here in the UK there were 8 million people employed in the manufacture of all of the things that we used on a routine basis, making up over 25 per cent of jobs and over 30 per cent of the economy. The manufacture of our everyday goods employed people in almost all towns and cities across the UK. We made the clothes we wore, the washing machines we washed them in, and the soap powder we used to clean them. We made the crockery and cutlery we ate with, the pans and toasters we used to cook our food, and the garden tools we used to help us grow it. In the early twentieth century all of the things we used in this way were made locally, and the work created prosperity and a sense of identity for millions of people.

My family like most others bought our everyday clothes from Marks & Spencer: socks, pants, shirts, jumpers. In fact they sold almost a fifth of all clothes in the UK. And at that time still over 95 per cent of those clothes were made here. St Michael clothing was spun, dyed, knitted, woven and sewn in the UK, helping sustain jobs for at least 1.5 million people. Manufacturing jobs, many of them in the Midlands and the North of England, in southern Scotland, in Northern Ireland, and in South Wales, in fact in almost every corner of the country. They had shops in even the smallest towns, supporting retail jobs for men and women of all ages, and these shops in turn supported other service jobs, the rents on the shops flowed to local landlords, and the passing trade of shoppers supported a further service economy. All of this activity created huge tax revenues, through the income tax paid by the people making and selling the clothes, through the business rates paid on the factories where they were made and the shops through which they were sold, and through the corporation tax on the profits of not only Marks & Spencer but of their suppliers, and all of those other local businesses their presence supported. The retail businesses from whom we bought our clothes and almost everything else we bought were mostly UK based, so their profits stayed in our local economy. So did the wages and spending of all their head office staff. And the tax revenues from manufacturing and retail funded our public service, paid for the art and culture that so many of us enjoyed, paid for art and crafts in schools and allowed every school pupil to have access to playing fields and to enjoy sport on a regular basis.

Today the number of people who make things for a living has fallen to just 2.6 million, which represents less than 8 per cent of UK jobs and just 10 per cent of the economy, and the regions where those jobs have been lost are the poorest, most deprived and most disenfranchised in our society. We're moving very rapidly towards a system of consumption of everything we buy that gives no benefit at all to the local population. Offshoring the manufacturing of the things we buy has cost us over 5 million jobs. And what were those lost jobs replaced with? Well, for a time people were employed in shops, selling the goods made overseas. But now those jobs are going too. Our steady migration from traditional retail to online has cost us another million jobs and this number is rising all the time. Our regional high streets are increasingly deserted. Retail jobs have been replaced by people picking goods and packing boxes in giant warehouses, and driving vans and scooters to deliver those boxes to our homes. Jobs with limited satisfaction and even less of a future, because those jobs are going too, to be replaced by robots, driverless vehicles and drones.

But we do have a choice. We can spend our money in ways which support employment within our own communities, which support our tax base allowing the continuation of our health, education and other essential services, which provide opportunity to decrease rather than increase levels of inequality, which do not destroy the natural ecosystem, and which provide opportunity for economic, social and environmental regeneration.

We can choose to reshape our economy around genuinely meaningful work for all our citizens, work which rebuilds community and restores a healthy balance with nature. Technology has greatly reduced some kinds of work, but it has created and increased others. In *Small is Beautiful*, Schumacher notes that 'the type of work that technology is most successful in reducing or even eliminating is skilful, productive work of human hands'. Philosopher Thomas Aquinas defined humans as beings with brains and hands, happiest when both brain and hand are employed creatively, usefully and productively. Skilled work, hard but satisfying labour, brought us simple pleasure, enhancing our physical and mental wellbeing. In advanced industrial societies such work, what we today call craft work, has become exceedingly rare, and the work that has replaced it is often dull and unfulfilling. It is a great irony that the rich now spend their leisure time doing for pleasure what were the everyday jobs of the past. They spend large sums and weeks of their lives learning to throw pots, to carve wooden chairs, or to cut and hand stitch leather goods. The work we removed from the ordinary man has become a great luxury and a plaything of the wealthy.

Many of us clearly yearn for work that is more physical and connected to natural materials. The followers and views on Instagram and YouTube of videos of men and women making things reach the millions. People working with their hands and simple tools, turning simple honest materials – wood, clay, metal – into beautiful things. 128 million people have watched a man make a chocolate cabinet. There are entire channels devoted to watching people make things in pre-mass production ways. Millions of us tune in every week to watch *The Repair Shop*, *Inside the Factory*, *The Great British Sewing Bee* and *The Great Pottery Throw Down* on television. As our lives become more digital, we become more powerfully drawn to work which is analogue and real.

The extent to which technology has taken over the work of human hands was demonstrated by a simple calculation done by Schumacher. He calculated that, collectively, we as a society spent just 3.5 per cent of all our time in what he called *real production*, the gainful employment of manufacturing, agriculture, mining and quarrying. The other 96.5 per cent of our time was spent on other things: eating, sleeping, watching TV, doing jobs that are not *directly* productive. Today, after half a century of offshoring, fewer than one in ten of us in the UK are engaged in *real production*, and just 1 per cent of our time is spent producing. Little wonder so many of us feel unfulfilled and disconnected from the real world. As Karl Marx put it, 'the production of too many useful things results in too many useless people'. And a large amount of the work of mass production has, as Schumacher put it, 'been turned into an inhuman chore which does not enrich man but empties him'. Technology has deprived us of the work we enjoy most, the useful work with hands and brains. In the past we spent most of our waking hours in the engaging, skilled work of farming, making and building. Today 15 per cent of us work selling people things, things they mostly don't need. A large and growing number of us – more than now work on the land – work in giant windowless warehouses packing and shipping the things people buy. Nearly a million of us work distributing and delivering things. And what do the rest of us do? About 15 per cent of those in employment work in health and social care, 10 per cent in education, 9 per cent in construction, and just 7 per cent of us now make things for a living. Most of what we buy is made by machines operated by poorly paid humans on the other side of the world.

We all need and want good work. Let's look again at the work of making and doing. Instead of seeking to reduce it, look to increase it, build an economy on doing things well. Let us seek again to build an economy which 'mobilises the priceless resource of our clever human brains and skilful human hands'. Such a low-volume, high-quality economy would be entirely compatible with modern ecological and environmental thinking, polluting less, using less of the earth's scarce resources, and allowing the use of all available natural resources, including the irregular ones passed over as unusable by mass production. A system which balances the need of humans for high-quality employment and the need of the planet for low levels of consumption of high-quality goods; which takes the best of the labour-saving technology, but forgoes the technology which reduces humans' skilled and thoughtful input.

We can all say no to more and more stuff, and no to growth which does us as citizens no good. Whilst some activities could happily be grown, some could stay the same, and any activity which is not universally good could be reduced. Replace bad economic activity with good. It may seem far-fetched, but a new lifestyle, where making and repairing work are central, is a realistic economic possibility.

A third of the work we have now will be gone in a decade. If nothing changes in the meantime that could leave half of all working-age people in the UK without jobs. We're already increasingly unhappy – how will we feel as a society when this comes to pass? Today charities and healthcare providers are prescribing time in nature and craft work as a cure for our rapidly growing mental ill-health. Our work could be our cure.

9

Why I Love a Factory

I've always really liked factories. I remember a school trip to the Forbo Nairn linoleum factory in Fife aged probably about twelve or thirteen. I was captivated by every single thing about the place: the huge materials stores, the smell of hot linseed, the jute, the bubbling vats of hot oil and the gigantic machinery that rolled out this amazing multicoloured flooring.

The landscape of memorable parts of my childhood was punctuated by the tall chimneys and monolithic mill buildings of the Scottish textile industry. When I was quite young, my grandmother remarried and moved to Galashiels, where my grandfather's family had deep connections with textile making. My Grandpa Ali had been a yarn designer at the now defunct firm of Laidlaw & Fairgreave. Later, as development officer for the Borders region, his job was to attract inward investment into the area to help rebuild it after the loss of so many textile jobs. I still remember their slogan of 'Fresh Air and Elbow Room for Industry', and have a box of matches with the words embossed upon it. Textiles was everything in the Borders. I would spend weeks during the holidays staying at my grandparents', and every activity seemed to take place before a backdrop of textile activity, in towns like

Galashiels, Hawick (the home of cashmere), Selkirk (now home to the finest tartans), Jedburgh, Langholm and the majestic River Tweed, a vital industrial artery which gave its name to the famous cloth.

Wherever you go in Scotland, the geography and the textile industry are inextricably linked. The pride of the people who worked in the textile industry was palpable, and the dignity in the work they did then feels at odds with many of the ways we earn our livings today.

I had a gap year between school and university and did a 'Year In Industry', a work-experience scheme which was quite popular at the time, working for Camerons brewery in Hartlepool. Established in 1865, it was one of the town's biggest employers, famous for brewing a ruby-red bitter called Strongarm that it was claimed contained the perfect balance of minerals and salts needed to rehydrate the thirsty workers who plied their trade at the steelworks in the town. The smell of the place was incredible. It was my first long-term exposure to a site of such a scale. There were over five hundred employees, doing many different types of jobs. Brewing was probably the most obvious, but there were labs with people in white coats, there were warehouse and distribution jobs, the forklift drivers, and the draymen who delivered the beer, sales and marketing jobs, HR roles and people who worked in the finance team.

During my undergraduate degree I did an Erasmus exchange, spending my second year at a French school of engineering in Orléans. The French students had to complete a three-month 'stage' or work placement, so I did the same. There were options in France, but I took a place at a ceramic tile factory in Coimbra in Portugal, working in the research lab. My job for most of the three months was to create little clay strips with different compositions, and apply different glazes to them, like a latter-day Josiah Wedgwood, in an attempt to understand why the tiles came out wobbly, and to find a solution. Shrinkage differential between glaze and body and too much glassy phase in the clay body rendered the tiles weak during the single-fired process they used, a relatively inexpensive but problematic method of making tiles. It was an astonishing place, full of furnaces and giant multi-ton tile presses which stamped out the tile shapes. One of the employees was a blind man who tapped his way around the factory, my Portuguese was never quite good enough to understand exactly what he did there. A man had recently lost his hand in the tile press during an afternoon shift, so the management had put up a sign in the works canteen which showed five glasses of red wine, three of which had a big X over them.

I began my professional career in 1995 at a blue-chip British manufacturing business called BICC. The hum of the shop floor, the factory bell and the chatter of the works canteen was the soundtrack to my early working life. BICC, or British Insulated Callender's Cables as it was before 1975, was formed through the merger of Callender's Cable & Construction Company, founded in 1870 in Erith, Kent, and British Insulated Cables, founded as the British Insulated Wire Company at Prescot near Liverpool in 1890. At their peak in the 1970s they had factories in Erith, Prescot, Kirkby, Leyton, Helsby, Leigh, Melling, Wrexham, Blackley, Belfast and Huyton. The BICC Prescot factory had at one time employed 28,000 people. Erith had their own brass band, for which the company supplied uniforms and instruments and which broadcast on BBC Radio in the 1920s and 30s. When I joined in 1995 they had still five UK factories, all in and around Merseyside, and employed 35,000 people, most of them in manufacturing roles. They also had plants in Italy, Spain and Zimbabwe.

I worked in a plant in Whiston, just outside Liverpool, which manufactured fibre-optic cables. Hair-thin optical fibres, protected by an extruded plastic sheath, were twisted together, then sheathed in a thin steel tube, which was then enclosed in twisted heavy-gauge steel wire, drawn and annealed on site. Another factory, in Knowsley, made aluminium power cables. Our factory in Leigh was steadfastly

Victorian in appearance as well as in its practices. In 1995 it still had three canteens – one for shop-floor workers, one for management, and a third (with silver service each lunchtime) for directors. All these plants were crucial to the social and economic fabric of the towns in which they were situated. All had several members of staff who had worked for 'BI' all of their working lives. I can recall at least a couple of gold clocks being given out for twenty-five years of service. These weren't just workplaces, they were communities, extended families. They looked after their own, they provided structure to people's lives, they gave purpose and identity, and provided mentorship and guidance to younger staff. Emotional support and social lives. They had societies, clubs and hardship funds. They would take staff 'on the chara' (named after the early charabancs in which staff were conveyed to the seaside or local beauty spots for subsidised – and sometimes paid-for – away days). Today not one of those BICC factories remains open, and none of those manufacturing jobs remain.

I've been very lucky to have spent time in lots of amazing car factories. Rolls Royce, Lotus, Jaguar, Land Rover, Aston Martin and McLaren – all the absolute best. As a science and engineering nerd these places are amazing. Not only are most of them in extraordinary modern buildings set in acres of beautiful lake-strewn parkland. But at car factories pretty much everyone is continuously involved in trying to solve problems and make things better. Toyota invented the concept of Total Quality Management, which turns every employee and small team into a dynamic problem-solving machine. Everyone is empowered to think and to act. You can't help but be inspired.

Our cars are about the only things we buy that are much better than they were fifty years ago. (Apart maybe from televisions, certainly the Japanese and Korean ones.) And I would argue that this is because the car industry still makes the cars it sells, and as a result everyone in the car industry is obsessed with quality. As an industry it has consistently invested heavily in science, engineering, production machinery, training, management practices. And it's a UK success story. We have amazing engineers. They are so good that most Formula One teams are based here, and some of the Indycar ones too. I remember on a visit to one of the newest Jaguar plants at Castle Bromwich being told that when they opened the factory they had had 3,000 positions to fill. They had advertised locally and received over 30,000 applications. People want to work if the job is good, the long-term prospects are excellent; if the product is cool, if the manufacturing process is state of the art, if the working conditions are great (shiny building, subsidised canteen). Car manufacturers are the absolute best in class at this. All other UK manufacturers need to take note of their example.

10

Made in Britain

By 2008 I'd achieved some small success with Norton & Sons and buyers from a couple of retail stores began to ask me if we might do a few ready-to-wear items for them, following the same philosophy of meticulous sourcing and uncompromising product quality. For Beams, the iconic Tokyo select store, we created a limited line of knitwear, made at the family-owned mill of William Lockie in Hawick, and a 'trotter's bag' (the trotter was the person who would run the cut cloth and other trimmings between the cutting room and the tailors' workrooms on Savile Row, originally in big cloth tote bags). The products were a success and they wanted more, but having only just got Norton & Sons working well I was reluctant to do anything which might upset the balance. And I feared it would be difficult for the company to be taken seriously for bespoke when it had a ready-to-wear line under the same name.

In the 1960s, when Norton & Sons had been enjoying a period of sustained success, it had first given a temporary home to, and then acquired, several other struggling Savile Row houses. After the Second World War many firms that had specialised in military or sporting tailoring had fallen on hard times and Nortons, like many of our neighbours on the street, bought a handful of these ailing houses and incorporated their businesses into its own. Those Nortons bought were E. Tautz & Sons, Hammond & Co., J. Hoare & Co. and Todhouse, Reynard & Co.

E. Tautz & Sons had been a hugely successful firm in the late nineteenth and early twentieth century. It had built its own flagship store on Oxford Street opposite what is now Selfridges, had a store on the Rue du Faubourg Saint-Honoré opposite the Elysée Palace, and had a royal clientele to go with them. Edward Tautz had been a pioneer in the world of sportswear as the inventor of the knickerbocker, and had made a name dressing Europe's sporting elite. Tautz had been Winston Churchill's tailor when he was a young man, with Churchill writing in his diary, 'send me Tautz breeches, they are the best'. The Churchill Archive in Cambridge shows that over the years, Tautz made a huge assortment of clothes for young Winston, including cashmere racing breeches and jockey silks (Churchill was rarely prompt at paying his bills). Tautz had dressed kings and emperors and notable men of style such as Cary Grant and America's Best Dressed Man (according to *Esquire* magazine), Anthony J. Drexel Biddle III. They had sold their own ready-tailored sporting clothes, so despite the challenge of restarting from scratch I decided to relaunch E. Tautz as a handmade ready-to-wear brand.

Finding Factories

The philosophy of the relaunched Tautz was straightforward: design and sell simple menswear of exceptional quality, made by the best UK manufacturers from the best British cloth. I'm still proud that every garment we ever sold was either made in the UK, or from British fabrics, and in many cases both. From the off a large and hugely enjoyable part of my job was to find and build relationships with the British makers. Back in 2008 this was less simple than it is today (Make it

British, the UK Fashion & Textile Association and others now have comprehensive directories), and every conversation with a factory would lead to information about others. I loved the thrill of discovery, and that first glimpse inside the factory of some unknown maker, the challenge of understanding how this organism of humans, tools and machines transformed materials into usable things. It was the sound of unfamiliar machinery, of never-before-heard accents in previously unvisited corners of our country. Sometimes it was a smell you'd never encountered, like boiling linseed, or warm cork, or vulcanised rubber and glue. Factories are sensory experiences, and finding and visiting new ones remains a great joy in my work. Over the first few years I developed a network of factories and workshops that extended from Somerset to Suffolk, from South Wales to the far north of Scotland, and with each new season I'd add some new gem to our roster of makers.

The very first E. Tautz collection was aesthetically far from ground-breaking: a small handful of simple tailored pieces, shirts, knitwear and a few silk and wool accessories taking their cues from the world of Savile Row, shown simply on a dozen assorted mannequins in the Nortons shop. But what was different was the provenance. Every piece had a story, each one could trace its creation from field to finished garment, and it was this which made it special.

Tailoring

Tailoring has always been a big part of Britain's cultural and economic history. Since the days of Beau Brummel we've been regarded as the home of the finest tailored clothes and until the early modern period there were tailors in every town and city across the country, as well as a good number of villages. In 1901 the *Tailor & Cutter* magazine, bible of the British tailoring trade, described our 'noble army of tailors', which then numbered 80,074 in London alone, out of a total population of 4,536,541. Just a century ago 2 per cent of the population of London were tailors, and *Tailor & Cutter* estimated that at that time there were 731,720 tailors working in Britain. Today the number of tailors in the UK must be no more than four or five hundred, with Savile Row employing the vast majority.

Throughout Tautz's long history it had been known for its exceptional sporting tailoring. It was important that this form a large part of the collection, but we couldn't carry out the Tautz tailoring at Norton & Sons because we didn't have the capacity. Instead I had the garments sewn in what was formerly the Chester Barrie factory, founded in Crewe in 1935 by a Russian immigrant named Simon Ackerman who had named it, inexplicably, after a nearby town and the author J. M. Barrie. They made beautiful tailored clothes, all hand finished, for many of the world's great department stores, including Harrods, Selfridges and Saks in New York, as well as luxury brands like Turnbull & Asser and Ralph Lauren for whom they made the prestigious Purple Label. The factory latterly passed into private ownership but sadly it has not survived. There were just two other tailoring factories left in Britain that I knew of at that time, neither of which could match the quality of the former Chester Barrie workshop, and of these I think just one remains. For the country that gave the world men's tailored clothes, it is a sad state of affairs.

Cloth

Whilst it was astonishingly difficult to find high-quality tailoring production outside of the small workshops of Savile Row, it was, and is still, easy to find the very best tailoring fabrics. Britain has a long history of making the world's best cloth. As early as 1130 the Weavers Guild is recorded in the Pipe Roll of Henry I, and in 1155 the Weavers were granted a royal charter by Henry II, making them the oldest livery company in London. In the 1300s, rival freemen weavers were authorised to compete with the guild, and later Edward III, recognising the value of a vibrant textile trade, encouraged expert Flemish weavers to come and set up shop in England. In the late seventeenth century close to 50,000 Huguenots fled persecution in France, bringing their exceptional weaving technology with them to England. Britain had established itself as the home of the most skilled artisans, and competition amongst them ensured a flourishing textile industry, enabling British cloth to sit at the absolute pinnacle of quality. Between 1733 and 1836, British innovations from John Kay's flying shuttle to James Northrop's power loom punctuated a period of technological advancement which dramatically reduced the cost and improved the quality of the everyday textiles used to make our clothing and home furnishings. By the 1850s Britain was not only producing the best woollen and cotton cloth on the planet but also in the greatest quantity, at its peak manufacturing over 70 per cent of the world's cotton textiles. Textile and clothing production accounted for over 20 per cent of jobs in Britain, employing over 2.5 million people.

In the twentieth century, the consolidation and globalisation of the UK textile industry, alongside the introduction of synthetics, marked another great upheaval. Over a period of less than fifty years, hundreds of UK manufacturers of lower and mid-market products were displaced, with the associated loss of hundreds of thousands of jobs. We went from making virtually 100 per cent of our own clothing and textiles to making less than 2 per cent.

What remains is that part which could not be easily replicated by less experienced manufacturers operating in the re-emerging Asian manufacturing regions. Everyday cotton textiles are relatively simple to spin, weave and finish, and indeed many countries in the developing world had been cotton textile producers for thousands of years in the pre-industrial era. But spinning, weaving and finishing wool and linen requires huge knowledge and skill. The woollen textile industry in the UK today, operating predominantly in West Yorkshire and the south of Scotland, is a highly differentiated collection of specialist mills producing the very finest wool, mohair and cashmere, worsted and tweed cloth for the world's most discerning customers, including the tailors of Savile Row and the luxury fashion houses of London, New York, Tokyo, Paris and even in some cases Milan. The British mills I have worked with over the past two decades make cloth for, amongst many others, Hermès, Louis Vuitton, Chanel, Prada, Gucci, Dior and Saint Laurent, and British textiles continue to enjoy significant cachet around the world.

For the first Tautz collection in over fifty years I sourced worsteds from Taylor & Lodge in Huddersfield, Pennine Weavers in Keighley and Bower Roebuck at New Mill, Huddersfield. We also used authentic RAF wool barathea. Huddersfield was and remains the traditional centre of production for the finest-quality worsted fabrics, whilst Bradford and other centres produced the still excellent but more everyday qualities used to sew suits for the mass of the UK population in the tailoring factories in nearby Leeds. Pennine Weavers, a relative newcomer, was established in 1969. Taking over an existing mill in Keighley, a town which at one time boasted fifty-six textile mills and was better known for more prosaic fabrics, Pennine specialised in the commission weaving of luxury fabrics. The oldest of the three, Taylor & Lodge, founded in 1883, has throughout its long history specialised in weaving high-end luxury worsteds. Bower Roebuck, with whom we worked most, were founded in 1899 and they too had established a reputation for weaving with the finest-quality wools; they were the first, in 1974, to weave with superfine 120s wool, and then in 1991 the first to weave even finer 150s. We worked with them and their sister design team at Savile Clifford for almost every collection we produced.

Our tailored clothes were without question as good as any available anywhere at any price.

Over the dozen years of developing the Tautz collections I worked with a lot of special British manufacturers, many of them centuries old, and many stewarded by generations of the same family: A. W. Hainsworth in Pudsey for melton cloth; Joshua Ellis, also in Pudsey, for cashmere overcoating; William Halstead, in nearby Bradford, specialists in worsted mohair; Johnsons of Elgin on the Moray Firth for tweeds; Reid & Taylor of Langholm, now sadly gone, for twist worsted. Often stories or images of the Hebridean islands and islanders wove their way into my thinking in the design studio and we worked with two wonderful independent Harris tweed weavers, Donald-John Mackay of Luskentyre Tweed, his weaving shed overlooking the vast white expanse of Luskentyre beach on the island's west coast, and Garynahine Harris tweed, a little inland, who produced a wonderful pheasant-eye fabric that Jarvis Cocker wore in a magazine shoot and liked so much he asked to buy it (I gave it to him). We sourced tweeds, either undyed, or dyed using local plants like the crotal which grows on the coastal rocks, from the weavers at Ardalanish; they were made using blends of natural black and ecru wools from their own farm on the Isle of Mull. For a collection inspired by photos of George Mallory's team on their ascent of Everest we needed soft tweeds in muted tones which I sourced from Breanish, a tiny, family-owned tweed business based in a small weaving shed in the very far north of the Isle of Lewis run by Ian Macleod and his father Zebo. And for one inspired by William Hogarth's *The Rake's Progress*, we used bouclé tweed from Linton Tweeds in Carlisle, now part of the Chanel iconography.

For that collection, in 2014, we worked with tutors and students at the Royal School of Needlework at Hampton Court Palace to create the hand-embroidered embellishments. We used a vast array of silk jacquards and lamés for the trousers and jackets produced by Vanners and Stephen Walters in Sudbury, combined by Christian Louboutin with meltons and other fabrics to make brothel creepers. No collection showed the versatility, creativity and exceptional skill of the fabric weavers and clothing makers of the UK better than this collection.

Shirtmaking

The British tradition of excellence also extends to shirts. Jermyn Street, a short walk from Savile Row, is still home to several of the world's best makers, and shirt factories were once commonplace in the UK, especially in and around Derry and Strabane in Northern Ireland. Here there was a long history of quality shirtmaking stretching back to the 1840s, and a history of outwork shirt production dating back a century before that. Desmond & Sons, which had begun as a small outwork shirt producer, went on to become Northern Ireland's biggest private business. Huge factories sprang up, taking advantage of the newly developed sewing machine to provide work for tens of thousands, mostly women, making shirts, pyjamas and shirt collars. Tillie & Henderson became the largest such factory in the world, employing 4,500 skilled hands, almost all of whom were women. By the 1920s there were forty-four factories in the area employing around 20 per cent of the local population. Tautz shirts were made in the Smyth & Gibson factory, one of very few remaining in Northern Ireland at the time, and were still produced entirely by hand to a standard every bit as good as those made on Jermyn Street.

Silk

Alongside the shirts we offered wonderful earthy-coloured, rustic-textured Shetland wool ties, the cloth woven in Selkirk by a small mill called Anthony Haines, and silk ties hand-cut and hand-sewn by the small but fantastically skilled team at Drakes in their old factory in East London, using Michael Drake's wonderfully off-beat and beautifully coloured designs. The silks were screen-printed by Adamley in Macclesfield, the last remaining silk printer in a town that for centuries was synonymous with the world's finest silk fabrics.

Before the seventeenth century Macclesfield had been known for buttons, made using wood from the abundant local holly trees and then covered in linen. When tastes changed and fashionable Britons began to wear silk-covered buttons the Maxonian button makers changed too, producing their own silk to meet demand. Initially hand-produced, it was later made in purpose-built mills, sited on the edge of the Peak District where the fast-flowing water from the River Bollin not only drove the mill wheels, but was perfect in its clarity and softness for dyeing and finishing silk cloth. The first silk mill opened in Macclesfield in 1743, and by the mid-eighteenth century the industry was the town's biggest employer with seventy mills producing the world's finest broadsheet silk.

What Macclesfield was to printed silk, Sudbury in Suffolk was to jacquard. Sudbury had been a weaving town since the fourteenth century, initially producing heavy woollen broadcloth before switching to the production of lighter fabrics during the sixteenth century. When persecution drove the French Huguenots to England, many settled first in East London, bringing fine silk-weaving skills with them. In 1774 tax rises in London saw them up sticks and relocate the short distance northeast to the Essex–Suffolk border. By the 1850s there were over two thousand silk spinners, dyers and weavers in Sudbury, operating more than six hundred silk looms. Stephen Walters began in Spitalfields in 1720, moving to larger premises in Sudbury in 1860. I worked with Walters regularly, making the most wonderful fabrics for ties, jackets and trousers, woven in mixtures of mostly wool and silk, but also cotton and linen. I still use them today for special projects like the interior of the GQ Mercedes created for London Fashion Week, or champagne bottle ties for Bollinger.

Two other silk weavers remain in Sudbury: Gainsborough, established in 1903, and Humphries Weaving, established by Richard Humphries in 1972, both world-leading specialists in fabrics like ottomans, damasks, brocades, tapestries and velvets, woven in silk and other natural fibres, mostly for interior furnishing. Sadly in 2022 the wonderful Vanners, founded in 1740, went out of business. They were tie silk weavers and the collapse of the giant Brooks Brothers saw them lose more than half of their business overnight. After a failed rescue attempt the doors were closed for the final time in 2022, with sixty-five staff losing their jobs.

Jumpers

I spent much of my early childhood in a hand-knitted jumper and have always loved the particular look and feel of a needle-knitted garment. And Britain, thanks to our occasionally cold climate and our abundance of sheep, has always been good at knitting. In our first Tautz collection we had some simple knits made for us in Sandness in Shetland by Jamieson's, a fifth-generation, family-owned knitting and spinning business established in 1893. Hand knitting is wonderful, but expensive and time consuming, impractical for most wholesale clothing businesses. But you can get close to the look and feel by knitting on small hand frames, and linking and finishing by hand. This was how we did it, working with the brother-and-sister team who run Corgi in Ammanford in South Wales. With hand framing you can make small quantities and specials, like the Z jumper we made for Elton John for his son Zachary. We produced ultra-fine-gauge merino and cotton sweaters and polos with John Smedley at their factory, built at Lea Mills on the River Derwent in 1784 and today one of the UK's greatest manufacturing success stories. We did two- and four-ply knits – what one new Community Clothing customer recently referred to as 'proper jumpers' – with William Lockie in Hawick. They make the best lambswool sweaters in the world, I have no doubt about it. I've a navy crew-neck two-ply Lockie sweater; it's had its elbows darned and patched, twice, and a few other darns here and there, but after well over a thousand wears it has never pilled or lost its shape. The lambswool yarns they knit with are spun in Yorkshire by the brilliantly named Zachariah Hinchliffe of Denby Dale, and the cashmere by Todd & Duncan in Kinross, whose founder had on his travels come across locals in Kashmir spinning ultra-fine goat hair and became the first to export this most precious fibre. Arguably the best quality yarn spinners on the planet, both spin yarn for the world's most famous luxury brands.

Raincoats

I worked with many iconic factories, few more so than the Mackintosh factory in Cumbernauld. Scottish chemist Charles Macintosh was credited with inventing a revolutionary waterproof material, sandwiching an impermeable layer of rubber between two layers of fabric. It was comfortable and completely waterproof and was such a great success that we now call a raincoat a mac. Mackintosh made trench coats for the British Army and waterproof clothes for the police and railway workers, and for anyone else who had to be outside in the rain. Uniquely the Mackintosh garments are not sewn; they are bonded using adhesive, applied with one firm finger. The factories – both the old one, and the new one now owned by Alexander Manufacturing – are full of old Quality Street tins containing wonderfully pungent glue. Two other outerwear factories we worked with were Cookson & Clegg, a former military outerwear manufacturer based in Blackburn and established in 1860, and Tower, a family-owned sewing factory in

Enfield in North London. Both made exceptional products. I now own the former, and still work with the latter.

Shoes

Although we had no intention of selling shoes, our models needed something on their feet. So we worked at different times with some of the brilliant British shoe factories still present in Northampton. The town has a long and rich history of shoemaking, dating back to at least the early thirteenth century – even today, the nickname of Northampton Town FC is the Cobblers. In 1213 King John is recorded as buying a pair of boots in the town, and Henry III bought shoes there to give to the poor at Christmas, Easter and Whitsun. Northampton had an abundance of cattle, for the leather, and of oak trees whose bark was used for tanning. By 1401 the town had established a Guild of Shoemakers, and its shoemakers shod Cromwell's army during the Civil War. In 1725 Daniel Defoe wrote that 'everyone's shoes, from the poorest countryman, to the master, came from Northampton', and the navy wore Northampton boots during the Napoleonic Wars. By the mid-nineteenth century there were 1,821 shoemakers in the town; almost half of all its men were employed in the trade, and during the First World War they made over 50 million pairs of boots for the allied forces. Dr Marten boots were made in Northampton (as their Vintage line still are).

We worked with John Lobb (the Hermès-owned one, not the bespoke shop in St James's), and with Trickers. Lobb can trace its history to the mid-nineteenth century when John Lobb became Bootmaker to the Prince of Wales. Hermès bought the brand in the 1970s and later acquired the original Edward Green factory in Northampton. Trickers, founded in 1829, is proudly the oldest established shoemaker in Britain and remains in the ownership of the original founding family. Both firms use the most painstaking methods and the most exceptional materials: oak bark-tanned leathers and natural cork, hand cut and stitched using the Goodyear welting process. Both offer a great repair service, from a resole to a complete rebuild (I saw a pair in the repair shop at Trickers recently that the owner's dog had chewed half to bits; they were remade good as new). When the then Prince of Wales, now King Charles, was having new evening dress shoes made by Trickers (he told me personally, Trickers would never reveal such information), they removed the grosgrain silk ribbon from his old pair and transferred it to the new ones. I have four pairs of shoes from each: Lobbs I wear as formal shoes, Trickers for everything else. All are now perfectly moulded to my feet and beautifully patinated through years of scuffing and polishing. Most of them have been resoled at least once. The dozens of years of wear and repair have made them very special to me.

Christian Louboutin, a customer at Tautz, happened to walk into the shop and overhear a conversation I was having with designer Nicholas Kirkwood about shoes for the show. Nicholas was in the midst of selling his business to LVMH and was struggling to find time for our shoes. With terrific gallic snobbery M Louboutin suggested he'd never heard of multi-award-winning Nicholas Kirkwood, proffering his own services instead. For our first season working together we made elegant evening pumps, some tasselled, based on the classic English design, sewn in the jacquard silks used in some of the clothing, and in simple black suede. Over the years all sorts of interesting shoes got the Louboutin treatment. Dodgy old-school plimsolls and 70s string-topped deck shoes, both charity shop finds, a pair of nineteenth-century leather-topped millworker's clogs I bought via eBay from a charity shop in Cheshire – all were reworked and given the famous red sole. The clogs came with a sweet handwritten note tucked inside the box, from a lady at the charity shop to her colleague, which read something along the lines of 'I think these might be quite old, and worth a few pounds'. They were part of an Autumn-Winter 2015 collection inspired by the Scottish poet Douglas Dunn's Terry Street poems about everyday life in Hull in the 1960s. Dunn's writing evoked a world captured in the photographs of the north of England by John Bulmer, of working men in places like Hartlepool, where I lived during my year in industry, and the Potteries, a world of smog and soot and cobbles. John kindly allowed us to use his images in the magazine we created to go with the show.

Alongside Louboutin in Paris we worked with a small number of other non-UK-based suppliers for items we couldn't source in the UK, including denim from Cone Mill in North Carolina, naturally dyed using plant indigo grown in nearby Tennessee by Stoney Creek Color. Cone later sadly closed their historic mill and moved production to China. We worked for many seasons with Loro Piana in Italy, who had perfected a process, akin to that of Charles Macintosh almost two centuries before, for bonding waterproof layers and membranes to beautiful wool and wool-blend cloths. It created textured, durable, waterproof and breathable fabrics that we used extensively in our rainwear.

Cotton

Incredibly, given the UK's global dominance of the cotton textile trade in the nineteenth century, by 2009 virtually no cotton fabric for clothing was produced in the UK. Just two mills, Mitchell Interflex in Colne and John Spencer in Burnley, have the capability to weave cotton clothing fabrics, but it wasn't and isn't a core part of either of their businesses. Instead we had to source our shirt cottons from Italy, mostly from Thomas Mason, an old English cloth house now owned and manufactured in Italy by the Albini group, or from the Albini range itself. We got heavier-weight cotton for our casual trousers through Brisbane

Moss, who formerly wove their own in Todmorden but now commissioned it from an Italian mill.

Storytelling

But British producers formed about 90 per cent of our main supply base. Making locally was important because the tangible quality of those remaining British manufacturers is exceptional. And vitally, because of our proximity, we could visit regularly and become familiar with their processes and capabilities, allowing us to design our products with greater understanding, and interrogate supply chains so that we could be absolutely certain of what was going into our products. Also, importantly, these factories, and the towns and regions where they were based, were rich in stories, rich in connection to a long history of making, the intangible quality that was so important. We told the stories of our makers through our various channels; we allowed the customer to peek inside the workrooms, to meet the men and women responsible for making their clothes. Because the precise provenance of every part of every garment was such an important part of the DNA of E. Tautz, on that first informal collection presentation I talked through the story of the garments and the people behind their making in person, with every buyer and fashion editor who came to see the show. And when, the next season, we moved to a bigger venue, with a seated audience, I narrated the show live, detailing each outfit, discussing its passage from fibre to finished garment through the hands of many makers, painting a picture for the audience of the land from which these clothes had come, and the people who made them. It became something of a signature of our presentations, and when the shows became just too big for the live narration to be practical there were a couple of editors who were kind enough to tell me that they missed the storytelling.

Provenance was all-important to me and to the Tautz brand. In 2009, these stories were not being told as they are today, and support for UK luxury clothing manufacturers was declining. I knew how precarious many of these businesses were and I wanted to do everything I could to support them. My friend Nick Sullivan, a sartorial giant of an Englishman who was then menswear editor (now creative director) of *Esquire* in New York, commissioned a film idea I pitched to him. We took a tour of our UK factories (as many as we could cram into a fortnight), and filmed the whole thing; ferries, cheap B&Bs and all. Ian Denyer, with whom I'd worked on the *Savile Row* and *Harris Tweed* documentaries for BBC Four, shot the film, and my good friend, portrait photographer Chris Floyd, invited himself along for the ride. We drove nearly three thousand miles around the UK in a borrowed Jaguar visiting many of the factories mentioned above. Over half a million people watched it on the US *Esquire* website in the space of a few months (you can still watch it somewhere on YouTube; look for 'The Makers of E. Tautz'). Not long after the film went live I was going through security at JFK airport when the giant security guy stopped me, happily he only wanted to ask if I was 'that tweed guy'.

The culture of everyday Britons was a source of inspiration throughout my time designing the E. Tautz collections. I loved the quirks and the oddities, and our collections mined the history and folklore of many of the places across the UK most closely connected with textiles and clothing. Turner Prize winner Jeremy Deller celebrates many of these same quirks in his book *Folk Archive* and I was absolutely honoured to work with him on an exhibition curated by *Esquire* magazine called 'A Singular Suit', which paired designers with artists and creatives across various fields. Jeremy's idea was to re-create Winston Churchill's 'Siren Suit' but cover it in an assortment of woven badges like a hiker's rucksack. Other inspirations included Jonathan Meades' astonishing documentary *Isle of Rust*, and the photos of Gus Wylie from his book *The Hebrideans*. The idea of slowing down and reconnecting ran through much of what we did; one show invitation featured a photo of a handmade sign in the Outer Hebrides which began, in hand-painted black letters, 'Remember the sabbath day to keep it holy'.

Whilst researching another collection I came across some wonderful photographs buried within a website devoted to the history of Morecambe Grammar School by a photographer called Peter Lane. A note beneath gave an email address to which I wrote, and to my great delight Peter responded. I went to see him at home and over a cup of tea he showed me his archive which contained photos of British seaside towns, mostly Brighton and Morecambe, taken over five decades working as a BBC in-house photographer. There were seagulls and strip shows and old ladies in tweed coats on beaches, the world Jonathan Meades describes as that of 'seedy private detectives and couples in flagrante delicto, of raffish bars peopled by ginny former Gaiety Girls, remittance men and bogus majors'. The photographs were so special that I decided to produce a book of them. We called it *Palace of Fun* and I was honoured when Martin Parr later told me he'd put a copy in his foundation's Archive of British Photography.

Some Success

At our peak Tautz had sixty-five global stockists, including some of the world's most iconic stores. We sold to Harrods, Selfridges, Isetan, Beams and United Arrows in Tokyo and Barneys' New York. In 2010 I won Menswear Designer of the Year at the British Fashion Awards, beating Burberry, Margaret Howell and Paul Smith. In 2015 I won the BFC GQ Fund – at the time the biggest cash prize in men's fashion – and was nominated for (but didn't win) another British Fashion Award, this time up against Tom Ford and J. W. Anderson. Our clothes were worn by many extraordinary people; musicians, artists, actors,

Donald-John weaving, Luskentyre, Isle of Harris

Desmond stenting, British Millerain, Elland, Leeds

The sewing team, 2015, Cookson & Clegg, Blackburn

Century Dyeing, part of British
Millerain, Elland, Leeds

Sewing a tongue, Walsh, Bolton

Family photo,
Hainsworth, Pudsey, Leeds

Inspection, British Millerain,
Elland, Leeds

Machine plates, Hainsworth, Pudsey, Leeds

Goods out, UK Piquet, Leicester

Chalk sharpening and marking out, Savile Row

Sewing trousers, Savile Row

Roy knitting, Riverside, Rugby

other designers. We helped other designers find British makers for their collections. All of this made my team proud. It was a great honour to be recognised for what we did, which was to design and make great clothes and support great British makers. The design philosophy at E. Tautz was much like the one at Volkswagen in the early days of the Beetle; make the best product you can, and with every new iteration strive to make it better, but never change it so much, cosmetically, that anyone who owned the previous model would feel embarrassed to be seen driving it, a philosophy in stark opposition to that of US car makers who'd change the appearance of their cars so radically that owners would feel embarrassed not to drive the newest model.

We had some small success. We designed beautiful, functional clothes, never compromising on quality, our clothes evolving slowly from season to season, our customers happy to wear them for years. Our field trousers achieved close to cult status in Japan, which made us feel proud. But fashion is about newness, and increasingly celebrity, and we couldn't, and didn't want to, compete this way. Add to this the small profit margins when selling wholesale and after a dozen years we had hardly made a penny (though we hadn't lost much either). But then in January 2020 Covid hit, our stockists slashed or cancelled orders, and our UK factories either closed or switched to making PPE. In March, Debenhams failed to pay us a huge amount of money owed for my Hammond collection and in early April 2020 they went bust. We didn't have the money to ride it out and in 2022 the E. Tautz name was mothballed.

11

Cookson & Clegg

There remain in the UK some exceptional clothing factories, but of these only a few are independent, producing clothes for the handful of premium UK brands that still make their clothes locally. Of these Cookson & Clegg, founded in 1860 on Mincing Lane in Blackburn, is in the categories it makes undoubtedly the best.

Cookson started life as a leather currier (the stage after tanning where the leather is coloured and dressed) and manufacturer of boot uppers and mill straps. By the 1930s this experience had seen them move sideways into the production of leather goods for the British Army and the RAF, including leather dispatch riders' jerkins and flying helmets. Throughout the later twentieth century, Cookson & Clegg were a major supplier of clothing and other sewn products to the Army, making combat pants, arctic parkas and an array of technical combat clothing, as well as other less obvious sewn products like tank camouflage covers. But in 2009 the Army had consolidated its kit contracts and to save money, had placed them with a company making this crucial kit overseas. Overnight Cookson lost about 95 per cent of their business. They had just one other customer, Nigel Cabourne, who loved that he could make his clothes in one of the factories that many of his archive military pieces had been made in, and from this one great client Cooksons tried to rebuild a business making civilian clothing for brands like Margaret Howell, Paul Smith and Burberry, as well as E. Tautz. They made lots for Tautz including our two bestselling products: the baggy, military-style heavyweight chino we called the Field Trouser, and a big 80s-cut shirt with amazing pockets inspired by an old railway workers' shirt, called the Lineman. But it was hard. Volumes were small, designs changed constantly and work was almost entirely seasonal. Three busy months would always be followed by three with very little work at all.

One Sunday night at the end of January 2015, I received an email from the CEO of Cooksons. Reading it at eight the following morning, I discovered that the owners had decided to close it down and that they were starting redundancy proceedings for all of their thirty staff with immediate effect. Saddened to read the news – the last time we met there had been talk of expansion and investment – I emailed him straight back. 'Should the worst come to pass,' I told him, 'I would be very interested in seeing if we could take on some or all of the workforce, yourself included. It would break my heart to see another great factory go to the wall.'

We spoke later that morning. Cookson & Clegg was at the time owned by a big manufacturer of workwear fabrics, the main suppliers of camouflage fabric to the British Army as well as other armed forces the world over. Whilst Cooksons had been one of the Army's main clothing suppliers they'd been strategically important to the group, but with the making contracts now overseas that was gone. Despite efforts to reposition they'd been losing money for years. Their owners no longer saw a future for making clothing in the UK. But I did.

We signed an NDA that afternoon and were discussing the outline of a deal within ten days, moving quickly to stop staff from being laid off, which would almost certainly have killed the business for good. We agreed outline terms on 23 February, and I began speaking to their existing customers and suppliers, their landlord and the staff. Final terms and staff and lease transfers were agreed, and by Sunday 12 April it was done. The following day I received an email from the now former CEO:

Congratulations. I am very pleased that Cookson and Clegg will get to live on under your ownership.

The deal was announced to our customers on 14 April and I packed a bag and shipped out to Blackburn. For almost a year I spent a good deal of time living at a B&B on the Preston New Road. In 2015, almost unbelievably, there was not one single hotel in a town that at one time had been one of Lancashire's and Britain's most prosperous.

Blackburn had been a thriving mill town with a flourishing textile industry which at one time employed close to 50 per cent of the population, but it was also a centre of engineering excellence, inventing, refining, building and exporting the machinery that much of the world's textiles were produced on. It boasted a fine technical college, grand civic buildings and a spectacular park, and had many claims to fame. The world's first motion pictures had been shot in Blackburn in the 1890s by two men called Mitchell and Kenyan. In 1931 Gandhi had visited next-door Darwen. And its football team, Blackburn Rovers, winner of the Premier League in 1995, had been one of the founding members of the Football League. The town had boasted a thriving nightlife: the Stones had played the Odeon in 1965, Bowie had played King George's Hall in 1973.

But by 2015, like so many post-industrial British towns, all that was in the past. There were brownfield wastelands where mills had once stood, the nightclubs were boarded up, the big shopping centre shut at 5.30 and locked its doors, leaving central Blackburn a ghost town.

Blackburn's professional classes had upped sticks and headed north to the beauty of the Ribble Valley and the Forest of Bowland. Young people with any get-up-and-go were getting up and going to Manchester or London. Topshop closed. And then Debenhams closed. The council and the owners of the main shopping streets worked hard to find ways to keep the shop fronts filled and the town centre lively. Blackburn market is always a-bustle, the food court is filled with great value, delicious, unique food. Darwen market is similarly wonderful, idiosyncratic and thriving most days. But it's no match for a Selfridges and a Wahaca. I love the team at the council, they work incredibly hard with almost zero resources to rebuild and regenerate a town they clearly love – even though a couple of times now they've allowed large empty buildings to be pulled down, which I strongly disagree with. You can do lots of innovative things with an empty building, you can do almost nothing with a patch of concrete where a building used to be, except park cars on it.

What post-industrial towns like Blackburn, and the dozens like it which are satellites to thriving cities like Manchester, have in great abundance – and which these cities increasingly don't have – is space, and with space and creativity and willpower you can do great things. With a couple of small exceptions a young person growing up in Blackburn, or one of the many towns like it, will have seen very little but decline during the years they spent there. No cranes erecting tall shiny buildings, no swish regeneration, no dockland renewals. In the North and the Midlands many cities are thriving. I have lived in Leeds, Liverpool and Manchester and they are boom towns. However, drive 20 miles from the centre of Manchester and you come to towns like Blackburn, away from the fast, subsidised urban transport networks and the mainline London train lines, away from the positive glow of the big universities. There are lots of these towns and they all need a future.

Cookson & Clegg, like many UK factories, faced a huge number of very significant challenges. The seasonality of the fashion industry, delivering Spring-Summer collections in January and Autumn-Winter in June, created huge regular gaps in the production schedule. In addition to these predictable gaps, the late delivery by our customers of the fabrics and trims from which we sewed their garments created additional smaller gaps even at busy periods. Some factories would hire and fire, some put staff on zero-hours contracts. I didn't want either of these, so I would take on work making simple pieces like aprons and tote bags and subsidise staff wages with my income from Debenhams. With newness the lifeblood of fashion, few garments were ever made more than once, meaning that there was no chance to optimise production and efficiency. Instead Cookson produced small one-off runs at low production efficiency. The seasonality also meant always waiting to start production until new styles had been developed and fabrics delivered, all of which tended to happen for every customer at the same time. There was no consistency of demand and no security of orders, meaning there was no chance to invest in the machinery and systems that would reduce cost, and no chance to grow the workforce to improve operating efficiency through better use of the overheads. We faced a severe skills shortage and the thorny issue that very few young people wanted to get into manufacturing, after years in which politicians on both sides had looked down on manufacturing jobs for anything but the most high-tech products,

I spoke often with the managers of manufacturing businesses like Cooksons, and I had acted in an advisory capacity for a potential rescue of the old Lyle & Scott factory in Hawick where I'd seen the books. Time and again I saw the same issues that C&C faced, but in some cases worse, dozens of fantastic factories crying out for stable year-round work. I knew just how efficiently a clothing factory like Cooksons could run if only it was full, and could afford to invest in staff, machinery and training. The cost of production could be reduced by as much as a third. These factories were, almost without exception, businesses vital to the economy and the identity of the towns in which they sat, towns that desperately needed a leg up. And in addition, I met endless consumers desperate to support local businesses if they could only afford what they sold; consumers who not only wanted to buy locally but wanted to buy better. But with the cost of cheap clothes so low, the price for British-made quality clothes seemed exorbitant.

And this was the big issue. There are a handful of excellent British brands who still make in the UK, but they are all expensive, well beyond the reach of most ordinary Brits. So their volumes are low and the factories they use run inefficiently; all are stuck in a negative Catch-22. Yet from all of this the little seed of an idea that would become Community Clothing began to grow.

12

Community Clothing

A lot of people talk about doing the right thing, many of them very famous and well paid, but very few actually do anything beyond talk. For those that do, and there is a small but growing list (I name a few of these good guys at the end of the book), I applaud you, whatever your individual motivations. I know how hard it is to run any business, let alone one which flies in the face of the 'profit-above-all-else' mentality. But I know too how rewarding and life-affirming it can be. Action is what is needed. To those who speak the words yet fly in private planes or take money from the brands who support terrible ethical or environmental practices, shame. You can do better.

I'm lucky to have been brought up frugal (thank you, Mother). I have no wish to be rich, or for the obvious trappings of wealth. I want to be happy, and the things that make me happiest are largely free. I drive a Prius, I ride a bike, I ride the bus or the tube and take the train. I buy very little, I shop second hand. I would feel like a fraud and a fool if I did otherwise. When in 2015, aged forty-three, I bought Cookson & Clegg, I was motivated by putting my money where my mouth was after fifteen years of preaching to others about the importance of high-quality manufacturing and supporting local jobs. Over the first five loss-making years it has cost me personally over a million quid, which is why the derelict house in the Forest of Bowland that I bought in 2017 still has no floors, no doors, no fireplaces and no kitchen.

How do you sustain and create jobs in the UK? Not in the places where there are lots, like London and the Southeast, but in the rest of the UK, in the former manufacturing and agricultural heartlands, the regions where economic and social deprivation is worst, where many people feel frustration and anger daily. How do you bring back quality? And make it affordable? And how do you encourage people to enjoy having less when having more is so much a part of our everyday lives? You have to do something that's different from what has been done for the past fifty years; something that is designed from the ground up to do good. As a society, and as businesses, we have to start by making the creation of skilled, fulfilling local jobs our goal. To prioritise the manufacture of top-quality things, objects that provide the longevity, and the lasting pleasure in using them, that allows people to stop buying the mad volumes of terrible stuff. We need to make these high-quality things affordable to many people, not just a wealthy few, and we could do with government spending our money on high-quality, locally made things too. Because all of this activity increases local economic value and the local tax pot, so that we can all enjoy top-quality public services and live in healthy, happy communities. These were my thoughts when I was thinking about the model behind Community Clothing.

I had been thinking about schoolkids' jumpers. In my day we all wore woollen jumpers which kept us warm in winter and served as goalposts in summer. They often came to us second hand via the school exchange and they would usually be passed on to some other lucky devil after we outgrew them. They weren't washed that often because frankly they didn't need to be (kids don't need to be that clean). And almost every single one of them was made in the UK, just like the blazers, school ties, shorts and woollen socks we also wore. In 1980, around

65,000 people were employed in the textile industry in Scotland. That figure had slipped to less than 40,000 by the end of the 1990s, and by 2010 fewer than 450 firms remained, employing less than 20,000 people. The majority of these jobs had been lost in fewer than half a dozen small towns in the Scottish Borders. The effects were devastating to the region, both in economic terms, and in the loss of enjoyable fulfilling work, personal identity and civic pride. My grandad, once a yarn designer at the now defunct yarn spinners Laidlaw & Fairgreave, had been one of these to lose his job.

In January 2016, less than eight months after stepping in to save Cookson & Clegg from closure, I was asked by Lord Digby Jones (the former head of the CBI) to advise a friend of his who was considering mounting a rescue bid for Hawick Knitwear (formerly the Lyle & Scott mill before they, like Pringle, moved their production to China), which had been placed into administration. But there was sadly no deal to be done. The machinery was sold and the business closed. I had done a back of a fag-packet calculation and had worked out that you could re-employ every person who had lost their job in the Scottish knitwear industry in the past decade if you got UK school kids wearing woollen jumpers again. This was the seed from which the idea behind Community Clothing grew.

Mission

Community Clothing has a simple mission:

- Create and sustain skilled jobs here in the UK
- Make fantastic quality clothes which sell at affordable prices

To achieve it I sketched out a business model that was radically different from those of other clothing brands. I asked myself what was needed and what was not. I simplified everything.

Cut Out the Middle Man

Selling your product in your own or other people's shops is really helpful, especially if you have a good product, because it allows people to see, feel and try on your gear. But it is very expensive, and gets more so as rents, rates, and energy bills rocket. By only selling online, which brings its own costs and challenges, we save as much as a third of our operating costs. We have sold for limited periods through a few other fantastic retailers, including Selfridges, Liberty and John Lewis, but this was because we like them and thought many of their customers would like what we do. But those partnerships were always on terms that meant we didn't make any money on those sales.

No Newness

Designing new styles every season, or – as is now increasingly the case – every day, is fundamental to getting people to want more. Not doing that means people might just buy what they need. And don't businesses need to grow, all the time, and make bigger profits? Well no, they don't. There are 66 million people in the UK and they all need clothes. Some of these clothes, socks and pants, might wear out after a few years; others, T-shirts, shirts and trousers, might last a bit longer. How many clothes do we need? Five hundred years ago we had just one set, maybe five garments. Fifty years ago the average person had fewer than a hundred items in their wardrobe. If, let's say, they need replacing every ten years, that's ten pieces a year, meaning every year the people of Britain *need* to buy 330 million pieces of clothing. If we had a business that was just 0.3 per cent of this then we'd be selling a million garments a year. That would be fine by me. And instead of finding temporary and somewhat limited fulfilment and happiness through buying things, we could instead find deep and lasting fulfilment and happiness through having a great job we loved.

So at Community Clothing we don't design new stuff every day, or even every season. We add a few things here and there that we think people might need, but otherwise, it's the same stuff this year as last year. Staples, classics, basics, whatever you want to call them, we make the everyday clothes that form the foundation of most people's every-day wardrobes. The jumpers and T-shirts and sweatshirts and jeans you keep and wear for decades, often for a lifetime. No one today makes good-quality affordable basics. You can have good quality, or you can have affordable. But the affordable stuff is *terrible*; cheaply made from nasty cheap materials. I think everyone should be able to afford good-quality clothes that don't harm the planet. So that's what we do. Our clothes are great quality *and* affordable.

Constantly designing, developing, sourcing and launching thousands of new styles entails huge cost. Our model radically reduces design and development costs, e-commerce and other costs, and ensures maximum quality, minimum price and zero waste. We design and engineer the very best version of every single garment we sell; we design great-looking clothes but we also design for comfort, function and a long life. We fit, test, review, refine and repeat until we think we have it right. Sometimes developments can take years. And then when it's right we make it in exactly the same way time after time. The same natural raw materials from the same farms, produced by the same spinners, weavers, dyers, knitters and garment makers, because that is the only way to ensure exceptional quality. At Community Clothing the socks you buy from us this year will be the same socks you bought from us last year, and the year before that, and the year before that.

And this consistency of design isn't just great for you, it's also great for the fantastic UK factories we work with. We work closely with our long-term partner factories to design products that are simple and efficient for them to make, meaning the highest quality and lowest cost. We always design our clothes with simplicity in mind: we add no unnecessary features which increase the cost, and we try to use as few different fabrics across our product ranges as possible. All of this means our business is efficient and easy to manage. And because we don't change our clothes from season to season we never waste any fabric or trims. It also means our fabrics and our clothes can be made at any time during the year, which is great for all of our suppliers. Other brands waste tens, if not hundreds of millions of pounds each year designing and launching new products. They waste millions of pounds more in unused fabrics, and they end up with millions of unsold garments each season which they waste more money disposing of in landfill or incinerating. Just imagine the cost of developing thousands of new products a month like some fast fashion brands do. Imagine how much testing they do (it's not a lot). Our model avoids all of that.

But this consistent approach doesn't mean we stand still. Far from it. We are always looking for ways to make our product better. Can we improve its lifespan, can we reduce its environmental footprint, can we work with our partner factories so that more of our supply chain is local to the point of consumption? Can we go right back to the soil, growing the fibres we need, regeneratively, right here in the UK? No seasonal collections, no weekly drops, no must-have items. Just great everyday clothes, at great everyday prices, every time.

Because we're not tied to launching new products at the start of every traditional fashion season, our factories can make product for us when it works for them, in what would normally be their quiet periods. Manufacturing is hard. You need to manage quality, efficiency, innovation, staff ups and downs, your supply chain, the crazy rises in energy costs. It's really tough, and only the best survive. On top of all of that, even the very best British textile and garment factories have downtime between the traditional fashion seasons, some of it significant, and this can be financially crippling. We place large rolling orders up to a year in advance which gives our partner factories total flexibility, meaning they can keep their production lines running at full capacity all year round. And it is great for our customers – they get amazing quality at the lowest possible prices. And as Community Clothing grows our partner factories grow, because they know we are with them for the long term, creating a further positive cycle of rising investment, rising employ-ment and rising efficiency, delivering better wages for workers, and greater economic stability for the manufacturers and the communities they support.

Engineered Clothing

My background is in engineering, where new designs take years, where materials are tested and verified, where every component and assembly is tested to destruction before it is launched to ensure it's really going to work. When I design clothes I take that same approach. I want to design and develop and test the clothes we make at Community Clothing so that we can be as sure as we can that they are always going to work, to last well and actually get better with age. I only want to make clothes that you want to keep and wear, we hope for decades. This doesn't mean that things will never go wrong, but it does mean that most things go very right. We use materials we've used for years, facto-ries, machines and techniques that are tried and tested. We do make exceptionally good clothing. I know, because I wear it almost every day. We use materials that won't quickly wear out, that we know the prove-nance of, that we've tested and worn for years. We source them from manufacturers who in many cases have centuries of experience making one thing and making it well.

Making good materials is difficult and expensive. You need to start with great raw product, and our yarn spinners are experts in sourcing the right raw fibres for the job. Consistency is important, so they use the same fibres, grown or raised on the same farms year after year. It then means spinning the best-quality yarn, and our spinners are the best in the business. They spin yarns for some of the best-known luxury brands on the planet and have centuries of experience and accumulated skill and knowledge in the workforces. And it's the same with the weavers and knitters who produce our fabrics with such great skill and care. Then these fabrics need to be cut with precision and sewn in a way that ensures the clothing is robust. That means felled seams on trouser legs and dresses, rivets on jeans, topstitching on sweatshirts. It can take almost twice as long to sew clothes this way, but we do it because we believe every garment should be made well. It's why we are confident to say that we don't think you can buy clothes as good as ours for even twice the price.

Repair, Swap, Resell

We encourage second-hand clothing sales and have run several trials of a second-hand shop for our own product with a view to bringing this in as a permanent part of our business. We absolutely encourage repair and the reclamation of fabrics for reuse. We've run several repair cafés, and we work with various clothes exchanges and zero-waste charities. We are working to encourage the restoration of a network of local repair and reclamation businesses, but for this to happen we have to build the making skills locally first, and as a business we are 100 per cent dedicated to local production and local skills training.

Local

Every single product we have ever made has been made in the UK. Almost every product we make is made using locally made fabric, and we're working hard to get this to 100 per cent too. We call this philosophy 'next-level local'. Local production is good on every level. Local means transparency and traceability, it means minimum environmental impact and maximum sustainability. And it means getting to work with people with whom you've built long working relationships. Making locally means we can be absolutely certain of exactly who is doing what in our supply chain, and that we are making our products sustainably. We inspect factories – check the fire escape, check the wage slips and employment contracts, check that the kettles work and that there are plenty of tea bags in the canteen (most important). We can make sure they are following the extremely tough environmental standards required here in the UK.

Supply chains in the fashion world are murky businesses. Many brands couldn't tell you hand on heart where their products are made, not every step. And if that's the case, how do you know how they're making your product? And we go much further. We aim to keep everything else we do local too. Wherever possible we work with service providers and suppliers who are based in the towns where we make our clothes. We use local label suppliers, local packaging suppliers. We use local graphic design agencies, local printers. It's about putting the greatest amount of economic benefit into the communities in which we work. Success for us means bringing 100 per cent of our supply chain local to the point of use.

Local supply chains mean:

- near zero shipping costs with no customs costs;
- minimised clothing miles and carbon footprint;
- total transparency and traceability;
- clean production systems covered by the tightest environmental standards;
- a growing skills base for garment repair and aftercare.

Low Impact

We make our clothes from the lowest impact sustainable natural materials, made to the toughest environmental standard, made using the cleanest energy, and made where they're sold, reducing transport pollution. And of course, every single garment is made to last, further reducing the environmental impact. I can confidently state you won't find a more environmentally sustainable manufacturing route for mass-produced clothing anywhere on earth.

Creating Jobs

Our long-term ambition is to directly create 5,000 textile and garment manufacturing jobs, and I think that if we are successful we can indirectly catalyse the creation of 50,000 more. We want to create opportunities for people of all ages living in these regions to build long-term, rewarding, fulfilling careers, not just in manufacturing, but in all the other areas connected with our business. But it is no good creating and sustaining jobs in these regions if nobody wants them. The governments who told us for decades that skilled manual work, blue-collar work, was no good, were correct insofar as in industries that for many years were declining there was certainly a lot less security. But manufacturing locally is vitally important for providing work that fulfils us, and for reducing our harm to the natural world. So we work to build pathways into work, and equally importantly we work to encourage people to see making jobs as great long-term fulfilling careers. I know from experience that people who make are on the whole much happier than people who do many other jobs. We work with education charities such as The King's Foundation, helping to deliver skills training and textiles education for both school students and adult learners. We work with local schools and colleges, helping build connections between them and local textile and clothing manufacturers, facilitating work placements and open days. We work with local colleges and universities, including Blackburn College, Burnley College, Manchester Metropolitan University and UCLAN in Preston, giving opportunities for students in photography, design, marketing and textiles to work on real projects.

Clothes That Speak for Themselves

Our entire philosophy is about keeping things simple, minimising costs and environmental impact, and maximising quality. Another way we do this is to let the quality of the clothes speak for themselves. Many clothing brands spend far more money on *marketing and selling* their products than they spend on *making* them. I've always thought this is crazy. Our philosophy is to spend most of our money making the best clothes we can. The advert we run on social media simply says 'This advert cost less than £1 to make because we'd rather spend our money making good clothes'. It has proven very effective. Every advert you see on Facebook or Instagram is written and created by us, not by a highly paid advertising agency. I write most of the emails. As we've seen, many fashion brands spend at least 20 per cent of their turnover on marketing and advertising. Expensive models, expensive photographers, expensive locations, and expensive post-production, because making average clothes look good is really hard. And then they have to pay celebrities and influencers to say they love the clothes. Their fees would shock you.

We don't do any of that. We think spending those kinds of sums is crazy. And if you make a really good product it shouldn't be necessary.

Many of the people you see in our films and our images are not professional models, they're lovely people from the communities where our partner factories are located. Students from local colleges, people we meet at events, local teachers, local artists, the guys from the local bowling club, the stallholders from the local market, and a cool guy we met in the Co-op downstairs from the studio where we shoot in Blackburn. We shoot in studios and locations in and around those very same communities, with local photographers, not in expensive sunny locations overseas. Our models mostly do their own hair and make-up on our shoots, and we don't retouch the images because that's expensive and we prefer our images to be honest and real. We currently sponsor two local grassroots sports clubs (and are in discussions to work with two more), and we shoot with their players and fans and volunteers. It's all part of telling the story of our communities, the factories, the makers, their families and friends, the clubs and societies, which make up the textile towns they call home; and the community of likeminded individuals who choose to buy our clothing.

Never On Sale

It's no good making clothes that last for ages if you're trying to sell people new ones every week. We never chase trends, we offer great clothes with enduring style, we design every piece with a view to it having a minimum twenty-year lifespan. Some of the pieces we design have been worn in largely the same way for over half a century and are likely to be worn in much the same way half a century from now. We don't have sales, or discounts of any description, to lure you into buying things you don't need. There's never anything that's going to run out of stock (unless we decide to discontinue a style for good). Selling clothes people don't need is the opposite of sustainable. But they're finding it a hard habit to break. At Community Clothing we never have a sale. Adding huge mark-ups then constantly reducing prices through offers and sales is just plain wrong. It drives needless consumption. But it is a necessity for most fashion and clothing businesses who need sales to clear out perfectly good stock to make way for the constant merry-go-round of new stuff. And it's all priced into their model. People are often surprised to discover that these fashion brands are still making a profit on their garments even at 70 per cent off. You might also be horrified to learn that around 30 per cent of all the clothing that is made is never sold. Last year the fashion world produced over 100 billion garments, so that's 30 billion garments that were made that nobody wanted; 30 billion garments worth of wasted energy and resources and pollution.

Discounts create want, they make us buy things we don't need. In the UK we only wear between 30 and 35 per cent of the clothes in our wardrobes. In other words we need about a third of what we thought we wanted. We waste money buying them, we waste money storing them, and we waste time and effort disposing of them, unless, like 80 per cent of people, we just throw them in the bin. Instead of over-inflating our prices and then discounting we sell our clothes at the very best price we can, every single day of the year. Our seasonless staples model means we never need to get rid of surplus stock. And because there are no discounts to tempt you, you only buy what you need, when you need it. So with our model there's no over production, no over-inflated want, no overconsumption, just great clothes at a great-value price every day.

———————

We are called Community Clothing for good reason: because we make clothing, we *don't* drive fashion. Where fashion is about newness and consumption and want, clothing is about enduring value and need. Clothing is cherished, cared for, repaired, passed on. Where fashion is fast, clothing is slow. Clothing is about making better and consuming less, and because of that, it is good for the people that make it, good for the people that wear it, and good for the planet. At Community Clothing, every piece of clothing we make is made well, made with pride and made to last.

The Price is Right (And Clear)

There are lots of brands that make great-quality clothing. What's so different about Community Clothing? Simple: the price. We charge about a third of what other premium brands for the same quality of clothing. We're confident you won't find clothes as good as ours at even twice the price. We can do this because our business model is unique. We cut out all the usual costs of designing and selling clothes, meaning we don't need to add anything like the same mark-up as most other brands. This means we can sell the same great quality at a fraction of the price. Let's take a few examples. Start with socks. Our everyday socks are £6. You can buy pretty much the same sock (same yarn, same factory) for £24 from another well-known premium brand. Our £70 lambswool jumpers are made from the same yarn, in the same factory, as a £250 jumper from a different premium brand. And our selvedge jeans are £90 where you can easily pay £250 or more for an almost identical jean elsewhere. Our clothes are not cheap, but their quality is exceptional. I am very confident that our clothes offer the best value for money in the UK.

Being honest and completely transparent about how the economics work is important. We need more of it in the world. We've always been very happy to share the numbers behind our business with our customers. This is because, unlike most brands, we have nothing to hide. We're so happy to do this we ran a full-page advert in *The Times* on Black Friday detailing the exact cost and price structure of our popular socks.

Where the Money Goes

One of the unique things about Community Clothing is where the money goes. Over half of what customers spend with us goes directly into the pockets of the people who make the clothes as wages. Of the remainder a portion is spent on local administrative costs, services like security, cleaning and transport, plus rent and utility bills, and the remainder is UK VAT and local business rates, which all goes to funding local services. In fact only about £1 out of every £10 spent with us leaves the UK, most of that going to pay the farmers in Australia, New Zealand and the USA who grow the cotton and wool we use. And even better, because local spending gets circulated and recirculated within the local economy its economic value gets multiplied, typically about three times. Our average first-time customer spends around £40. This will generate over £100 of local economic value. That's business that does good.

A Good Start

In 2016 I launched Community Clothing with a crowdfunding campaign and three products. We hustled every day for three weeks pressing every connection we had to get the campaign over its target. We sent emails, we badgered press contacts, I went on QVC, or something very like it. At just before midnight on Friday 11 March 2016, thanks in large part to a big article in the *Evening Standard*, we shot past our target with over a thousand backers. Just five weeks later the first clothes were in production at five UK factories. And we set the counter in motion, counting the hours of skilled UK work we created.

We've since been covered in every major newspaper and magazine in the UK, and some in the USA and other countries. We've been on the BBC, on *Countryfile* and Radio 4's *Open Country* talking about growing textiles in Lancashire. We've done projects with some fantastic retailers, and supplied our clothes to some fantastic brands. His Majesty the King sells our aprons in the Highgrove shop. I've talked about our idea at TEDx, the Royal Geographical Society, B Corp, the Business School at Oxford University, and the Adam Smith Business School at Glasgow University. We've done lots of great things within the various communities in which our partner factories are based. We're a founding partner in the Festival of Making and the British Textile Biennial, and in 2023 were delighted to be part of the new We Invented the Weekend festival in Manchester.

And we are growing quickly: not because we spend lots of money trying to convince people to buy our products, but because we do it the old fashioned way – by making something good, and selling it at a decent price. What's not to like about that? John Molson, founder of Canada's oldest brewery, used to say something along the lines of, 'An honest brew makes its own friends'. That's how I feel about our clothes: they're honest, and they're making their own friends. People like what we make, and what we do, and they're glad to spread the word.

Welsh Pants

In September 2023 we launched a campaign to restart the production of underwear in South Wales, a region once famed for it. At the peak two thousand mostly women sewed pants and bras in the valleys, but by 2020 the number was just thirty. If 5 per cent of Brits wore high-quality Welsh-made pants we could rehire every one of those two thousand women. In many ways it was the Community Clothing story in miniature, perfectly encapsulating everything that the brand was about: the preservation of a long tradition of regional making; job creation; and making a high-quality piece of everyday clothing (and nothing is more everyday than the humble knicker).

It was also about engaging a community of supporters behind the idea to help tell and spread the story. As we set about building the campaign I wrote a short overview explaining the history of underwear making in the region and telling the story of its subsequent decline, and the associated loss of jobs, and sent it to a bunch of Welsh friends. Without exception they were hugely supportive. The Wonderbra had been made for many years in the Gossard factory in Pontllanfraith, a few miles from our partner factory in New Tredegar. I remember vividly the traffic-stopping 'Hello Boys' campaign of the early 1990s starring Eva Herzigova, giant billboards that according to perhaps apocryphal stories caused cars to swerve and crash when they were erected. I thought it might be fun to run our Welsh pants under the heading 'Hello Boyos', but I wasn't sure if it was lazy Welsh stereotyping, so I rang Kiri Pritchard-McLean, who is both Welsh and funny, and asked her opinion and she gave it the nod. Wynne Evans, the wonderful Welsh opera singer most famous as Gio Campario from the Go Compare adverts, sang us a version of 'Bread of Heaven', substituting pants for bread, and added a couple more entirely ad-libbed pants-based songs for good measure. We got dozens of Welsh models of all shapes and sizes to appear on video and in stills.

We launched to loads of great coverage, BBC Wales giving the campaign a huge boost. We had hoped to sell 5,000 pairs of pants in a month. We sold 3,000 in two days and reached over 10,000 pairs before we had to stop the campaign because we'd far exceeded the initial capacity of the team we had lined up to sew them. I believe in the role of business in shaping better societies, and I believe all businesses have the power to increase the common good. I believe Community Clothing is an example of such a business.

Part IV

LESS

13

A Different Way

We are pushed relentlessly to want more. And in having more we've accepted, perhaps unwittingly, ever-diminishing quality in the things we consume. And by wanting more and ever cheaper things, we've been responsible for the disappearance of millions of skilled, fulfilling jobs, leaving many in our society without work, and many others with jobs they find mind-numbing and unfulfilling.

But it would be simple, and would cost no more, for us to consume differently. We can simply choose to buy less, to buy better, and to support local businesses which sustain good local work. Put simply, we can choose to live by a philosophy of less, better and local.

Buy fewer things, own a *lot* less stuff, use less of everything, wean ourselves off our manic consumption. Buy better things, ensure everything we buy is of the highest quality: objects which are pleasurable to use or to wear, durable objects, made without polluting or destroying nature, made where possible with regeneratively produced or recycled materials. Better things will cost more, but will last longer, so we will need fewer of them, and they will be more enjoyable to use. We need to make, swap, resell, repair, remake and recycle all the things we buy locally, creating a vibrant skills- and knowledge-based local economy. Local production means traceable and transparent practice; where possible let's encourage a return to artisan production where maker and buyer are directly connected, so that the money we spend goes directly to the people making and growing.

Let's re-engage with craft, where skill and knowledge matter, where the work is meaningful and respected, where consumers can once again feel connected to the product. We must re-establish networks of skilled repairers, enable widespread local collecting of discarded objects and materials, and remake from them. All of this would redistribute jobs country-wide, increasing prosperity in every town and city, and catalyse the creation of a fit-for-all education system, preparing everyone for these newly created jobs. It would allow us to reinvest our personal spending into our local economy, supporting businesses which are rooted in and supportive of their local community, businesses which give rather than extract.

It is possible to imagine a completely different form of industry and commerce across many of the things we buy; it is certainly achievable in textiles and clothing. This new form would be of benefit to the individual, whether user or maker, to society, whether at a local, regional or national level, and to nature and the environment, enabling the regeneration of the natural systems which support our life on earth.

We need to find new ways to make ourselves happy. Fashion, and the ideal of a luxury lifestyle, was sold to us as a way of increasing our happiness, but in a society where the luxury life is constantly and deliberately shifting beyond our reach, it can never be attained and will only make us anxious and unhappy. Can we instead find a new and more permanent happiness elsewhere, away from consumption? Through having good pleasurable work around which to structure our lives? Through being made to feel it's enough just to enjoy the simple pleasures in life? Through the everyday enjoyment of using and cherishing well-made things, enjoying the connection both to the object and the

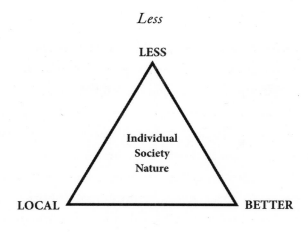

Less

Figure 3

story of its making, the good its creation has done? Like the Japanese, we can find ever greater value in things the more they have aged, and worn, and been repaired. Rediscover the great satisfaction of making your own clothes, ceramics, wooden objects. Find joy in hand-me-downs and clothes with stories and meaning, in the great skill and creativity of new clothes made from old. A happiness that will come from knowing that we are improving the lives of those people who live in our community, by valuing their skill and hard work, and in knowing that the way we live is helping to stabilise and reverse the damage we have been doing to the natural world.

The idea of less, local and better applies equally to every type of consumer good we buy and use: furniture, crockery, pots and pans, cutlery, bedlinens, towels, small electrical goods, etc. We used to make all of these things in the UK, and make them well, and make them to be repaired and passed on.

In November 2021 I gave a lecture at the Royal Geographical Society in South Kensington as part of their regular Fellows and Members' lecture series. It was titled 'Happy Planet Clothing' (I've given more detail in Appendix 2). For the talk I very roughly modelled what a completely reshaped clothing industry might look like; one which dramatically reduced the volume of consumption of new products, and in which all of those new products were made well from high-quality materials, and where possible made locally. The new model would require a dramatic increase in the sale of second-hand clothing, a trend that is already growing rapidly. However, it would also see the return of a secondary clothing economy, in the repair, reuse and recycling of clothing and textile products, which would create significant numbers of local jobs. Making some quite conservative assumptions, it is possible to envisage a system that sustains more local jobs, many of these being more stimulating and rewarding than the jobs they might replace (shelf stacking, warehousing, delivery), overall higher local economic activity, dramatically reduced consumption, and a reduction in the overall carbon and pollution footprint of our fashion and clothing system by as much as 90 per cent. I'm pretty sure an economy like that would make most of us happier.

14

Less

We *need* a certain amount. We *need* clothing, food, shelter, warmth, and probably transport, to exist comfortably. But we *want* a great deal more. This want is tied to our drive to make ourselves feel better about our lives; we mistakenly think that by having more our happiness will increase. Philosophers and theologians have struggled with the idea of human happiness for over two thousand years. For Aristotle, 'Happiness is the meaning and the purpose of life, the whole aim and end of human existence.' And if the number of bestselling self-help books are anything to go by then happiness and contentment are equally as important to us today, and our struggle to achieve them increases as our society evolves. Roman poet Horace devoted a large chunk of his work to discussing the issues of personal fortune and individual contentment. 'Measure and moderation', he claimed, were the means to bring about and secure a happy life. 'To marvel at nothing is just about the one and only thing, that can make a man happy and keep him that way'; 'There is a proper measure in all things, certain limits beyond which and short of which right is not to be found. Who so cultivates the golden mean avoids the poverty of a hovel and the envy of a palace.' And he cautioned against envy, saying that 'no greater punishment than envy was devised'. Another Roman, the philosopher Seneca, agreed: 'A wise man is content with his lot, whatever it may be, without wishing for what he has not.'

And work was important. 'You will not rightly call him a happy man who possesses much; he more rightly earns the name of happy who is skilled in wisely using the gifts of the gods.' It was not what a man had, but what he did, that Horace believed was the route to happiness. Others made the same point, Frederick Donaldson, Archdeacon of Westminster, stated in 1925 that 'Wealth without work' was one of what he called 'The Seven Social Sins'.

Many writers have made the link between an obsession with money and material things and unhappiness. Douglas Adams wrote in *The Hitchhiker's Guide to the Galaxy*, 'This planet has – or rather had – a problem, which was this: most of the people living on it were unhappy for pretty much of the time. Many solutions were suggested for this problem, but most of these were largely concerned with the movement of small green pieces of paper.'

And many more have written of the pleasure in simple things. Sylvia Plath found happiness in a nice view: 'I felt my lungs inflate with the onrush of scenery – air, mountains, trees, people. I thought, "This is what it is to be happy."' Being nice to others. Mark Twain: 'The best way to cheer yourself is to try to cheer someone else up.' Martin Luther King Jr: 'The surest way to be happy is to seek happiness for others.'

We can find great pleasure in real simplicity. Nikos Kazantzakis wrote in *Zorba the Greek*, 'I felt once more how simple and frugal a thing is happiness: a glass of wine, a roast chestnut, a wretched little brazier, the sound of the sea. Nothing else.' J. R. R. Tolkien wrote, 'If more of us valued food and cheer and song above hoarded gold, it would be a merrier world.' And we can find happiness in a quiet life of usefulness. In the words of Leo Tolstoy: 'A quiet secluded life in the country, with the possibility of being useful to people to whom it is easy to do good, and who are not accustomed to have it done to them; then work which one hopes may be of some use; then rest, nature, books, music, love for one's neighbour – such is my idea of happiness.'

Perhaps most important, and most easily achieved, is simply learning the difference between need and want. Epictetus the Greek philosopher wrote, 'Wealth consists not in having great possessions, but in having few wants.' Chinese philosopher Laozi said much the same: 'Manifest plainness, embrace simplicity, have few desires.' G. K. Chesterton went further: 'There are two ways to get enough. One is to continue to accumulate more and more. The other is to desire less.'

Less is easy. Everyone can afford less, everyone has room in their life for less. Everyone has the time for less. It is also practical. Why have three low-quality things when you can have one high-quality one instead? We never need to waste time and energy making a choice. We have that one thing, and if we consider its purchase correctly it will be a good one and the right one always.

Simple pleasures too are within the reach of us all. In Britain we were once the masters of enjoying the simple things in life: a cup of tea; a nice sit down. In his 1995 book *Notes from a Small Island*, Bill Bryson describes what he sees as a uniquely British ability to be happy with almost nothing. Spotting a couple sitting in garden chairs outside a hut on a windswept beach, he writes:

> The man was trying to read a newspaper, but the wind kept wrapping it around his face. They both looked very happy – or if not happy exactly, at least highly contented, because at any time they wanted, they could retire to the hut and be fractionally less cold. They could make a cup of tea and, if they were feeling particularly rakish, have a chocolate digestive biscuit. And this was all they required in the world to bring themselves to a state of near rapture.

Bryson believed us Brits to be the happiest people on earth. He noted that we love to smile or laugh, and are incredibly easy to please; we like a scone, a crumpet, a Rich Tea biscuit. 'Offer them something genuinely tempting,' he says, 'a slice of gateau or a choice of chocolates from a box – and they will nearly always hesitate and begin to worry that it's unwarranted and excessive, as if any pleasure beyond a very modest threshold is vaguely unseemly. "Oh, I shouldn't really," they say. "Oh, go on," you prod encouragingly. "Well, just a small one then."' Bryson was absolutely right. But if it was true just thirty years ago in 1995, what has changed to make us all so unhappy?

In the past thirty years the speed and intensity with which our wants are encouraged has increased exponentially. Our greed and envy have been stoked and unleashed in a way those pioneering American capitalists could only have dreamed off. Greed and Envy, the twin forces unleashed upon us by those intent on making us want more, for their enrichment not ours, far from increasing our happiness are in fact doing the opposite. We suffer from anxiety and feelings of insufficiency; no matter how well we do, or how much we acquire, we can never be free from the awareness that others have or seem to have more and better. Greed and Envy are much cautioned against in almost all world religions, except the religion of Capitalism. Envy is the distress or resentment we feel when others have what we have not. Envy (*invidia*) is characterised by an insatiable desire like greed and lust, a resentful covetousness towards the traits or possessions of another. Bertrand Russell says that envy is one of the most potent causes of unhappiness. Greed is the insatiable desire for material gain, an inordinate desire to acquire or possess more than one needs. In the words of Henry Edward Manning, avarice 'plunges a man deep into the mire of this world, so that he makes it to be his god'. The great problem with want is that it is limitless. At what level does my want stop? At the level of the richest person in my friendship group? At the richest person I see in my town? At the richest people on the planet? I don't have any means of really calculating what I want, and this fills me with anxiety too.

Need, on the other hand, is easy to determine. I need enough socks and pants to last me between washes. I need a thick jumper to keep me alive in my mother's freezing cold house. I need a mug from which to enjoy a cup of tea, and a comfortable chair to sit in whilst I drink it.

What I don't need is a new jumper every few weeks because someone on Instagram tells me the one I have is no longer in fashion. Even as little as forty years ago fashion wasn't such a bad thing. Of course, it encouraged needless (literally) consumption, but at a comparatively low level, and it brought a great deal of beauty and happiness into many people's lives. And at that point fashion was a small industry, centred around creativity, artistry and craft. The materials used were almost universally natural, and the clothes made, whilst they had a short aesthetic shelf life, were durable and held their value for a very long time. Second-hand designer clothes that are twenty, thirty or even fifty years old are still much coveted, and much worn.

But today, 'Fashion' – which is dominated by fast fashion – is a $3 trillion industry, double the size it was just ten years ago. Smartphone-based e-commerce, automated warehousing, a dramatic fall in the price of new clothing, and the co-opting of a large section of the everyday population into becoming want-inducing 'influencers', has caused consumption rates that dwarf all previous frenzies. In 2023 over 100 billion garments were produced globally. The fashion industry consumes 350 million barrels of oil annually and produces 282 billion kilograms of greenhouse gas, equating to 10 per cent of all global emissions. It accounts for 22 per cent of global insecticide use. Its production systems release carcinogens, neurotoxins, heavy metals, phenols, phthalates, hexavalent chrome, formaldehyde and carbon disulphide, leading to eutrophication, acidification, and toxicity in the air, water and soil. It consumes 20 trillion gallons of water annually in the production of its textiles, producing 2.5 billion gallons of waste water. This amounts to 20 per cent of global water pollution. Up to 34 per cent of the microplastics found in oceans are from textiles lost into the air and water during wearing and washing our clothes. And the fashion industry exploits human beings on a gargantuan scale. It is common for workers to be paid as little as $50 a month. I have personally seen pay rates of just 80 pence per day, or around 8 pence per hour, and that was in a factory making garments for well-known designer brands. The industry pays poverty wages, operates under deeply unsafe working conditions and offers no workers' rights. And when wages or labour costs rise, it simply moves elsewhere. In the UK between 1970 and 2020, 1.5 million workers lost their jobs when the industry was moved offshore, with communities (and in some cases whole regions) devastated, and 25 per cent of the population left out of work. Our clothes may be cheap but they come with a very heavy cost.

In order to reach the global reduction in emissions required to control climate change, the UN has set a target for the fashion industry of a reduction of its greenhouse gas emissions of 90 per cent. This seems a spectacular undertaking, but unlike food, we don't need fashion, we just want it. The simplest and most obvious way to achieve it is simply to reduce consumption.

We only wear 27 per cent of the stuff we buy, so let's just not buy the stuff we don't wear. Think very carefully about the clothes you buy. With clothes so cheap as they are now, there is little economic incentive to think hard about the purchase we're considering making, but there is a huge environmental and human cost. Consider that. If you don't think you'll wear it at least a hundred times, don't buy.

If we all bought just 20 per cent of the new clothing we buy now, topped this up with second-hand or remade items, and only bought good things which were made without harm to people or the planet, we'd still have more clothes than we would ever wear and we'd have reduced our carbon footprint and our pollution footprint by at least 80 per cent. With a few tweaks to this formula we can reach that unreachable 90 per cent target with almost no difficulty at all. And as a bonus we'll create lots of space in our cluttered homes.

The fashion and clothing industry currently sits in two broad camps. First there's Big Fashion, the want pushers, who have a lot to lose and who need us to carry on buying at the volume we are buying now (or higher). Of this camp, some are doing very little and simply saying they are sustainable (there is no industry body or country that checks these claims), but a smaller number do seem genuinely interested in at least trying to reduce the harm they cause. Mostly this is through the adoption of new technology, particularly in the materials side which, whilst it won't make a huge difference, could at least see double-digit percentage reductions in some areas. Included in this camp are most of the luxury houses, who are small in the grand scheme of things and have a relatively low footprint anyway. And some of the bigger, cheaper businesses do have good people working to change at least a small part of what they do.

But it's not enough. A few years ago I had the pleasure of having dinner with the erudite and charming Stefan Persson, the now former chairman of H&M, and his wife, and we discussed sustainability in fashion. He asked what I thought might be the biggest improvement H&M could make, and I suggested, in good faith, that closing it would arguably be the very best course. He asked what he might do with all of his staff in Sweden (they're the second largest employer there). I suggested that he might invest in new ventures to employ all those very smart and talented people in ways that were exclusively plant positive (he is after all worth a quoted $27 billion and is a generous donor to may good causes). But so far H&M live on.

Then there is the second camp, a small but growing one, who have no vested interest in the status quo because they sit outside of the big financial-industrial complex. All advocate for a shift to a radically new paradigm – a completely fresh system based on the best of the past and the best of the present and future. There are lots of interesting schools of thought here.

What if we just cancelled all of fashion? Would that be ridiculous? That's what Extinction Rebellion advocate. Do not buy any clothes for a year was their campaign in 2023. Lots of people I meet are opting out of the consumption of new clothes altogether. Many others are opting to only buy second hand. The organisation Fibershed offer a different solution; only wear what can be made locally from fibres grown or raised within your bioregion (roughly a few hundred miles in most cases). Great if you live in California where founder Rebecca Burgess is based, where cotton grows naturally, and merino sheep thrive, and flax grows well. Here in the UK it's tougher, but not impossible; we managed it for 30,000 years. The majority of our native sheep yield a slightly courser wool than we've become accustomed to wearing, and we could only grow cotton in greenhouse conditions (although in Holland this is becoming a reality), but flax for linen grows well. In our 2021 Homegrown/Homespun project we grew, hand-spun, naturally hand-dyed and hand-wove a piece of indigo denim in Blackburn. And a friend of mine, Allan Brown, relearned the ancient craft of making textile from nettles, something poor agricultural labourers would have been relatively familiar with in the UK before the Industrial Revolution. He produced a dress for his daughter in what became something of a labour of love, made from handwoven cloth, itself made from hand-spun yarn made from fibre extracted entirely from foraged nettles. A beautiful film was made about it called *The Nettle Dress*.

Earth Logic advocate for the consumption of less, and for new local systems of production and repair, and Fashion Revolution pushes for huge reforms to labour practices, but also advocates for major changes to consumer behaviour via reduced and more informed purchasing. All of these, and many other organisations thinking along similar lines, are right, and are contributing significantly to the debate.

The very idea of 'Fashion' is the great big elephant in the room. Fashion, the idea that we get rid of one set of clothes and adopt another at the whim of some arbitrary external actor, designer, tastemaker or influencer, is obviously completely at odds with the idea of reducing the harm we are doing to the planet. We don't need Fashion. There is a fundamental part of our human nature that sees us wish to adorn ourselves, to dress in a way that expresses something about ourselves; it is linked to tribalism and status and all sort of other things. The process of dressing up is an enjoyable one, and I am not a killjoy, and I don't want to do away with that fun. And we do of course need clothing. It is cold and rainy in the UK and we need to stay warm and dry. And we need to save other people the embarrassment of seeing our naked bodies. We also need jobs, which in this country fashion provides a lot of. But the average person in the US buys 2,604 items of clothing in their lifetime. The UK number is unlikely to be very different. This is a staggering number.

In one of his autobiographies, David Niven describes how when he moved to Hollywood he did so with just one small suitcase of clothes. He had four suits (one a dinner suit) and a few shirts. Niven, owner of one drawer full of clothes, was considered one of the world's best-dressed men. I was a teenager in the 1980s, before cheap fashion had really taken off. I loved clothes, but I never once thought 'we don't have enough fashion in our lives'.

Whilst it is of course natural for us to get a bit bored with the things we have, constructed systematic fashions in all the things in our lives

– the clothes we wear, the interiors of our homes, the cars we drive – are artificially created to make us consume more. Resisting the want is difficult when those creating it are so skilled and so ever-present in our lives. We need to deal with it consciously. Maybe every time you decide not to buy something, give yourself a pat on the back.

The truth is we really don't need much in order to look and feel great. Find what makes us happy, what makes us feel good about ourselves, and stick to it. I look at what my friends who work in fashion wear, and it's the very opposite of fashion. I have never seen one well-known designer wear anything but an old pair of faded jeans and a navy sweater; another only wears black trousers and a black jumper. It's almost as if the more talented the designer, the less concerned they are personally with fashion. Today at the age of fifty-one I wear the same things pretty much all the time. For the past six months I've really only worn one pair of trousers and one sweatshirt, swapped for a heavy wool jumper during the colder winter months, a few navy T-shirts on rotation, and socks and pants. It makes my life very simple and I feel happy and content in my clothes every day. As the Roman Emperor and philosopher Marcus Aurelius said, 'Very little indeed is necessary for living a happy life'.

15

Better

Filling our lives with fewer but better objects will improve our lives. William Morris, the leader of the Arts and Crafts movement, famously declared, 'Have nothing in your house that you do not know to be useful, or believe to be beautiful.' The great jumper that will keep us warm, a good chair that will give hours of comfortable rest and be a joy to behold, the good mug that will increase our enjoyment of a simple cup of tea.

If an object is reliable we will never have cause to feel the frustration of it not working when we need it to. If the things we use don't fail – the brakes on our bike, say, or the handles on our pans – then we will meet with fewer accidents. If an object lasts I will not have to waste my time replacing it, and I will grow more attached to it the longer I have it. In the case of good clothes or good shoes, they will mould to me and fit better the more I wear them. I will look forward to using or wearing those things knowing they will always do a great job. One of the things I look forward to in winter is wearing my great thick heavy-ribbed fisherman's jumper. I come back to it year after year like an old friend.

Buying things that we know have not harmed, and will not harm, the planet, or things that have been made by people who are well paid, valued and respected, makes us feel better too. How do the buyers of fast fashion cope with the guilt of knowing the harm the things they buy do? The stories behind our objects make them special to us and will increase our pleasure greatly. Every time I wear my plum sweatshirt I think of my much-loved grandma, every time I drink from my green hand-thrown Tin Shed mug I think of the joy my sister had in choosing it for me, and of the beautiful Isle of Mull.

Better quality is better for our working selves, sustaining jobs that are a source of individual fulfilment and pride. And it's better for nature too. If I have an object that is twice as durable, which lasts twice as long, its environmental footprint will be effectively halved. If it lasts five times as long you can divide its pollution footprint by five. I will have used one-fifth of the amount of raw materials. I will produce one-fifth of the amount of waste. If it is made using natural materials it will cause less harm.

Scientists and engineers have spent centuries, and collectively millions of hours, making things that work brilliantly, using the least amount of precious material, and which continue to work well for a very long time. They arguably perfected the manufacture of most of the objects we used in our everyday lives, and then with the quest for ever-growing profit greedy businesses threw all of that away. For 30,000 years the question that manufacturers wrestled with was 'How can I make this better?' Now the only question for the very great majority of them is how they can make it cheaper. In a hundred years we have undone the work of thirty millennia. It's simple maths. I can sell you one good thing, for say £50, that will last ten years. Or I can sell you a cheap thing for £10 that will last you a year. If I am a profit-driven business I will choose the latter option every time. But if I care about human happiness, and the value of human labour and the health of the planet, then the former is my only choice.

With so much bad quality it has become increasingly difficult to find the good. So where buying less could not be simpler, buying better is far from easy. The intangible quality is easy for most of us to make a good judgement on: do I like how it looks, do I like the story behind the product (if it has one)? And this subjective quality is of course different for everyone. But tangible quality has many components and is much harder to discern. How is this object constructed, how and in what order are its constituent parts joined together? Are the materials from which it is made high quality? Do I know enough to tell high-quality wood or plastic from poor? Buying online makes such judgements more difficult and has arguably been a factor in allowing lower-quality products to proliferate. If we can't judge them side by side, quality judgements are harder. Often only through handling or use will an object reveal its true quality. So how do we buy better? How do we navigate the dizzying amount of information available via the web? How do we gain the practical knowledge we need? Who do we trust?

Trust

We set a lot of store by trust in my business. We place trust in our suppliers, our customers place trust in us. Reliable, consistent quality, year after year, is the fundamental principle behind the way we think of product. Designing and engineering a good product takes time, skill and commitment. If you change your product every six months, or in the case of the fast fashion brands every day, it is unlikely that you have spent the necessary years designing, sourcing, prototyping and refining the product to make it excellent. The Burberry classic trench coat has been sold in roughly its current form for around a century. It was designed and tested in the trenches of the First World War, its fit and function was refined over decades, and they still weave the gaberdine cloth that goes into it in their own mill. Most of what they sell is made by other factories, but this one coat is probably as good as it gets (their

Scottish-made knitwear is great quality too, it's made in one of the factories we use at Community Clothing).

Buy from people who make their own things, both large and small, because they can usually be trusted to make them well (I've included a list of as many of such businesses as I can think of in Appendix 1). We are slowly returning to the artisan tradition, where we buy directly from the maker, in lots of areas of our lives, particularly our food. We buy from artisan bakers, and directly from farmers' markets (if you can find a real one). As little as four hundred years ago everything we bought would have been bought directly from the person or small business that made it. The direct relationship mandated high quality. And with no intermediaries your money is paying only for the skilled labour of the manufacture, and for the materials.

The same is true for most maker businesses: you get quality, and you get value. Staffed from top to bottom by people who care greatly about the product, because that product is their whole work, their personal reputation, their source of pride. At Community Clothing we do not own our partner factories (although I personally own one of them), but we act exactly as if we do. We are effectively a cooperative, helping to market and sell the goods that our factories produce. We leave them to the business of making, at which they are expert. We take care of the design and selling, at which many of them are not.

Trust businesses that just do one thing. It is likely that if they didn't do a good job of that one thing then they wouldn't be in business. The same goes for brands that have been doing just one thing for a very long time. Even if they no longer make their products in their own factories, it is likely that they will have found partners who uphold at least the majority of the standards they previously set under their own roof.

Build relationships with brands you trust. Start by trying to understand the essence of the brand, their story and their people. Do they sell based on price, or do they sell based on quality? There is a very well respected and much used management theory developed by a man called Michael Porter. When I studied economics in the early 2000s this theory was still being taught, and I suspect it probably is today. Porter says there are only two viable long-term sources of competitive advantage: low cost, i.e. be cheaper than your competition, or be differentiated, be better or be unique. Over the long run, no business can find sustained success in the middle ground. Which of these is your chosen brand's strategy? Have a look at their website; start with the History page, or the About Us page. Do you get the feeling this is a place where people love their product, where they live and breathe it? Or is it a place where sales and discounts and aggressive promotions dominate, where products come and go? Look at their history. Fifty years of doing one thing well is usually a good sign. On the homepage of the Trickers website is a video called 'everything you need to know about Trickers', the opening line of which is 'This is where you come to buy the very best footwear'. That really is all you need to know.

Look at the churn of the business's product range. How often do new products appear? Bootmakers Hunter made three types of wellies for 95 per cent of their existence; they didn't need others because their existing range was so good. Then they were taken over by a private equity firm who wanted to rinse the name for profit. They expanded the range exponentially – it was mostly pretty bad, and within a few years they'd gone bust. The best welly boot maker on the planet, gone. Barbour built their reputation on about five iconic products, which are still made in their South Shields factory. I would love them more if that was still all they did.

Price is helpful only in one sense. If a new product is really cheap, it's very unlikely to be good. But paying a lot is no guarantee of quality. You could easily just be paying the 99 per cent modern brand premium.

Labels

Read labels. They are supposed to be there to help us. They will tell us where, in theory, something has been made, and what it has been made from. But exercise discretion and caution, because often a label will not tell the whole story.

The label currently only tells you where the final step in the manufacturing process took place. 'Made in the UK' means simply that the last substantive process in the production of a thing has happened in the UK. The rule is designed to allow for products which are built from sub-assemblies; for example Bentley and Rolls Royce cars are made in Britain, but their engines, transmissions and gearboxes are built in Germany. That feels okay to me. You visit Rolls Royce, one of the greatest factories in the world, and a huge amount of highly skilled work is taking place. What they are doing there definitely feels like making cars. But some brands, both expensive and cheap, cheat. They choose to define 'substantive' by the monetary cost of the work. Let's say they've made a garment somewhere really cheap, say for £1 in Asia, and then they ship it to the UK, take it out of the box, iron it and label it here in the UK, and and with the high UK labour costs that final bit of work also cost £1, they say that this is 'substantive', and thus claim that the product is legally made in Britain. Boohoo were caught out for doing this in early 2024.

Another dumb attempt to misdirect consumers I have seen become more prevalent over the last few years is the labelling of products as 'Designed in Britain', which you should take to mean '*Not* Made in Britain'. I saw it on a mug that one of my builders left in the kitchen. It was a black mug. Someone in Britain 'designed' it by choosing to make it black. I suggest a total avoidance of anyone labelling a product as such.

Interrogate the product or the brand. Dig deep into their website, ask questions. Where is this product made? And don't be fobbed off with a simple answer (unless it's a really simple product). Drill right down. Even something as simple as a T-shirt goes through between six and eight major stages. If it's a polyester one, this starts with extracting oil. If the brand won't, or can't, tell you (lots simply have no idea where their stuff is being made), then that should be a warning. If they volunteer very limited information, or none at all, then assume it's bad because anyone who does things well will be shouting it from the rooftops. On our website there's a section called 'Materials We Use (and Materials We Don't)' which tells you everything about our sourcing, right back to the individual cotton and wool farmers. But if something is genuinely made in a high-wage country like the UK, or the USA or Germany, it's probably a good sign. As a rule, a brand is unlikely to make things where it's expensive unless their strategy is to sell on the basis of quality.

In food, because we eat it, the smallest trace of a substance must be included because of the direct effects some of these ingredients can have on our health, and labelling is routinely checked. But labelling on clothing is poorly regulated and far from rigorous. There is no mention of the lead, arsenic, toluene, hexavalent chromium, dimethyl fumarate and other toxic substances that are found in some cheap synthetic clothing. Clothing can be labelled as 100 per cent cotton yet be sewn with polyester thread, and contain small amounts of polyester in things like the neck rib and zip tapes.

And even if a label does accurately tell you the percentage of the materials in it, this is only part of the story. It tells you nothing of the provenance, nor the grade or quality, of any material that's in it. Where is the material mined or extracted? Is this work done by children under slave conditions? How is the oil in our synthetic fabrics processed? All synthetic materials are not the same. Some are well made in countries with very clean energy, like much of the EU or the UK, and where emissions and effluent are tightly controlled. But most is made in countries where coal is routinely burned to generate electricity, like China. Neither are all natural fibres the same. Much of the world's cashmere, for example, is now of poor quality, farmed in a way which is not good for the goats and is turning the natural grazing habitats across central Asia to desert.

Labelling is a start. And there are moves to legislate for greater information and tighter control. Not in Britain, where we put business before all else, but in the EU, which seems to have a greater concern for the wellbeing of its citizens, and be less susceptible to the lobbying of business. Their recent Textiles Strategy report states that by 2030 products placed on the EU market must be long-lived and recyclable, to a great extent made of recycled fibres, be free of hazardous substances and be produced with regard to social rights and the environment. This is a gigantic step, very much in the right direction. They go further, expressing a wish to see fast fashion go out of fashion, and economically profitable reuse and repair services become widely available. The *producer pays* principle may also finally find a legal footing as the EU takes steps to ensure that businesses take responsibility for their products along the whole value chain, including the disposal of them as waste.

A revision of textile labelling will introduce mandatory disclosure of sustainability and circularity parameters on the textiles' labels. According to MEP Delara Burkhardt, 'The EU must legally oblige manufacturers and large fashion companies to operate more sustainably. People and the planet are more important than the textile industry's profits.' They have already made it law that all white goods must be repairable, and parts made easily available. This is a positive move. But we as consumers need to ask more searching questions, and only buy from businesses that give us good answers.

Accreditation

Third-party accreditation can point us towards businesses that we can trust. One of the oldest and best known, certainly amongst my generation, is the British Kitemark, a quality trademark issued and certified by the British Standards Institute since 1903. The Kitemark on a product confirms that a product or service has been tested by experts and that any and all claims it makes have been verified. I worked with the BSI during Covid on certification of the PPE we made; they are the real deal, rigorous, infallible. This is the gold standard of standards. The Woolmark is another, a wool industry certification that since 1964 has ensured that all products which carry it meet the quality standards set by the Woolmark Company. These standards not only include the quality of the wool, they also include the quality of life enjoyed by the sheep who produce the wool, and the system by which the wool is processed. You will find the Woolmark label on many of our products.

New standards are being created which deal with other aspects of a business's activities beyond the tangible quality of their products, including social and environmental standards. B Corp is one such; founded in the US in 2006, its strapline is Make Business a Force for Good. Its accreditation process requires adherence to sustainable social and environmental practices throughout a business, including the treatment of staff and suppliers, and insists on significant business transparency. I did a talk about Community Clothing at one of their early UK conferences, held at a bug farm in Pembrokeshire, and met many businesses all doing amazing things for the betterment of society. I have worked with several B Corp companies since, and enjoy the products of a couple of others. Our standards are their standards, which are well thought through and incentivise good behaviours. It's a three-year process to get formal accreditation and my tiny team wouldn't thank me for the extra workload just at the mo. But it's on the long to-do list.

And beyond formal accreditation there are agencies like Which? who exist to provide impartial everyday advice on products and brands – everything from electric heaters to chicken soup, insurance to credit cards. Which? runs on a subscription model, important because it hugely improves corporate impartiality. Be aware of how any agency you turn to for advice is funded. Many of the supposed arbiters of sustainable practice in my industry are funded by the bad brands they should be warning against. Much the same caution should be exercised around the impartiality of online influencers who are entirely funded by the brands they promote. Interestingly, sufficient numbers of young people are now so sick of being lied to by influencers that we have a rising world of de-influencers, people who have taken it as their mission to debunk the bullshit being peddled. Online reviews are equally likely to be filled with misinformation, with brands paying agencies to puff their own products, and rivals writing scurrilous negative reviews. Numbers count: if there are 10,000 positive reviews stretching back years you might be onto a winner. A healthy dose of cynicism might avoid you being parted from your money for a bad product or service.

Curation

Allow others with the knowledge to curate selections for you. Place your trust in the care and knowledge of buyers of both new and second-hand items through reputable shops and marketplaces. A well-established local hardware store or garden centre is more likely to sell you good-quality tools or plants because it is likely to be run by a person with a real love for the product, probably someone who uses what they sell, who buys the goods as well as selling them, and for whom their personal relationship with you as an individual customer is meaningful. The further you go from these intimate relationships with customer and product, the less likely you are to be sold something good. Giant retail buyers are driven by cost reduction targets, not by a love of product or by valued long-term relationships with customers.

In Japan, where the retail environment feels very different to the UK, there is a great tradition of what are called Select Stores. Here individual buyers look after small departments; they work on the floor of the stores, they meet the customers, they use the product, they check the quality of every product that comes into their store. They are almost like a collective of small individual shops under one roof, working with the same care. Good department stores should also employ experienced staff with good product knowledge, but it is becoming rarer. One of my favourite stores is Tokyo Hands – in Tokyo, unsurprisingly – which sells super high-quality homewares, tools and stationery, many of the products unique to Japan. The entire store is perfectly curated.

Auction houses too are a great place to find well-curated objects, their auctioneers all specialists in the things they sell. Most will only consign high-quality goods, because again, their personal reputation is on the line. Specialist dealers should be a better bet than mass generalists. On eBay there are many great sellers who have built a reputation for sourcing and selling the best quality second-hand items in certain niche categories. And increasing numbers of small stores are taking eBay shops in order to sell to a wider audience.

Saturday Clubs

Who knows about quality? People who make things, and people who used to make things. So let's gather the former carmakers, and weavers, and engineers, and all the people who worked in practical careers and get them to teach younger people. Harness the power of the skilled older generation. There are increasing numbers of programmes connecting young adults with retired seniors, teaching all sorts of great skills but also passing on intergenerational wisdom and life lessons, helping younger individuals to gain greater personal insight. The brilliant Men's Sheds programme was set up to tackle isolation and loneliness in older men. Here men, mostly retired, get together to do practical things – woodwork and metalwork, lots of nature projects – providing camaraderie while also doing valuable work within their communities. But now they're beginning to open their doors to younger men, who gain a practical skill set and at the same time benefit from the wisdom and life lessons of their older mentors. It's what used to happen when young people were apprenticed. I think there's a place for a version of national community service in which practical skill and volunteering go hand in hand. I'll discuss this in more detail in the 'Local' chapter.

Making Better

We have to consume with much greater care, responsibility and commitment. As consumers we need to demand better, make informed purchase decisions not impulse buys, and buy what we need, resisting the lure of offers and discounts.

Everything we buy should be of the highest possible quality we can afford. A heavy hand-forged carbon steel pan, a hand-turned old-wood hand-built chair, a hand-thrown earthenware mug. Return to a way of making that captures the very best of every material used: traditional methods, assisted by clean modern machinery. There are very easy ways for brands to make better clothing, we all know in theory how to do it. We simply turn the clock back fifty years. Heavier fabrics, pure natural materials, longer coats, heavier pure cotton denim, run and fell seams not overlocking ones, hand linking. All the stuff that our grandparents would have known. But of course making in this way is expensive, so we all need to become comfortable with the idea of having less. If consumers demand greater quality, then the brands which sell such things will thrive, and those which do not will either have to adapt or fail.

If we cannot improve the tangible quality of an object, we can at least reduce the harm it does to people and the planet. We are not, without significant legislative intervention, going to wean people off fast fashion any time soon, so we urgently need large-scale alternatives to the system we have now – a system which uses 70 per cent oil-based synthetics. Whilst some of these might be made of recycled material, none are currently recyclable in an economically viable way. We need clothing systems that are either:

- *circular* – endlessly recyclable, industrially, using renewable energy; or
- *soil to soil* – regeneratively produced and biodegradable.

Circular vs Linear; Recyclable vs Recycled

Whilst a massive reduction in the amount of synthetic clothing we buy is by far the best solution, in a world where most people are hooked on high volumes of super-cheap clothes such a change is unlikely to happen quickly. Better synthetic options are very much needed, and needed now. As consumers we are currently being fobbed off with 'recycled', but we need to demand that brands move towards 'recyclable', towards the development of completely circular systems of textile recovery and reuse. They will only take this step if we reject their current linear offer.

Industrial chemists, and the materials scientists working at universities and for textile manufacturers around the world, are working hard to find scientific solutions. And scientific solutions are of course preferred by the big fashion businesses who would like to keep us consuming at the same rate, just with a less harmful version of what they are producing today. Many are already making the switch to different materials, driven by the need to appear at least to be acting in a sustainable manner. The fibre most commonly used for clothing globally is polyester. Many are switching to recycled polyester (rPET), which is claimed to have 35 per cent to 50 per cent less energy use than virgin polyester. Which sounds impressive. But it actually still generates more CO_2 than any of the natural fibres, and there are widespread reports that the performance of the recycled material is lower than virgin polyester. That means it will fail earlier, so we'll need even more of it. And where does the recycled plastic come from? Well, that's a bit murky. They claim it comes from post-use plastic water bottles, the scourge of the oceans. But buying water in plastic bottles is a terrible idea in the first place and should be ended. We lived perfectly well before bottled water; until the late 1970s we drank water from taps and we still have those. Recycled polyester only works if we carry on creating crazy amounts of single-use plastic waste.

And there is more bad news. Plastic bottles can be recycled, and if they are turned into other plastic bottles they can be recycled again and again, meaning we could stop generating virgin plastic for bottles. But if you turn a plastic bottle into polyester textile that's the end of the recycling road, for the foreseeable future at least. For recycled polyester to be a sustainable solution, we'll need a continuous supply of plastic bottles. So all you've done is made the supply chain longer. You still need the oil.

But if we can't recycle clothing, what happens to the clothes we stick in those textile recycling bins in high street clothing shops? Is that not recycling? Not as you or I understand it. It's not like recycling glass or aluminium cans, where new usable material is created. Recycling clothes means selling them to – or dumping them on – someone else. When you put your clothing into those 'recycling' bins, it goes to be sorted locally. The best stuff stays here and is resold, but a large percentage of it gets put on container ships and sent to sub-Saharan Africa or

South America. There it's sifted through again and a small proportion will be resold. But a lot is simply incinerated or dumped. There is a clothes dump in Chile that's now so big it can be seen from space. In fact these poorer countries have taken so much of our discarded clothing in the past few years that in 2023 many of them stopped accepting it. Literally no one wants our cheap discarded plastic clothes. It's the dead end of a linear system.

Why can't you recycle polyester clothes? Well, in theory you can, but there are several big problems that mean right now it doesn't work. In order to recycle you need a single material, and many clothes are made with blends of materials. Many also have zips, buttons, etc., which are made of other materials, and all are sewn with thread which is also typically a different type of polyester. So to recycle you need to mechanically remove, i.e. cut off by hand, all the zips, buttons and sewn seams. The whole process is very costly. It currently costs significantly more to recycle polyester than it does to make new, whether that's making virgin polyester from oil or making it from water bottles. There are currently no economically viable routes to recycle polyester. Also, and significantly, when you recycle polyester textiles the resultant material is brown, which means it can only be dyed darker brown or black. This is a very big problem, for quite obvious reasons. We have spent thousands of years developing dyes which never fade and never come out; now we need to work out how to do the opposite.

New legislative frameworks such as those being envisaged by the EU must penalise the sale of polluting, non-recyclable products. The principle of 'Polluter Pays' has to finally be established firmly as a fundamental principle of all human activity, whether for profit or otherwise. Those who benefit financially from the activity must be made to bear the total cost of exhausting non-renewable materials, the pollution caused in extracting and processing them, and the waste created from their disposal.

Scientists in many countries are working to make recyclability an economically viable option. They are researching alternative synthetic materials to polyester which are more easily recycled and are compatible with new dyeing technologies which make dyes more removable. At Leeds University, and their partner institutions, work is taking place on a system using a bio-based material called cellulose diacetate, which shows some promise. It can be dyed using techniques which allow the dye to be easily removed, and can in theory be endlessly recycled. It can be produced in a way which makes it feel more like cotton than many other synthetics, and there is huge capacity to produce it globally; it is used to make cigarette filters. However these new technologies, if successful, will require a rethink of the entire design and production process, such that every product is designed and made to be easily recyclable. As well of course as building the global apparatus for textile recycling.

Scientists are also attempting to cure the oil dependency of the fashion industry by developing new plant-based textiles, which are increasingly touted as an answer to the sustainability issues that the fashion industry faces. Traditional natural fibres have a very low carbon footprint, wool and linen have very low water consumption, and all are naturally biodegradable. But linen and wool are relatively expensive to produce, and the intensive production of cotton is problematic because of its conflict with the land needed for food production, its heavy water consumption, and in non-organically grown cotton the use of fertilisers and pesticides – so much so that some within the EU now see its long-term future as very much in doubt. Long-established plant-based synthetics such as viscose are well understood and do offer some advantages over oil-based synthetics, but there is a lot of obfuscation around supply chains and in many cases they are responsible for major deforestation. Having been told as much by big fashion, most people think viscose is a nice happy natural plant material; whilst some European-made viscose is good, however, across the world 70 million trees are felled annually to provide feedstock for its production; a third of this is from ancient and endangered forest, leading to soil erosion and topsoil depletion.

Bamboo viscose, sometimes erroneously called bamboo, or bamboo silk, is enjoying a huge rise in popularity, partly because a lot of people assume it's a natural fibre like cotton or linen. But it is not, it's a synthetic viscose. As a result of the rising demand for bamboo as a feedstock, farmers in developing nations are cutting down ever more native forest to plant it, and using fertilisers to promote more rapid growth. Viscose is, under the correct conditions, biodegradable, though claims as to the degree and speed of its biodegradability vary significantly, but it also has twice the CO_2 footprint of cotton.

New plant-based synthetic alternatives to oil-based materials are being developed all the time, but their development has been far from straightforward. Bio-based textiles are defined as containing a minimum of 20 per cent renewable carbon content (not much really, though some have 100 per cent), mostly from corn, sugar cane, sugar beets, and plant oils such as castor oil. Bio-based polyamide (nylon) is synthesised and polymerised using a multi-stage industrial chemical process which uses about 20 per cent less energy than standard polyamide – so a small improvement – and the makers of one bio-nylon claim it will biodegrade within a year. Elastane, a synthetic stretch material made from oil (Lycra is elastane), is ubiquitous in modern clothing. Some running tights and leggings contain 22 per cent elastane, stretch jeans contain up to 5 per cent, and it is in almost all our underwear. It doesn't biodegrade over any timescale we know about, and even with chemical intervention it does not completely break down. It's really bad stuff. All attempts, and there have been many, to synthesise it from renewable plant material have so far achieved only modest improvements over oil-based sources. Their reduction in water and CO_2

footprint is relatively small, not more than about 20 per cent, and there seems to be limited evidence of complete biodegradation.

Bio-based polymers do offer a partial solution to dependency on oil, but the jury is still out as to their overall environmental credentials and their performance characteristics. So far they have managed about a 20 per cent reduction in carbon footprint, nowhere close to the 90 per cent target set by the UN. Their cost is currently significantly higher than standard oil-based synthetics, making it prohibitive for the fast fashion brands. And, crucially, growing plants to make more synthetic clothes removes land from the growing of food which is already in short supply, and will be even more so in the future with world population increasing exponentially. It's no good having plant-based leggings if we have nothing to eat. Every potential avenue leads to the same conclusion. It's the volume which is the real problem. The answer is less.

Regenerative and Biodegradable

There is also a growing movement in favour of a return to completely natural and symbiotic textile practices, and, in a parallel with the more developed bioregional food movement, to bioregionalism in textiles; to only wearing clothes made from fibres grown or raised using regenerative farming practices within your bioregion. At present this is limited in scale, and prohibitive for most ordinary people on the grounds of both cost and time. You also have to live without any synthetic materials or dyes – which of course we did for 30,000 years, but we're pretty hooked on them now. But it is a compelling proposition in many ways.

In 2000 I got together with my old friend Justine Aldersey-Williams, a natural dyer and co-founder of the Northern England chapter of Fibershed, and the arts-led regeneration charity Super Slow Way, with whom I've worked for many years on the British Textile Biennial.

Together we mapped out the idea behind a novel regenerative textile system with far-reaching benefits for the health and cohesion of the community, for the environment and nature, and for the stimulation of a local green economy. We called it Homegrown/Homespun, running a pilot in 2021 with funding from the National Lottery Communities Climate Action Fund. Homegrown/Homespun is a reimagined textile system, borrowing heavily from the practices of the past, growing, processing, spinning, dyeing and weaving textiles from plants grown locally in the Lancashire textile regions. It aims to build a vibrant and sustainable long-term regional textile system based on nature and climate-positive principles. It has repurposed disused urban and semi-urban spaces using regenerative principles, to create vibrant green spaces for citizens and nature. It will focus on creating products which can be repaired, repurposed and recycled locally, and all products will biodegrade cleanly, allowing a return to the soil at end-of-life in a naturally beneficial closed-loop system.

Such a system would create local jobs, engage, inspire and reconnect communities and enhance the natural environment, helping to address the climate emergency, restore nature and reduce social inequality by creating long-term sustainable economic growth. It has huge numbers of benefits for different constituents. First for the community, where it would improve the physical and mental health of those involved in the project, reconnecting citizens with nature and with each other; enhance the natural landscape; provide educational activities in art, science and engineering; and create opportunities for green economic regeneration, thereby reducing social inequality. Second for nature: it would create and enhance natural spaces in the urban environment; reduce textile industry greenhouse gas emissions; eliminate pollutants; increase biodiversity (our little field was filled with butterflies and bees); regenerate soil and water systems and sequester carbon. And finally for the local economy, where it would directly stimulate the development of small and medium-sized natural textile, garment, bio-composite, and bio-extraction/refining businesses, and catalyse the development of other novel green technology businesses.

Back in 2019 I began working on an idea for a range of sports clothes made with no synthetic material at all. I played all sorts of sports as a kid. I was pretty good at athletics, taking to the track and the cross-country course in cotton shorts and vest. I played rugby until the early 1990s, and the kit I wore was still made of natural materials: durable woven cotton shorts, heavy knitted cotton rugby jerseys and leather boots. They all got a bit sodden if it was raining hard but it didn't stop us. Now, almost thirty years later, rugby, like pretty much every other sport, is played in synthetic kit: plastic, non-biodegradable, and made from oil. Some of the greatest sporting feats of the twentieth century, Roger Bannister's first sub four-minute mile, Pele's 1,279 goals, Bob Beamon's 29ft 'leap of the century', were all achieved in natural cotton and leather kit. We don't need plastic kit.

In January 2024 we launched Community Clothing Organic Athletic, a range of 100 per cent plastic-free sportswear. It will establish, we hope, a whole new paradigm, and show that, much as it was in the past, making sportswear without plastic is a realistic proposition. It took us five years to develop, because every single part of every product had to be redeveloped from scratch – elastane-free elastic made from natural rubber, polyester-free fabrics made from cotton, cotton threads, water-based printing instead of polyurethane logos. We're moving on to waterproofs next, looking at plant dyes in place of synthetic dyes, and elastane-free leggings. There's lots to do. But those years studying materials science are paying great dividends. It may be the thing I'm most proud of across my twenty-year career in clothes.

Making from Old

There is a growing movement in the making of new from old. It's another idea that is far from novel, but had been made largely redundant by the cost of new clothing dropping so low. Now it has gained fresh impetus as a means of reducing the consumption of resources, and of keeping material from landfill.

In the past every item or garment would be cared for and repaired, but when it had reached the end of its useful life in its current form any useful material would be reclaimed and something new made from it. An adult's dress might be cut up and a child's dress made from it. That might in turn be reworked to make a dress for a toddler. I have a bird table I made from two old chairs found in a shed. It was all done domestically, with used materials shared between friends and family. On *Sewing Bee* our second challenge is to make something new from something old. They've made dog coats from festival tents, and raincoats from shower curtains, inspired by a collection of Esme's which she and the Swanky Modes girls made in the late 1970s. It has thrown up some incredible and inspiring garments, requiring skill, knowledge of materials, and great creativity and vision.

In 1990 in Venice Beach in California I bought a bag that had been made from old truck inner tubes and a 1970s car seatbelt, with buckle. About fifteen years ago I bought a pair of sandals in the Jemaa el-Fnaa in Marrakesh that had been made by the guy who sold them to me, simply assembled from two pieces of old tyre, a length of cotton rope and some leather scraps.

In 2020 we made shirts for a forthcoming E. Tautz collection out of fabric recovered from discarded men's shirts. I sourced a few sacks full of second-hand white cotton shirts (apparently there is an almost inexhaustible supply) from Astco, one of the UK's largest textile recyclers, run by a friend of mine. Most, besides a bit of discolouration and the odd bit of fraying at the collars and cuffs, showed little signs of wear. We cut all the usable fabric from the seams, the fronts and back and the two large sleeve pieces, and then reassembled them, seaming them together to form large usable lengths of fabric at the same width as standard cloth. We then laid our standard patterns on top and cut out and sewed the clothes as usual, letting the seams of the reassembled fabric, and the variations in texture, fall as they may.

The New Remakers

Today there is a growing wave of remakers. Individual designers or makers, small businesses and collectives are springing up, reclaiming the materials from old clothes and turning them into new items. These artisan remakers are popping up across the UK, the US and other advanced industrial nations, seeking to create a new paradigm around reduced consumption of new materials, hyper-localism and a community focus, both in terms of the makers and their customers. Mostly established by young founders, they're popularising remake, repair, environmental education, building engaged, happy communities and are making upcycling very cool. Their ideals are garnering significant support, particularly amongst young people, who not only want to buy their product but are keen to join their business as makers, making making cool.

In 2005 Elvis & Kresse began making belts, wallets, bags and homewares out of reclaimed firehose, which is manufactured of an incredibly strong double-wall-coated woven nylon. The hoses are washed, cut and sewn. Since their foundation they've kept hundreds of tons of old firehose out of landfill; in fact for a long period no London firehoses went to landfill at all.

Nathan Hughes founded Restrap in 2010. With his mum's help he started by making bike pedal straps out of recycled car seatbelts on their sewing machine in the back bedroom, first for himself and then for his friends. Word spread and interest grew, as did the business, branching out to develop into bags, luggage and accessories. They took a workshop in Leeds and built a team of young hip sewing artisans with a shared passion for bike riding and functional kit. They now run workshops teaching customers how to make their bags; they offer repairs and a buyback programme – all of which has helped to build a strong community of customers who share the ethos of the brand. They employ a very healthy fifty-five staff. Trakke was also founded in 2010, by Alec Famer, and also began with a single cycling-based product, in his case the bike messenger bag. Alec too started with a recycling ethos. He and his art school pals raided local skips rescuing advertising banners and old sofas; they'd salvage zips and buckles and anything else that seemed like it would be useful, and would turn them into bags.

My friend Seren Colley started BidiBoon in 2020. A former menswear designer at Burberry and Tom Ford, she sews childrenswear from repurposed old adult denim jeans. Carefully deconstructed by hand, the reusable fabric pieces, and details such as pockets, are unpicked or cut out before being carefully assembled, piece by piece, balancing colour, fade and wear across the new garment. Seren's unerring eye enables her to maximise character while minimising waste, with each garment then being sewn by her. It is a perfect example of how skill and design talent can make something beautiful, useful and new from something worn and discarded. Assuming her sewing machine is powered by green renewable energy, her footprint is near zero.

Cloth Surgeon, founded by former professional footballer Rav Matharu, also makes new clothing from old. Rav, a graduate of Leeds College of Art and Design, deconstructs and then recombines street and sportswear to make high-end menswear. He has a huge celebrity client list and now has a great store on Savile Row. Another remaker making big waves is Nicole McLaughlin, who started off mostly making hilarious sliders from old sports clothes. She now makes irreverent and sophisticated garments from almost anything: bras from croissants, shorts from bags of Haribo, gilets from garden refuse bags – all with exceptional skill and finish. She works with some of the biggest brands and has over 800,000 followers. The UK's fashion colleges are turning out increasing numbers of young designers whose work puts remaking using found materials at the heart of their design practice.

The sportswear world has spawned several fascinating remakers, largely because as an industry it is so synthetics/plastics heavy, and consumption of sportswear is going through the roof. The RE-ACTION collective was founded by Gavin Fernie-Jones, who whilst working in the Alps was appalled at the amount of perfectly good skiwear that was being dumped after a few years' use. Today the collective, loosely assembled under shared ideals of material rescue, keeping outdoor wear out of landfill, includes over forty individual or small practices, like Tentshare, Sheffield Clothing Repair (Gavin's mum) and Little Re-Creations, doing everything from making coats out of salvaged festival sleeping bags to gloves and bumbags from old running tops and finisher's medal ribbons. ReTribe combine elements of all of these, making brilliant new from old in Sheffield.

Re-Run and Rubbish Shoes were both the brainchild of Dan Lawson, who set up his business to make runners more aware of their environmental impact. He started re-homing old running kit, but found that old shoes were the big issue, so he decided to cut them up and, in his term, 'Frankenstein' them, reassembling the bits into new shoes and sliders which have acquired something of a cult status.

And there are a growing number of others, both in fashion and sportwear and in other product categories, like Clement who makes chefs' knives from waste metal and plastic, or Juli Bolanos Durman who makes her products from waste glass. There are new like-minded businesses springing up across the UK, US, France, New Zealand and Australia.

There are many special elements about these individuals, small businesses and collectives: their commitment and willingness to act rather than just talk, mostly with very limited resources, some with, initially at least, a somewhat restricted skill set but with vision, a clear and genuine passion and a bit of bravery. All seem to be thriving emotionally in what they are doing, many are embedded within strong and highly supportive communities, and most are remaking at the point of consumption, devising solutions specifically for people they know, marrying creativity, care and community.

Moving away from standardised mass-manufacturing production methods allows us to make use of the materials we find around us – windblown trees complete with knots and branches, old jeans, old seatbelts, or simply everyday stuff from the skip. It places the value of the object firmly back in the domain of the maker's skill. We are paying only for the adaptability and ingenuity of their design and their skills as a maker. This is the sort of economic activity that needs to be encouraged – activity where the distribution of value is radically reshaped, where the value from that economic activity goes to those who grow, or in the future recover or recycle, the primary materials needed, and to those whose skilled labour produces the product. In the world of less we will want fewer things, made with minimal amounts of virgin materials, made to the very highest standard for maximum durability and enjoyment, and where if possible all of the money we spend goes to the maker or collective of makers. Where we return to the idea of paying for human skill. A society built on such principles would take little from the world, and would be significantly more equal economically.

16

Local

A prosperous, happy and healthy society needs to be underpinned by good work for all: work which is emotionally fulfilling, fairly paid and financially sustaining, and offers prospects for people of all outlooks and abilities, in every corner of the country. We need to do work which is good for us, good for our local community and our broader society, and good for the planet. The key questions we should be asking ourselves are, what work needs to be done within our society for us all to enjoy living well within it? What work would we personally like to do? And how can we change the way we consume to support good jobs within our local community?

If we want to be successful as a nation we need to be good at what we do. And we need every citizen to have the opportunity to contribute, to be useful, not only for the economic good but for our greater emotional wellbeing. To be really good at something it helps to really enjoy it. As Aristotle said, 'pleasure in the work puts perfection in the job'.

We need, as a society, to talk seriously about what work we value, which jobs we need more of and which we might do just as well without. And we need to talk about the future, what technology we encourage and what we suppress. We allowed mass production and offshoring to rob us of 5 million skilled making jobs, a loss that destroyed whole regions across the country. We need to collectively decide if we want to allow robotics and AI to take away another 5 million jobs in the next decade, because giving our money in the form of tax breaks to billionaire-owned companies so that they can invest in robots in their UK warehouses that take our jobs away might not be what we want to see happen. Do we care about individual people's jobs? Some of us might prefer instead to see our money spent creating a whole new wave of fulfilling and emotionally rewarding work.

We might not rebuild the 5 million making jobs that we've lost, but we could bring back a lot of them, in the places that need them most. What kind of jobs can we create in towns like Blackburn and Hawick and New Tredegar? As a nation we've been obsessed with service industries, but you can't start there. Service can't serve itself. There has to be some primary making and doing to kick things off.

And we need people to do jobs that can't be replaced by robots or AI, like fixing leaky roofs or repairing your boiler. There will never come a time when we do not need somewhere comfortable to live. Today, because we have failed to plan our education system properly, we have an acute national shortage of builders, which has led to an acute national shortage of housing, which has led to us all paying three times as much of our income on housing. Skilled builders, plumbers, plasterers, joiners and electricians are better paid than many university graduates, so why are we sending so many people to university? There are currently 9 million working-age Britons without jobs and 140,000 vacancies in the skilled construction trades. Surely 1.5 per cent of those people could be trained to do that critically needed work?

As we have seen, the loss of manufacturing jobs has ripped apart towns right across the UK. And it is not just the loss of income that has destroyed these communities. It is also the loss of a sense of purpose, identity and pride. The textiles industry has been particularly hard hit. Over the past fifty years, employment in the sector has dropped from around 1.6 million to just 100,000. In some towns, textile jobs accounted for almost 50 per cent of all employment. Today, in the former textile heartlands of Lancashire and Yorkshire, almost one in four people of working age are what the government classifies as 'economically inactive'. Essentially 25 per cent of people are not in work.

The loss of UK manufacturing jobs correlates directly with a significant rise in social inequality, which in the UK has never been greater. Social equality is important because it is a big contributor to our overall sense of happiness. People in more equal societies enjoy better mental health, children perform to a higher standard in school and enjoy increased educational prospects, people trust each other more and community life is stronger. People live longer, and there are lower rates of crime.

The feeling that others have it better has been growing in Britain for a long time now. In the period from the end of the Second World War until 1979, the UK had become a much more economically equal nation. If we look at income, the share going to the top 10 per cent of the population fell from 34.6 per cent to 21 per cent between 1938 and 1979, while the share going to the bottom 10 per cent went up to around 4 per cent. But since 1979 there has been a sharp reversal of this trend. Today, the top 10 per cent of the population receive 31 per cent of the income and the bottom 10 per cent just 1 per cent. In terms of wealth, the statistics are equally damning. In 2010 (the latest year for which data is available), 45 per cent of all wealth in the UK was held by the richest 10 per cent. The poorest 10 per cent held only 1 per cent.

And that's just the wealth that we know about. The Panama Papers gave us a small glimpse into the scale at which wealth is taken offshore and hidden. The UK has a very high level of inequality compared to other developed countries. On top of that the wealth is geographically unevenly spread, further exacerbating the feeling of inequality. Households in the Southeast have an average total wealth of £387,400, over twice the amount of households in the Northwest (£165,200).

Civic identity and personal identity are intertwined. The importance of place in creating a sense of happiness for citizens is greatly underrated. And it's not just how a place looks, although this is important, it's what a town *does* that defines and characterises it. Birmingham was the 'City of 1000 Trades', Manchester was 'Cottonopolis', Newcastle and Glasgow made ships, Stoke made ceramics, Sheffield made cutlery. This industrial heritage is preserved in the nicknames of football teams (the Potters, the Blades). Work created shared experience and bonded communities. Fathers followed sons, and daughters followed mothers, cementing family bonds. The work was respected, the workers had dignity.

When I first began living and working in Blackburn I was recommended William Woodruff's book *The Road to Nab End*. It is a simple story of mill-town life in the 1920s and 30s. There is one line that particularly stuck with me:

> 'Men and women were not judged by what they did at home but by what they did in the mill. People respected Skill. Pride of Work meant a lot. Work was everything.'

That line has shaped so much of what I am trying to achieve in my professional career. It is about giving people back work that they can be proud of, and rebuilding positive communities that they can feel proud to belong to. I enjoyed a privileged upbringing, and in my early years never had cause or opportunity to think about anybody who might not share the same sense of optimism about life to come. In my late teens I read *The Ragged Trousered Philanthropists* and *The Road to Wigan Pier* and I remember for the first time understanding that this was far from everyone's reality. I went to university in Leeds, then lived in Manchester and Liverpool. All three were cities with significant areas of deep-rooted economic deprivation. When I lived in Liverpool in the mid to late 1990s it was on the EU's Objective One funding list, and was amongst Europe's, let alone Britain's, poorest regions. I lived in one of the first buildings repurposed with money from the EU. All around me were whole streets which looked as though they had been locked up forty years before and untouched since, shop fronts in some cases still filled with sun-bleached goods. Whole warehouses lay empty, buddleia growing from their ledges and cracks. But Liverpool, Leeds and Manchester have long since shaken off any trace of their grim northern industrial heritage and reinvented themselves, with the help of significant government support, as thriving urban centres, attractive places in which to study, live, work or build a business. In Leeds in the early 1990s, the part of the city known as The Calls was a red-light district and a solid no-go area. It's now a bustling restaurant quarter.

Moving to Blackburn in 2015 I was shocked by the difference. In stark contrast to nearby Manchester, the smaller towns and cities which surround it have endured significant and persistent economic and social stagnation or decline since the start of the de-industrialisation process. This is characterised by a feeling of intractable social breakdown and in many cases deprivation, leading to low confidence, low aspiration and an inability to attract or retain talent. I have recently worked with Blackburn Council on an initiative specifically aimed at trying to keep talented youngsters in the borough. It is a huge issue, but without big change an intractable one. It's hard to make someone stay and start a career in Blackburn (or Burnley, or any other similar town on the fringes) when Manchester, just 25 miles away, seems like another, better world. It might not be an exaggeration to suggest that if things don't change soon then these towns might simply come to the end of their useful lives, just like Detroit in the US, the abandoned ruin of a once-great industrial and cultural powerhouse. We need a plan that gives our industrial towns a future before it's too late.

In the UK, there are 900 towns with populations of between 10,000 and 100,000. Nearly 33 million people live in towns in England and Wales, roughly half the UK population. Between 2001 and 2019, the population in major cities grew rapidly; London by 27 per cent, Manchester by 30 per cent. In nearly a fifth of all towns the populations declined. The cost of living in cities is rising rapidly, too. Most people living in them are priced out of owning their own home and rents have risen significantly faster than wages in recent years. There is a nation-wide shortage of housing, and yet across the towns in which I work all I see is space. Empty buildings, empty plots. And with the environmental crisis looming, and net zero targets to hit, we have to move away from a model which requires people to commute long distances to work, especially if that commute is by car (even with electric cars).

We need to create good work in every town and city in this country, allowing people to live and work where they can enjoy the support of family and close friends. We have to be able to work where we live and live where we work.

Brexit

In 2015 I took over an ailing clothing business in the Lancashire town of Blackburn. Once a thriving manufacturing town with a buoyant local economy and a strong sense of community, it had, like many other very similar so-called post-industrial towns, become a town with a declining economy, rising unemployment and an increasingly broken and divided community. The wealthy had fled, leaving behind a population with increasingly low educational attainment and diminishing health, surrounded by rising levels of crime, addiction and antisocial behaviour.

In his book *Little Platoons*, David Skelton discusses Brexit and its foothold in post-industrial Britain. He refers to Consett, a former steel town in County Durham that my dad and I would pass as he drove me to school in Barnard Castle. Skelton writes, 'When the Royal Navy ruled the waves this was the town that produced its steel, and built bridges around the world as a monument to the craft of steelworkers in England's "far corner". Workers at the Consett Iron Company took pride in their trade and that Consett Steel was a symbol of quality around the world.' When the steelworks closed the town lost everything: jobs, identity and pride, in a story echoed in similar towns right across the UK. Consett, once a steel town, was now a town of bookmakers, discount stores and empty shops. Like many other similar towns, it had lost its reason to exist.

In a paper published in August 2016, Atif Shafiq of the Royal Society of Arts described how the biggest losers from economic restructuring (or what Thatcher called 'modernisation') had been Britain's traditionally industrial regions, places historically reliant on mining, steel and textiles. These industries had collapsed under pressure from lower-cost goods imported from countries with lower labour costs and had been written off as 'lame duck' sectors by the UK government. Shafiq describes how many of these places went from close to full employment in the 1960s, to mass unemployment through the 1980s and beyond, a phenomenon hidden by Thatcher's decision to fudge unemployment figures by redesignating hundreds of thousands of laid-off workers as 'economically inactive'. Those on incapacity benefit went from under 400,000 in 1963 to close to 2 million by 1999. These communities were left to rot by an indifferent government. It is no surprise that forty-one of the forty-two former coal-mining communities voted for Brexit.

This is not a uniquely British phenomenon. America's Midwestern rust belt suffers from the same problems as Britain's industrial north. In 'Youngstown', a song about another former steel town in Ohio, Bruce Springsteen describes the pride workers felt in their work and its contribution to the American war effort, and notes the feeling of anger felt by a working population used and then tossed aside. Inequality and the loss of pride sit heavily upon the working-class populations in the post-industrial regions of all developed nations.

These post-industrial towns (I find it sad that we call them post-industrial) have lost their identities. What are they for? What future do they have? Without answers to these questions it is very obvious why large numbers of people would vote for something that promised a fresh start, a renewed sense of identity, the nebulous concept of sovereignty. You cannot blame anybody for feeling this way. When life feels hopeless and seems with every passing year to become more so, it is all too easy to be drawn in by the promise that everything can be made better, however scant the evidence.

Skilled Work

Skill makes us feel good. Working with our hands and with our senses makes us feel alive. As Richard Sennett writes in *The Craftsman*, 'The working human animal can be enriched by the skills and dignified by the spirit of craftsmanship.' Craft work can be meditative and challenging, keeping our brains in good shape, and the constant, even if low-level physical activity is great for the health of our bodies. Craftsmanship connects us to others and teaches us how to govern our lives. The earliest humans were constantly making and doing, mastering their ability to use their hands, creating and adapting tools for specific uses. Using our hands and even simple tools to work and shape the materials we find around us satisfies some deep inner urge that brings great satisfaction. No one who ever whittled a stick was left unhappy.

Skill, broadly, is the ability to do something well. Malcom Gladwell discusses the idea that anyone with a very high level of skill has achieved it through a minimum of 10,000 hours of specific application. This is almost exactly the number of hours, forty per week for five years, that it typically takes to become a Savile Row cutter. Skill does not come through experimentation, it comes through application and very specific learning, taught one to one from master to apprentice. It requires young people with a readiness to forgo their own wishes and feelings about an action and be willing to follow. Our schools need to prepare young people for this rigour. I think perhaps they do so less now than in the past.

The learned skill is a reward, the ability to make the hands do what the brain has asked of them, perfectly, every time. I watch my friend Keith Brymer Jones throw pots and I see this. He learned by throwing pots, thousands of pots, over and over again, under rigorous tutelage. Like Diego Maradona's pre-match keepy-uppy warm-up, or Lewis Hamilton driving go-karts, repetition after repetition after repetition until perfection is achieved. In Savile Row it begins with the needle and thimble, which must be worn and held in a precise way, needle between thumb and forefinger, thimble on second finger resting lightly behind. If the tailoring apprentice cannot make their hand attain the form then hand sewing will never be mastered, so a master might use a cotton wrap until the fingers and hand learn to hold the form. The same is true of holding the bow when playing a stringed instrument, or the forms held in ballet. Dedicated application is required to achieve mastery of skill.

Our bodies, and especially our hands, are capable of wonderful things. The writer Julio Ramón Ribeyo puts it thus: 'we find only one tool, neither created nor invented, but perfect: the hand of man.' Of all the human limbs, the hand is capable of the most varied and complex movements, movements we learn to control with extraordinary precision. Science has long revered the hand, a gift from God, perfectly designed. Our hands, their range of motion and the variety with which they allow us to hold objects, gives us, uniquely amongst animals, the ability to hold an object with one hand whilst working on it with the other. We are a making animal.

Craftsmanship offers a lifelong career, in the old English sense of the word as a well-laid road. The craftsperson nurtures and develops a single ability throughout the course of their working life, refining it through practice and through teaching. In the old guild system, an apprenticeship would last for at least seven years, the apprentice being required to prove his skills before being declared a journeyman. We run a similar system on Savile Row today, holding a ceremony to celebrate this moment of passing out twice yearly, a moment of great pride for apprentices, a recognition not just of skill earned but of application given. The journeyman would then practise and evolve his craft for at least seven more years before he could apply to be made a master. On Savile Row you are generally considered to be a master tailor after twenty years in the profession. Mastery is a great honour.

And what do we mean by good work? Good work is doing something the way it should be done. It is correctness, it is quality. The difference can perhaps be explained by imagining the conflict between doing something right and merely getting the job done. Too often in our modern working lives we are constrained, forced to do functional rather than good work, and this is a source of great frustration and anxiety. The desire to do good work is natural in us and the craftsman is not satisfied with just good enough. As much as we might desire to do good work, this is often frustrated by the conditions and pressures under which we work. It has been my great privilege to work for almost twenty years on Savile Row, where quality work is given the time and space to flourish. I have many friends who are doctors, nurses and dentists in the NHS, an institution once run in a way that allowed good work to flourish. Now, in the target-driven contemporary health service, many of those friends feel prevented from doing so, by lack of time and the correct resources.

There is also the sense of an innate goodness in craftsmanship. It is humble, peaceable, and works in harmony with nature's gifts. It is not an accident that Jesus was the son of a carpenter. Many of the craftspeople I meet and know find great contentment in their work. I recently had the great privilege of being asked to appear on BBC Radio 4's *Desert Island Discs*. One of the castaway's tasks is to select a luxury item to take with them to the island. Practical items are not allowed, but I requested a set of woodworking tools. Learning and practising a skilled craft, I argued, would be a great and enduring luxury.

Make Your Money Do Good

It seems astonishing to me that spending locally is not a more fundamental principle in the way both we and our government buy things. At Community Clothing we can tell you exactly where your money goes, because our supply chains are local and transparent. When you shop with us, 90p in every pound you spend stays in the UK economy and around half of the money you spend is going directly as wages, mostly to people living in regions of very high social and economic deprivation. It really is thinking about where you want your money to go. To Jeff Bezos, or to your bezzy Jeff. But even better, any money we spend locally creates even more value through a well-understood local economic multiplier effect. At CC our local suppliers tend to spend their money locally in the day-to-day operation of their businesses. They'll buy materials and equipment from local suppliers, use local services like cleaners, landscapers or waste services, and of course there are employee salaries, most of whom live locally. And then in turn all of those local businesses who supply to them spend their income locally, recirculating the money again. All those employees and business owners spend their income in the local economy too. This eventually adds up to around a three times multiplication of the original economic value. So for every £1 you or the government spend locally, almost £3 of local economic value will be created. And this of course makes a huge difference to struggling communities. Local spending and local production, and a return to smaller, owner-led or artisanal business, directly reduces wealth inequality. Labour is valued and correctly rewarded, surplus profits are either reinvested or else spent locally, and geographic inequality is likely to be reduced, with many UK making businesses being away from the more affluent Southeast.

I lived for a few years just outside Preston in Lancashire. Recently, the local council made the decision to try and buy everything locally, in a policy that they call Community Wealth Building. The idea is simple: buying from local businesses benefits the local economy. And it is hoped that in time they can encourage more of the primary manufacture of the goods being bought locally, effectively using government spend to support investment in productive economic activities for the shared benefit of the entire local community. It follows pioneering work by Manchester City Council into keeping spending within the local economy. Looking back over the work, it is clear that there have been huge benefits to the local economy, and Manchester is now seen as an example of best practice when it comes to progressive procurement for increased social value. The proportion of money spent with organisations based in, or with a branch in Manchester, went up from 53 per cent to 74 per cent between 2008 and 2016; and when you took greater Greater Manchester into account the number was 91 per cent, almost half of it with small and medium-sized businesses. And as this money is spent and re-spent within the local economy it is multiplied. Re-spend by suppliers back into the Manchester economy increased from 25p in the pound in 2008 to 43p in the pound in 2016.

Lots of other places across the UK are working with variations on this idea, including Birmingham, Oldham, Salford, Kirklees, Islington, Enfield, Southampton, Wakefield and Bristol. There is a clear desire to see government spending find its way back into the local economy, for the benefit of the local community, and not into the pockets of global corporations.

Local manufacture also means transparent and traceable manufacture, both of which are increasingly important not only because the customer is slowly beginning to value such things but also because it allows for much greater control over the potentially harmful stages in production, and over the pay of workers and the conditions in which they work. UK made means cleaner energy for production, lower transport cost, lower emissions from transport, much tighter regulation around industrial effluent and much greater general adherence to such regulation. In many countries where clothing is produced there is very little regulation, while in others regulation exists but the enforcement by local officials is patchy and in some cases anecdotally non-existent.

Covid was a catastrophic event for the UK economy, but it could have been an opportunity to kickstart the process of reshoring manufacturing. The supply of the scrubs and disposable gowns and masks used by the NHS represented a huge opportunity. Buying such items from UK manufacturers would have put money into areas of the UK economy which greatly needed new jobs. Much of the cost of these goods is in the labour, so the money spent would have flowed directly back into the economy as wages, as income tax, NI and local taxes, and all of this would have been recirculated, generating more economic benefit through the local economic multiplier effect.

A simple calculation shows the difference between local and overseas sourcing. It was estimated that at the time, UK mask consumption was 3 billion units per annum. Buying the required masks from China cost £150 million, benefiting the UK economy by just £9 million (the money made by the UK importer) and giving a net economic *loss* to the economy of £141 million. But whilst buying masks from the UK would have cost more, around £240 million, it would have benefited the UK economy, after local economic recirculation, by around £545 million, giving a net economic *gain* of £305 million. Choosing overseas versus UK-made masks cost the UK economy £446 million. Choosing UK-made supplies would also have created at least 5,000 local jobs, manufacturing a product we can never imagine not needing within the NHS.

Thanks to my interactions with the Cabinet Office during the Covid response I learned a lot about the way governments buy things. Much of it makes no sense, unless your intention is simply to hand profit to companies you like. Rather than buy things themselves, our government pays companies to buy for them, and in return gives them large amounts of risk-free money for doing so. It's either lazy, stupid or corrupt.

The NHS in England spends around £23 million every year on uniforms. In addition it uses gowns, which in the past were durable and made to be washed and reworn a hundred times. Today they are disposable, and made of plastic; the largest trusts use between 4,000 and 7,000 single-use plastic gowns per day, and there are 215 trusts. Even assuming an average daily consumption of 1,000 per trust, that's well over 70 million disposable gowns a year. During Covid several trusts, those with laundries, switched back to reusable gowns, made locally (we made some for our local trust). But when Covid ended it was back to buying disposable gowns from China. Most of our NHS supplies are made in China; so are our school supplies and our military uniforms (which seems beyond stupid). In the year to September 2022 the UK gave almost £72 billion to Chinese manufacturers of goods and services, a policy many people are increasingly questioning. The procurement of the things we need to run our health and social care sector from the other side of the world seriously diminishes our ability to respond in times of crisis. And the decision to buy all the things we need from cheaper manufacturers overseas may have saved individual departments, or parts of departments, money in the short term, like the procurement budgets of the Departments for Health and Defence, but it is robbing Peter to pay Paul.

The government buys a lot of steel, for building roads, railways, schools and hospitals. Its Steel Public Procurement 2023 report says it needs to buy 7.2 million tons of steel a year across all departments. We need around 6 million tons just to build the offshore wind turbines that are planned. The UK currently has capacity to make almost exactly that amount, around 7.2 million tons. The Port Talbot steelworks in South Wales, currently threatened with closure, produces about 5 million tons of this. The steel industry supports 33,400 UK jobs. The government's steel report notes that this is just 0.1 per cent of jobs, as if this is an irrelevance, proudly announcing that China makes 996 million tons a year. But no job is irrelevant. That's 33,400 families, maybe 120,000 people, many of them in the poorest parts of the UK. And if we let the steelworks close, it could cost nearly half a billion pounds a year in benefits. What's more, not having local steel production leaves us entirely at the mercy of other nations, most notably China. The other big European countries produce a lot of steel, Germany about five times as much as us, and whilst our output has fallen by about 75 per cent over the last fifty years, theirs has remained the same or grown. The cost arguments about British steel apply similarly in Europe, but they've made it work.

So much of what we use every day could be made here. With the right investment in state-of-the-art kit, and the right skills training, those things could be made well, made cleanly, using clean power and clean processes, and made cost effectively – if not quite as cheaply as they can be made in some places where the cost of labour, rent, building, insurance and so on are lower. But again, the money spent on rent and so on flows into the UK economy, so it's not money lost.

But, most importantly, the return to a full-employment economy would also create happy, thriving, healthy, lower-crime communities for people to live in. Average salaries for manufacturing staff are between £20,000 and £25,000 depending on whose data you believe, and average salaries across all jobs in the manufacturing sector (including management) are over £30,000. Statistically, manufacturing jobs are highly productive, 12 per cent higher than the UK average and the second most productive of all sectors. So, in a world where our government talks about increasing overall productivity, would it not be sensible to invest more in a sector with already high levels of productivity? It would create jobs in the communities which actually need it most and would catalyse a huge reduction in inequality. That would really be levelling up.

Education at School …

It would be to our enormous benefit, both individually and as a nation, for every young person to receive a school education as varied and effective as that offered by the best schools, private or otherwise. If our education were to give everybody the start in life that the children of the richest in society receive, then our economy would be significantly better off. How much better off might be difficult to quantify, but the net benefit has to be *enormous*. Education needs to work for every kid; kids with science brains, arts brains, practical brains, kids with sporty brains, so that every kid gets a chance to leave school knowing what they're good at and knowing that they can be a useful part of society. Leave school happy. Leave school confident.

When I was in school, pretty much every child learned how to make things during term. Not only did it make school more fun, it promoted the creative thinking that I've used in different ways throughout my adult life. But not long before I left school these classes started to disappear. Educational budget cuts and a well-meaning but absolutely ill-judged desire to raise the aspiration of all people to achieve a university-level degree, meant that school became a place purely for academic learning.

As a nation it was decided that manual, technical work was not for us. We binned the brilliant technical training that underpinned industry until the 1970s, closed the institutes of science and technology and the colleges of advanced technology, turned the polytechnics into universities. Our tertiary educational system was getting us ready for 'knowledge work', focusing on churning out undergraduates in ever greater volume.

I have a brilliantly successful and very highly paid ex whose head hurt if she looked at numbers. For many people maths and science are boring and incomprehensible (I really liked both), and for others the maths of carpentry and joinery is a much more engaging proposition. The idea that all young people should study theoretical mathematics until the age of eighteen, as our prime minister recently suggested, feels like a waste of a lot of people's time. For a decent chunk of young people an education that focuses purely on academic subjects is an education which serves them badly. We are desperately short of people in all of the manual trades in this country, yet each year tens of thousands of promising young people leave school having failed to find the thing that, if not quite igniting a passion, at least arouses an interest in a skilled job that might fulfil them throughout their life.

By law children in England must stay in school or college until they're 18, but evidence suggest most gain very little during the extra school years. Almost one in five children (18 per cent) now leaves school as a 'low achiever', without the governments benchmark of five good GCSEs, and this number is rising fast. We have a huge mental health crisis amongst young people. In the US 40 per cent of children have seen a therapist. Unsurprisingly, the young people suffering from the greatest levels of reported mental health issues are those who leave school with minimal qualifications. People need to leave school feeling they have a place in the world. The technical colleges set up by former education secretary Kenneth Baker in 2010 teach hands-on practical skills with impressive results. Only 4 per cent of graduates fail to find employment or further training a year after they leave.

Education is an investment in the future, both near and far. We have to accept that to get things started we'll need to pay more tax. We should be happy to pay more tax. Let's all pay more tax. We've tried avoiding paying higher taxes and it has destroyed our economy. A good educational standard would, in the medium and long term, earn us all a fortune and save us all a fortune.

... and Education Beyond School

As much as I'd love to see us cram as much making and doing into the national curriculum as possible, there is only so much school can offer. How then do we really unlock all that potential, engage every valuable young human and ready them for the world of work? And how do they gain the life skills, and the knowledge of quality, they will need to live happily? I'm far from the first to suggest it, but there is a case for some form of mandatory national community service with an emphasis on practical learning and civic service. It could comprise the best bits of three types of programme: national service, volunteering and practical learning.

From military service we could extract the bits where participants discover the wellbeing that comes from physical and mental hard work, developing self-reliance, self-discipline and respect for others, the basic medical training needed to maybe save a life in the street. Learning to cook, and learning how and when to eat, to wean ourselves off the bad habits many have developed. And learning to appreciate and care for our everyday possessions – the basics of washing up, ironing, boot polishing and bed making. How to patch and darn. The armed forces basic training tends to create disciplined, practical, healthy, mentally agile young people, something schools seem often not to do, and it's worth noting that four of the happiest European countries have mandatory national service.

Take elements from voluntary work programmes like that of the National Parks, the RSPB or NHS youth volunteering, or overseas schemes like VSO or Raleigh, the volunteering bits of the Duke of Edinburgh Award scheme, where we'd learn the benefit to our emotional wellbeing of giving and caring for others and for the natural environment.

And the best of the practical learning programmes: the much-maligned Skillcentres and YTS, or proper apprenticeship schemes, programmes like the King's Foundation which teaches many traditional heritage building and making crafts, like sewing, weaving and dyeing, stonemasonry, carpentry and joinery, bricklaying, blacksmithing, plastering, thatching, roofing and tiling, painting and decorating. Many of these are on the endangered Red List of the Heritage Crafts Association, and all are offered free via scholarships and with a monthly bursary to cover living costs. Or the 2006 National Skills Academy programme, supported by some of the biggest names in British manufacturing including Rolls Royce, Caterpillar, Ford, BAE Systems,

Airbus and Nissan, intended to create a new generation of much-needed highly trained, highly motivated manufacturing workers.

Maybe after GCSEs everyone might take a year off to attend. And if A levels or university are not immediately in your plans maybe you can stay for two, to concentrate in the second year on preparation for a practical career focused on the industries that exist in your region, one that allows you to stay where you were raised, connecting you with the history of your town and with your ancestors. Maybe for every year of voluntary community service you do you could get a free year of university?

I wasted the academic opportunities of my last year of school. I had been at good schools all my life, I'd had discipline and structure and lots of support, yet I was demotivated and had no thoughts of furthering my education. My year doing practical work in a big brewery in the post-industrial northern town of Hartlepool straightened me out, remotivated me and improved me a bit as a human. I went to every lecture and lab as an undergrad at Leeds and narrowly missed out on a first. After university I spent two more years working and travelling in the US. I took on a mix of cushy and tough jobs, I did physically hard outdoor work, I grew up enormously. Undergraduate education would have been wasted on me as an eighteen-year-old and I would arguably have been even better placed to gain the most from it had I gone after a couple more years away. Certainly, when I went back to university again as a thirty-year-old postgrad I was an absolute sponge for learning and thinking.

What might we learn during our voluntary community service? Let's keep it solidly practical. Car mechanics and maintenance – basic stuff, changing wheels, checking and changing the oil; changing tyres and adjusting brakes on bicycles. Some practical skills that will serve you well enough to prevent you being ripped off by the garage, and enough to excite the imagination of someone who might want to do this as a career. A bit of metalwork: welding, soldering, casting – learn to discern good from bad, learn how good is made and cheap is made and how to spot the difference; learn how to make a spoon. Woodwork: make a chair or a bookcase, use lathes, drills, chisels and planes. Learn electrics and plumbing, enough to avoid calling in an expert every time a simple thing goes wrong in our homes.

On Savile Row we used to run a pre-apprenticeship scheme with a college in East London. Students spent three years learning to make waistcoats, trousers and jackets to a fairly modest level. After the first year they would come and work in the workshops on Savile Row a day a week, where they would see first hand the reality of the job, the discipline required, the style of learning (do as you are told). We would get to know them, see who had the most natural aptitude or the best work ethic, who was the most fun to be around. Placements often lead to permanent positions in full apprenticeship schemes. For us it was invaluable. First, we knew that anyone we took on through the scheme would really know what the job was all about and had had ample chance to change their mind. Then the training would shorten the time it took for us to train them by at least a year, in some cases more. The students themselves were a little older and a little wiser, and they really knew what the job entailed, enabling them to make good decisions.

As I observed earlier, many young people grow up only ever wearing cheap polyester clothing and plastic trainers. We need to know what good clothes feel like, and we need to know what the materials they are made from mean: cotton, wool, linen, polyester, nylon, elastane, acrylic, polyurethane, viscose (both bamboo and wood). I remember Joe Lycett, who is very smart, asking me during the filming of the second of his seasons on *Sewing Bee*, 'What is polyester?' No one at any point in his life had ever explained it to him. If we don't know what our clothes are made of, we can't make good choices.

School is failing huge numbers of young people, leaving them adrift and helpless in a world of knowledge work that simply does not suit their talents. We all have the ability to learn to make, we are already desperately short of making trades, and for our future economic sustainability we need to rebuild, not let go of the manufacturing industry we have. We desperately need something to unlock the potential of young people, and more importantly to show them how rewarding making and living with quality can be. *Back in Time for School* was a brilliant show on the BBC in which Sara Cox took a bunch of young people from the West Midlands and sent them back to school through the ages, starting in Victorian times. In one episode the girls had to learn embroidery. They complained bitterly about the idea, but after an hour of quiet needlework a Zen calm had descended. It was astonishing, pure mindfulness in action.

The King's Foundation

Growing up in the 1970s I recall Prince Charles being considered something of a hippy for his love of organic farming, his support for old crafts and his warning about the dangers of plastics. Today King Charles gets invited to speak at COP and is one of the most knowledgeable and forthright champions of the environment. He is the patron of the Heritage Craft Association, and a vocal champion for the education of young people from all backgrounds in the traditional making arts.

Back in 2013 he had begun expressing concern about the decline in sewing and textile skills in the UK and as work progressed on renovating Dumfries House in Ayrshire, newly acquired by the Dumfries House trust, the team at what is now the King's Foundation did not know what to do with the large attics in the house. Kenneth Dunsmuir, then administrative director, was a fan of *Sewing Bee* and thought about putting a textiles school in the attic, using it to offer sewing and textiles classes to young people from the southwest of Scotland, a region with a proud textile heritage. I have for the past seven years been delighted to give some small assistance in helping shape the direction of this brilliant initiative.

What is now Future Textiles has run workshops, schools competitions, industry placements and conferences attended by over six thousand twelve- to eighteen-year-olds from some of the most deprived communities in Scotland. There is an adult education programme, a local knitting group and, more recently, initiatives such as a natural dye garden inspired by Homegrown/Homespun. Dumfries House and the King's Foundation is now the biggest private employer in that part of Scotland. It offers training programmes covering sewing and textiles, heritage building crafts, stonemasonry, food, and regenerative farming, filling in the huge gaps that now exist in the school curriculum, and providing an enormous boost to the local economy.

Hometown

It was reported in 2023 that 83 per cent of young people think that they will need to leave their hometown to have a good career. It often amazes me that so few people are aware of the things made where they live, and the history and importance of those things to their town. Some of these businesses have made brilliant contributions, some have changed the world. Yet I talk to people from Bolton who don't know that the running shoe, one of the most ubiquitous objects on the planet, was invented there by a firm called Foster & Sons, a business which later became Reebok. Whilst Reebok has gone, Foster's legacy lives on in the running shoe factory built by Norman Walsh, their most famous employee, the man who made the shoes that Roger Bannister wore when he ran the first sub four-minute mile. Cookson & Clegg, my factory, has been in Blackburn since 1860, and I haven't stopped talking about it for the past decade. Yet I still regularly meet people who love clothes and well-made things, but have no idea that this is going on right under their nose. We need to get to know the things that are made in our home town, city or region. All schools should teach younger children what's being done in their backyard. There should be practical days when people from industry visit schools and show the pupils what they do. We had our first class of fourteen- and fifteen-year-olds come to Cookson & Clegg recently for a day in the factory. We hope in a few years' time we might see one or two of them again. Not only do local firms form an important part of a town's cultural heritage, they could provide that great career without having to leave friends and family behind. Maybe we need a yourhometown.com to show us all the things made where we live. If you want to make your town better, support the people who support it by keeping great jobs alive.

Efficiency

One of the very great issues faced by UK manufacturers is scale, and consistency of work. In purely economic terms we are making very poor use of our assets, the factory buildings and the machinery we own. It is a sad irony that we do not buy British-made goods because they are too expensive, since if we bought more British-made goods they could be made a lot more affordably. This is a pattern we are trying to break with Community Clothing.

If UK factories had a lot more work, they would work much more efficiently, in two significant ways:

1. Work efficiency.
Everyone who works in my factory is highly skilled. But the difference between an efficient week and an inefficient week is substantial. Our staff work most effectively when they work in a

smooth uninterrupted flow, when there is always work on hand to do, and always the right work: the work for which their skills and their machinery is optimised. In our terms, that might mean a line of staff who make just moleskins, cords and denim jeans, much the same operations, on the same machines, and a similar weight of fabric, where every run of work lasts at least a *month*, so that their speed of handling, their one-ness with their tools, their ability to pick up, manoeuvre (from the Latin for hand and work), align, adjust, sew, stop, lift, manoeuvre becomes innate, an effortless ballet of mind and hand. You can hear the hum, the focus and concentration, at the end of the day you sense the satisfaction. Instead in some *weeks* a line might switch from jeans, to shirts, to hoodies, to shorts, never having time to develop their flow. In the most efficient weeks they might be doing productive work for 70 per cent of the time they are on the clock. In the least efficient, when they are stopping and starting, the figure might be as low as 20 per cent.

2. Overhead efficiency.
My factory is a 14,000-square-foot, modern, bright building on an industrial park in Blackburn. Whatever I do in it I pay the same rent (to a very nice local man), the same business rates (to the very supportive Blackburn Council) and the same costs (maintenance excluded) on the machinery inside it. In addition we employ a couple of people to manage the whole operation – to organise production, to find the work – who are paid roughly the same whether we make a lot or a little. These overhead costs of running my business are the same whether I employ fifty people in a single shift four days a week making small runs – say 50,000 items a year – or two hundred people over three shifts, five days a week, on large runs making 400,000 items a year. In

the former setup my overhead per item might be £10; in the latter it would be just 65p.

This huge disparity accounts for a not insubstantial amount of the difference between many UK manufacturers and most of those in Asia. If UK factories had the same volume and consistency of work as those in Asia, they could be more than twice as efficient as they are today. And there are easy ways to provide such volumes, such as the government uniform contracts that my own factory had until 2009.

Future Jobs vs Today Jobs

In the foreseeable future we will not stop wearing clothes, nor will we stop sleeping in beds, drinking from mugs, sitting on chairs or eating with knives, forks and spoons. Indeed, little bar the quality of these things has changed in the best part of a century. And if we want the very best quality in all such things, as we should do, then we will continue to need skilled human beings to make them. Manufacturing jobs, despite what many politicians might say, are jobs both for the present and the long-term future.

Politicians like to divide manufacturing jobs between advanced and non-advanced, a distinction which is infuriatingly dumb. No good manufacturing business is not advanced. Although my own factory makes simple clothes, we use state-of-the-art digital management technology to track operations. We have many highly advanced machines including one laser-guided robot, and we practise Six Sigma quality management, a standard that many of the best car companies use. If we were not advanced we would not be in business.

Harrison Spinks makes mattresses in Leeds; they made them for the Queen. Despite the high level of human skill involved they're also one of the most advanced manufacturers I know. They don't just make beds, they employ engineers to make the machines that help make the beds. The idea that as a nation we should only be interested in making what politicians imagine are leading-edge products neglects huge viable chunks of our economy which are making the simple things that we know how to make, and for which there is a large market, here, today – industries which at worst would have decades of viability.

As the technology in our everyday lives becomes more complex, our understanding of the things about us becomes increasingly tenuous. Doorbells, washing machines, bicycles have become smart objects, existing in a realm a million miles away from their mechanical beginnings. There's an ever-increasing danger that we won't understand anything in our lives, leaving us feeling helpless, stupid and adrift. There is a large and growing trend for people, many with advanced tertiary education, to return to simpler, what might be seen as old-fashioned ways of making a living. People are taking up trades that in the 1990s we decided were no longer good enough for us – joinery, painting and decorating, baking, thatching – because they offer us a more direct sense of fulfilment, the ability to look back upon a day's work with great satisfaction, to see the tangible result of our labour and allow us to feel straightforwardly useful.

The UN has seventeen Sustainable Development goals, and in at number eight is 'Decent Work and Economic Growth' – specifically, inclusive and sustainable economic activity offering 'full and productive employment and decent work for all'. I'm not convinced by the growth bit; I think a stable global economy, with better distribution of the benefits, would work just fine. But decent work for everyone should be a fundamental goal of all nations.

CONCLUSION

W e buy an incredible amount of rubbish. We'll buy more this year than last year, and next year we'll buy even more still. We've more of everything than we know what to do with, yet we've never felt so dissatisfied with what we have. Partly this is because the quality of these things has never been worse. Millions of people today have never known the enjoyment that comes from wearing or using or living with great-quality things, watching them improve with age and develop a character that tells of their use. And by buying cheap, low quality things, millions of people are being denied the chance of fulfilling, rewarding work.

We are befouling nature. Our wild places are littered with our waste, many of our beaches are more plastic than sand or pebble, and the mountains of discarded synthetic clothing we're building, slimy plastic monuments to our greed, are now so big they're visible from space. We're poisoning our precious soil, seas and rivers with the cocktail of chemicals used to produce our clothes and all of the other things we buy with so little thought. We're blighting the air we breathe, while the oil-driven fast fashion industry's emissions contribute significantly to the changing of our climate, the effects of which are fast becoming catastrophic. We need to stop.

Switching from a low-value, low-quality, high-consumption economy to a high-value, high-quality, low-consumption economy would positively transform our society and the environment. Living with less but better would make us healthier, wealthier (comparatively) and happier.

We simply need to stop buying so much stuff. Buying a lot less would improve our enjoyment of everyday life, increase our mental and physical wellbeing and reduce our ever-growing anxiety by allowing us to refocus our time on the simple pleasures in life, the things that actually make us feel better. There is no downside to us buying less but better, unless you own Amazon or Shein. Our current globalised, high-volume, low-value economy is a taking economy, but a local, low-volume, high-quality economy could be a giving economy.

Do anything but buy more of this garbage. Delete the shopping apps, go outside, meet a friend for a walk, plant some veg or a nice tree, go to a gig, eat a sandwich up a hill and just look at nature. Spend time with your family, give them the gift of your company instead of buying them more mostly meaningless things they don't need. Go to your shed, put the radio on and make a bird table from an old flat-pack chair that broke after five minutes of sitting on it. Stick it in your garden or on a windowsill and enjoy wildlife returning to your home. Simple pleasures cost nothing.

By buying locally made, high-quality things we would create loads of highly skilled, highly fulfilling jobs right across the UK, reversing a half-century cycle of economic decline, taking the 'post' out of 'post-industrial'. We'd significantly reduce the pollution we cause and the waste we create – in fashion and clothing it could easily be a 90 per cent reduction or more. We could reduce both wealth and income inequality, and begin to heal the fractures in society, rebuilding more cohesive, fairer, more collaborative communities.

Take stock of what you wear and what you own. Imagine you're moving to Leeds for two months: genuinely, what do you take? Which things do you really love, what would you save from a burning building, which are the objects in your life that make you happy every time you use them, or see them? Remember William Morris. Not useful, not beautiful, not meaningful, then not needed. Be ruthless. Then take what you don't need, or no longer like, to a charity shop if you can afford to. Let it do some good for others; let it have a new life where it is needed. One man's trash is, after all, another man's treasure. Or stick it on eBay or Vinted and earn a few quid. We don't have to go the full sixteenth century on this, but maybe go 1950s, when the relationship between quality and value and the number of things we had seemed like it was in some sort of equilibrium. And then only repair or replace, don't add.

And when it does come time to replace, choose quality. Think about what the things we own are made from, where this material comes from, what it does to the planet, to other humans and wildlife, when it's made, and what happens to it when its useful life is over. Buy things made from great natural, renewable – ideally biodegradable or recyclable – materials: wool, linen, wood, metal, stone, ceramic, glass. Choose local craftsmanship over remote mass production, choose the two-hundred-year chair and the thousand-wear jumper. And choose to spend your money where it does good for your community, where it supports taxes that pay for the public services we would like to see flourish. Choose to spend your money so it does good for you too.

Teach every school pupil how to make. Unlock the inventive, creative and mechanical parts of their brains that book learning doesn't touch. Give every person the tools to fix and repair, and to discern quality from rubbish. Value makers, and doers, builders and menders. Let's end this idea of 'knowledge' work. There is knowledge in abundance in well-executed manual work. And what they mean by knowledge work is not for all; let's support the creation of millions of jobs that have meaning, that enrich and enhance people's lives, that improve their mental and physical health, that make them feel useful, and proud, and happy. Physical work makes us happy, craft work fulfils a basic human need to show our skill and to be useful to our society.

Until not so long ago we cared a great deal about every single thing we owned. Every purchase was made with great thought, every object's usefulness to us carefully calculated. As a young man I'd go back week after week to the same clothes shop, trying on some garment over and over as I tried to decide if I liked it enough, whether it would form a useful long-term part of my wardrobe. Now, with clothes costing less than cups of coffee, no one takes this care. We need to rediscover how to care about the things we buy. We need to go back to being thoughtful instead of thoughtless.

Having less but better would be a path to a healthier, more equal society, a source of hope for a better future for the many people of all ages living in what we call our post-industrial communities. Living with fewer, better things is an act of goodness and kindness to people and the planet, and it would make us all happier.

APPENDIX 1

The following is a list of British artisan makers. I use the term in its original sense, as people or businesses who manufacture *and* sell a product directly to the public. All of these businesses make their products in their own factory or workshop in the UK. This list covers manufacturers of those products discussed in this book, grouped broadly by material.

Those marked with a single asterisk (*) sell some products under their name which are made in other factories, either in the UK or overseas. Those marked with two asterisks (**) make only one or a limited number of the products they sell in their own workshop or factory.

I know many of these businesses personally. I have used their products, or visited their workshops or factories, or both. Others are known by people I trust to give an honest account of their facilities and products. I have done my best to make this list as comprehensive as possible and my thanks go to several people who have reminded me of a good number of firms I might otherwise have forgotten. My apologies to those who I have missed off: if you think you should have been included, please let me know so I that I might include you in any future list.

Clay and Glass

1812, Stoke-on-Trent, tableware

Anta, Fearn, tableware

Bentham Pottery, Bentham, tableware

Brickett Davda, Brighton, tableware

Caverswall, Stoke-on-Trent, tableware

Craven Dunnill Jackfield, Ironbridge, tiles

Curiousa, Wirksworth, lighting

Dartington, Torrington, glasswear

Decorum Tiles, Wadebridge, tiles

Duchess China, Stoke-on-Trent, tableware

Elizabeth Renton, London, tableware

Emma Bridgewater, Stoke-on-Trent, tableware

Emma Lacey, London, tableware

Froyle Tiles, Hambledon, tiles

Gillies Jones, Pickering, glassware

Halcion Days, Stoke-on-Trent, tableware

Henry Holland, London, tableware

Ingot Objects, Glasgow, tableware

James and Tilla Waters, Llanwrda, tableware

Joshua Williams, Galloway, tableware

Josie Walter, Bolehill, tableware

Karen Downing, Norfolk, tableware

Leach Pottery, St Ives, tableware

Lefroy Brooks, Hoddesdon, bathroom ware

Linda Bloomfield, London, tableware

Lindean Mill Glass, Lindean, glassware

Louisa Raven, Harborough, glasswear

Michael Ruh, London, glasswear

Nick Membery, Llandeilo, tableware

Patia Davis, Ross-on-Wye, tableware

Portmeirion, Stoke-on-Trent, tableware

Royal Brierley, Torrington, glasswear

Royal Doulton*, Barlaston, tableware

Samantha Sweet Glass, London, glassware

Sasha Wardell, Trowbridge, tableware

Silvia K Ceramics, Brighton, tableware

Sue Paraskeva, Ryde, tableware

Sue Pryke, North Kilworth, tableware

Tin Shed, Mull, tableware

TKJ Ceramics, Stroud, tableware

Tricia Thom Ceramics, Edinburgh

Wedgwood*, Barlaston, tableware

Whitebirk Sinks, Blackburn, sinks

Winchcombe Pottery, Cheltenham, tableware

Wychwood Pottery, Whichford, planters

Clothing

Anderson Knitwear, Shetland, knitwear

Barbour**, South Shields, rainwear

Begg, Ayr, scarves

Blackhorse Lane Atelier, London, jeans

Bridgedale, Newtownards, socks

Burberry**, Castleford, Rainwear

Community Clothing**, Blackburn, clothing

Corgi, Ammanford, socks

David Nieper, Alfreton, clothing

Dawson Denim, Hove, jeans

Deema Abi-Chahine, London, shirts

Drakes**, London, clothing

Ellipsis, Glasgow, clothing

Emma Willis, Gloucester, shirts

English Fine Cottons, Dukinfield, clothing

Eribe, Galashiels, knitwear

EROSA, Holywell, clothing

Graeme Bone, Auchinleck, clothing

Harley, Peterhead, knitwear

Herbert Johnson, Cambridge, hats

Hiut, Cardigan, jeans

House of Cheviot, Hawick, socks

Isabelle Pennington Edmead, Warrington, clothing

J Alex Swift, Hathern, socks

Jamieson, Shetland, knitwear

John Smedley, Lea Bridge, knitwear

Johnstons of Elgin, Hawick, knitwear

Joshua Ellis, Pudsey, knitwear

Kashket, London, military uniform

Kinloch Anderson, Edinburgh, highlandware

Laird, Colliers End, hats
Lochcarron, Selkirk,
  highlandware
Lock, London, hats
Mackintosh*, Nelson, raincoats
Margaret Howell**, London,
  shirts
Mars, Leicester, knitwear
McNair, Slaithwaite, shirts
Mountain Method, Millom,
  rainwear
Old Town, Holt, clothing
Paul James, Leicester, knitwear
Peregrine*, Manchester, clothing
PHD, Stalybridge, down
  clothing
Private White, Salford, rainwear
Robert Mackie, Stewarton,
  knitwear
Stewart Parvin, London,
  clothing
Sunspel**, Long Eaton,
  underwear
Superlove Merino, Stavely,
  clothing
The Kiltmakery, East Lothian,
  kilts
Turnbull & Asser, Chard, shirts
Wendy Keith, Probus, socks
William Lockie, Hawick,
  knitwear

Wm Blackhall, Tarland, kilts
Yarmouth Oilskins, Great
  Yarmouth, clothing

Leather

Armitage Leather, Yoxall,
  accessories
Barker, Earls Barton, shoes
Bonner, Cirencester, accessories
Cambridge Satchel, Cambridge,
  bags
Carradice, Nelson, cycle bags
Carv, Bideford, bags
Cheaney, Desborough, shoes
Church's, Northampton, shoes*
Cornelia James, Lewes, gloves
Crocket & Jones, Northampton,
  shoes
Dents, Warminster, gloves
Edward Green, Northampton,
  shoes
Ettinger, Walsall, accessories
Glencroft, Clapham (Yorkshire),
  sheepskin
Iseabal Hendry, Strathcarron,
  bags
John Lobb (St James), London,
  shoes
John Lobb, Northampton, shoes
Lamont, Braemar, sporrans
Launer, Warlingham, bags

Loake*, Kettering, shoes

McRostie, Glasgow, belts

Mowbray, Melton Mowbray, accessories

Mulberry**, Shepton Mallet, bags

Nursey of Bungay, Bungay, sheepskin

P Kirkwood, Brighton, bags

Skye Skyns, Isle of Skye, sheepskin

Swaine, Sawston, leather

Trickers, Northampton, shoes

Tusting, Olney, bags

Walsh, Bolton, trainers

Metal

A. M. Experimental, Willenhall, locksmith

Aga, Telford, cookers

Alex Pole, Broadoak, blacksmith

Arthur Price, Sheffield, cutlery

Barber Wilsons, London, taps

Chalk Pit Forge, Amberley, blacksmith

Clement Knives, Newton Stewart, knives

David Harland, Porthyrhyd, blacksmith

David Mellor, Hathersage, cutlery

Dualit, London, toasters

Ella McIntosh, Manchester, pewtersmith

Ernest Wright, Sheffield, scissors

Esse, Barnoldswick, stoves

Falcon/Rangemaster, Leamington Spa, cookers

Hallis Hudson, Preston, curtain track

Longdog Smithy, Eastlands, blacksmith

Melissa Cole, Pewsey, blacksmith

Michael May, Sheffield, knives

Netherton Foundry, Highley, cookware

Owen Bush, Welling, knives

Rayburn, Telford, cookers

Robin Wood, Sheffield, axes

Samuel Groves, Birmingham, cookware

Sherwood Tinning, Little Wymondly, tinning

Skye Knives, Skye, knives

Steve Rook, Balfron, blacksmith

The Leaf Man Forge, Chelmsford, blacksmith

The Silver Duck, Bristol, cutlery

Twisted Horseshoe, Wetherden, knives

Willslock Forge, Rugeley, knives

Wrought Iron and Brass Bed Company, Swaffham, beds

Other Textile Products
Aiguille, Kendal, rucksacks
Anaglypta, Gainsborough, wallpaper
Anstey, Loughborough, wallpaper
Armadillo Sun, Hawkhurst, beanbags
Atom Packs, Keswick, rucksacks
Axminster Carpets, Axminster, carpet
Beds Direct, Batley, beds
Brigg, Sawston, umbrella
Brintons*, Kidderminster, carpet
Brockway, Kidderminster, carpet
Bronte, Guiseley, blankets
Chapman, Carlisle, bags
Dusal, Glenrothes, bedding
Fermoie, Marlborough, homewares
Forbo, Kirkaldy, linoleum
Fox Umbrellas, Croydon, umbrellas
Glencraft, Aberdeen, mattresses
Globetrotter, Hoddesdon, luggage
Graham & Brown, Blackburn, wallpaper
Harrison Spinks, Leeds, mattresses
Heirlooms, Bognor Regis, bed linens
Hypnos, Princes Risborough, beds
James Cropper, Burneside, paper
James Ince, London, umbrellas
James Smith, London, umbrellas
John Atkinson, Pudsey, blankets
Lancashire Textiles, Burnley, bedding
Lockwood, London, umbrella
Luna Textiles, Hebden Bridge, bedding
Melin Tregwynt, Castlemorris, blankets
Natural Bed Company, Sheffield, beds
Paper Foundation, Burneside, paper
Peter Reed, Nelson, bedding
Putnams, Plympton, pillows
R U Comfy, Great Harwood, beanbags
Sanderson, Loughborough, wallpaper
Silentnight, Barnoldswick, beds
Sleepeezee, Rochester, beds
Summiteer, Kendal, rucksacks
Trefriw Woollen Mills, Trefriw, blankets
Ulster Carpets, Portadown, carpet

Zoffany, Loughborough,
    wallpaper

Remake/Repair/Exchange/ Share

Ahluwalia*, London, clothing
Ancuta Sarca, London, shoes
ApparelXchange, Glasgow,
    clothing
Benjamin Benmoyal, London,
    clothing
Bethany Williams, London,
    clothing
Bidiboon, Lewes, clothing
Cloth Surgeon, London, clothing
Connor Ives, London, clothing
Cric-kit, Leeds, clothing
Dirtbags, Kendal, bags
ELV Denim, London, clothing
Elvis & Kresse, Painters Forstal,
    bags
Jawara Alleyne, London, clothing
KitUp, London, outdoor gear
Leeds Community Clothing
    Exchange, Leeds, clothing
Little Re-Creations, Biggleswade,
    bags
Mallin & Sons, Wakefield,
    reproofers
Pair Ups, Seaford, running shoes
Paolina, Russo, London, clothing

Pre Loved Sports, Malton,
    sportswear
Rebel Patch, Bristol, repair
Repair Café at DoES, Liverpool,
    repair
Re-Run, Bristol, clothing
ReStrap, Leeds, cycle bags
ReTribe, Sheffield, clothing
Retrouvious, London, reclaimed
    material
Reworn, Swindon, remaker
Salisbury Clothes Swap,
    Salisbury, clothing
Sheffield Clothing Repair,
    Sheffield, clothing
Snowdonia Gear Repair, Y
    Felinheli, outdoor gear
Tentshare, Royston, outdoor gear
The Little Loop, Andover,
    clothing
Trakke, Glasgow, bags
Utilifolk, London, clothing

Tailoring

Anderson & Sheppard**,
    London, tailoring
Andrew Musson, Lincoln,
    tailoring
Antich, Huddersfield, tailoring
Campbells of Beauly*, Beauly,
    tailored clothing

Carl Stuart, Ossett, tailoring

Chittleborough & Morgan, London, tailoring

Chittleborough & Morgan, London, tailoring

Chris Kerr, London, tailoring

Classic Cuts, London, tailoring

Craig Fetherstone, London, tailoring

Davies & Sons, London, tailoring

Dege & Skinner*, London, tailoring

Desmond Merrion, Castleford, tailoring

Emma Cope, Birmingham, tailoring

Frank Hall, Market Harborough, tailoring

G. A. Shepherd, Hope Valley, tailoring

G. Livingston, Castle Douglas, tailoring

G.Livingston, Castle Douglas, tailored clothing

Gieves & Hawkes**, London, tailoring

Henry Poole*, London, tailoring

Huntsman**, London, tailoring

Joe Hoslgrove, London, tailoring

Kathryn Sargent, London, tailoring

Kent Haste & Lachter, London, tailoring

Lawrence Robinson, Alcester, tailoring

Lee Marsh, London, tailoring

Macangus & Wainwright, London, tailoring

Meyer & Mortimer*, London, tailoring

Montague Ede, London, tailoring

Nicholas Simon, Northampton, tailoring

Norton & Sons*, London, tailoring

Redwood & Feller, London, tailoring

Richard Anderson*, London, tailoring

Ritchie Charlton, London, tailoring

Samuel Brothers*, Aldershot, tailoring

Solomon Browne, Margate, tailoring

Souster & Hicks, Woburn, tailoring

Steed, London, tailoring

Stewart Christie, Edinburgh, tailoring

Taillour, London, tailoring

Territo, Bristol, tailoring

Wood

A little furniture Shop,
Shrewsbury, furniture

A. Nash, Tadley, Brooms

Alexander White Workshop,
London, furniture

All About Willow, Isle of Eigg,
baskets

Ambrose Vevers, Ashburton,
furniture

Bibbings & Hensby,
London, furniture

Bobby Mills, Braunton, furniture

Cameron Fuller, Honiton,
curtain poles

Chris Eckersley, Birmingham,
furniture

Colin Norgate, Petersfield,
furniture

Dalesbridge, Settle, furniture

Eastburn, Eastburn, furniture

Ercol, Princes Risborough,
furniture

Galvin Brothers, Beverley,
furniture

Gareth Neal, London, furniture

Hilary Burns, Devon, baskets

Hunter & Hyland, Leatherhead,
curtain poles

James Trundle & Isobel Napier,
London

Jones, Nottingham, curtain
poles

Laurence Veitch, Glasgow,
furniture

Linley, London, furniture

Luke Hope, London, tableware

Mountain Oak Woodcraft,
Witherslack, timber structures

Odd Chair Company, Preston,
furniture

Paparwark, Shetland, furniture

Par Avion, Norwich, furniture

Parker & Farr, Nottingham,
furniture

Petrel Furniture, Pulborough,
furniture

Robin Clarke, Leominster,
chairs

Sebastian Cox, London,
furniture

Sheahan Made, Edinburgh,
furniture

Slow Sofa, Settle, furniture

Stout Duck, Skipton, furniture

Studio Amos, Lewes, baskets

Takahashi McGil, Cockington,
tableware

The Orkney Furniture Maker,
Orkney, furniture

White Castle Furniture,
Abergavenny, furniture

APPENDIX 2

The Economics Of A New High Value, Low Consumption Local Manufacturing System

In November 2021 I gave a lecture at the Royal Geographical Society. In the lecture I outlined a radically different, locally focused UK textiles and clothing economy based upon a philosophy of 'buy less, buy better, make local'.

The central pillars of this reshaped economy were:

- Redistribution of value from brands to manufacturers and makers
- A shift from consuming high volumes of low quality new clothing to low volumes of high quality new clothing, and increased volumes of second-hand clothing
- The creation of sustainable, long-term jobs in making, remaking, repairing and recycling clothing and textiles.

Redistribution of Value

Those who make and grow receive the greater share of the value, and those who simply do the selling and marketing receive less. This is the case with most of the artisan businesses listed in Appendix 1. At Community Clothing, 65p of every pound you spend with us goes to the makers and growers.

Economic Redistribution

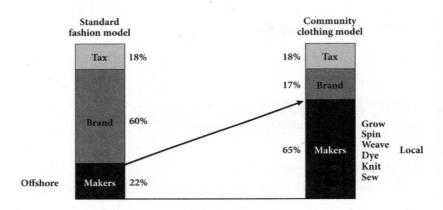

High Value, Low Volume

Buy less than 25 per cent of the new clothes currently bought and supplement with the same number of second hand. Shift high volumes of low quality new clothing, made with mostly oil-based synthetic fabrics, to a fashion and clothing system designed to be sustainable at low volumes, selling high quality new clothing and increased volumes of second hand clothing.

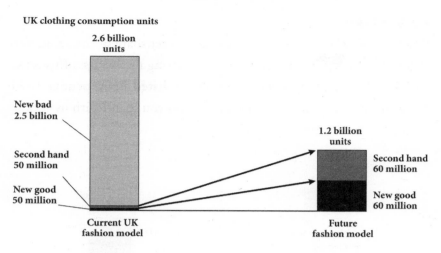

UK clothing consumption units

2.6 billion units

New bad 2.5 billion

Second hand 50 million

New good 50 million

Current UK fashion model

1.2 billion units

Second hand 60 million

New good 60 million

Future fashion model

Spend roughly the same amount of money on fewer, better new clothes and an increased volume of higher quality second hand clothes, too.

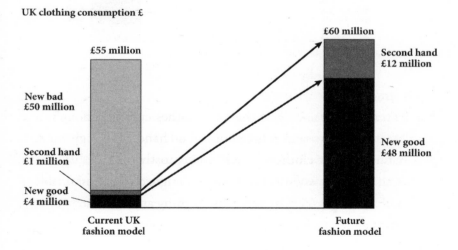

UK clothing consumption £

£55 million

New bad £50 million

Second hand £1 million

New good £4 million

Current UK fashion model

£60 million

Second hand £12 million

New good £48 million

Future fashion model

Local Making

Replace jobs selling low quality new clothes with more rewarding jobs selling higher quality locally made clothes and curating and selling second hand clothing. Increase jobs making, remaking, repairing and recycling high quality high value clothing and textiles five-fold.

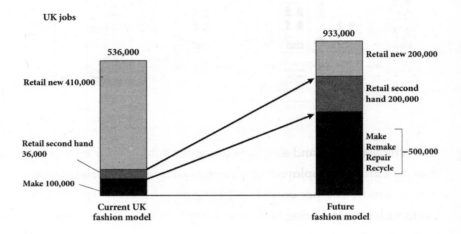

- Grow – fibre growing and processing: natural fibres such as linen, hemp and wool, natural dyestuffs, growing and extraction.
- Extract – fibre and dyestuff processing and extraction.
- Make – yarn spinning and extrusion using new and recycled natural and biosynthetic fibres; dyeing including natural dyeing; textile weaving and knitting; traditional garment and shoe making, as well as new remade garment and shoe production.
- Sell – selling new and second hand, curation of second hand, new and used clothing exchange and loan, repair.
- Recycle – broadly distributed textile and clothing collection and sorting, textile recovery and reuse, fibre recovery and reuse, mechanical and chemical recycling, composting.

Local Textile System

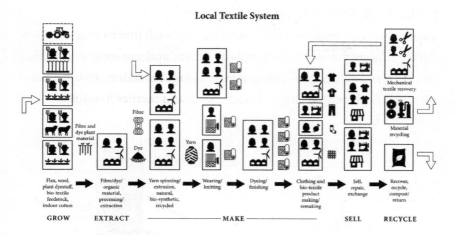

GROW	EXTRACT	MAKE				SELL	RECYCLE
Flax, wool, plant dyestuff, bio-textile feedstock, indoor cotton	Fibre/dye/ organic material, processing/ extraction	Yarn spinning/ extrusion, natural, bio-synthetic, recycled	Weaving/ knitting	Dyeing/ finishing	Clothing and bio-textile product making/ remaking	Sell, repair, exchange	Recover, recycle, compost/ return

This reshaped textile and clothing economy would employ *more* people than are currently employed, increasing UK-based textile and clothing jobs by almost 100 per cent and offering more stimulating rewarding work, with pay rates being higher on average, and economic value more evenly distributed.

Barriers

Buying one good thing will cost consumers less money in the long run than buying five low quality ones. But even if individual consumers can be convinced of this first-time cost of higher priced clothing, the increasing energy, housing and food costs could prove a barrier for people buying that 'one good thing'.

Some of this can be alleviated though an expansion of clothing swaps, loan or buy back schemes and uniform exchanges. And increased employment through the reshoring of manufacturing jobs will raise household incomes.

Once scaled up, high quality new clothing would be around 3–4 times the price of the cheapest, worst quality clothing. For example, a high quality cotton T-shirt might be £15, versus £4 for a low quality poly/cotton t shirt. However its worth noting that the price of cheap clothing is not sustainable long term, with oil prices and wages in developing countries set to continue to rise. It should be expected that the price of second-hand clothing will rise too: scarcity of high quality second hand clothes being the main factor, but also an overall increase in demand.

Residual resistance to wearing second-hand and repaired clothing, especially amongst those in the lowest income brackets (as highlighted by recent work at Glasgow University), will need to be overcome.

Benefits

- Reduce greenhouses gasses.
- Reduce consumption of non-renewable resources.
- Increase UK clothing and textile making jobs.
- Sustain UK clothing retail jobs.
- Reduce clothing waste.
- Increase overall economic value of the sector by almost 10 per cent.
- Future proof the economy against coming exhaust of materials.
- Safeguard jobs for the future.
- Achieve a more equitable distribution of economic value.

LIST OF ILLUSTRATIONS

Less

Sewing a tongue (*courtesy of Jack Bolton*)
Inspection (*courtesy of Tom Bunning*)
Family photo (*courtesy of Jack Bolton*)
Machine plates (*courtesy of Jack Bolton*)
Goods out (*courtesy of Ella Thomson*)
Chalk sharpening and marking out (*courtesy of Chris Floyd*)
Sewing trousers, Savile Row (*courtesy of Chris Floyd*)
Roy knitting (*courtesy of Ella Thomson*)

ACKNOWLEDGEMENTS

I'm so pleased to have had the chance to write this book so I must give the biggest thanks to Jo Thompson who watched my ten minute Ted talk and thought it might be possible to turn it into a half-decent book. To everyone at Williams Collins who read my outline and wrote such wonderful and encouraging things about it, your offer was one of the nicest things I've ever received. And a very big thank you too to Arabella Pike for taking this book on, and for being understanding of the conflicting pressures of running a business and writing this (and another) book. Your no-holds-barred comments in the margins made me laugh a lot and made your many encouragements mean so much more. Thanks to everyone who has worked to make this book as good as it possibly can be, especially Steve, Katy, Sam, Lizzie, Julian, Colin Thomas and the rest of the extended team at William Collins. I am very proud in every way.

Thank you to Ariella Finer for your skill in refining my outline (and your patience) and for working so hard to make this happen. Thanks to Matt Nicholls: when you called me to tell me about Collins' interest in doing the book I was untethering my bike from a lamppost outside a church after a carol concert. If I were religious I might say it was a sign. Thanks, too, to Amber and Tom, and everyone else at United.

I am incredibly fortunate to have had the chance to meet and to work with a huge number of wonderfully generous, smart, dedicated and forward-thinking people over the past 30 years of work, a mix of practitioners (manufacturers, craftspeople and artists), business leaders, academics, politicians and many ordinary people who share a love of doing things well. Collectively you have brought the ideas shared in this book to fruition, so a heartfelt thank you to all of you.

Huge thanks to the just over a thousand people who supported the Community Clothing Kickstarter back in 2016, and to everyone who worked on, and starred in, the campaign. Without you we wouldn't exist. Thanks to the over fifty thousand people who've ordered clothes from us since we launched, and to the over ten thousand people who supported our Welsh pants campaign in 2023 (and massive thanks to Wynne Evans and Kiri Pritchard-McLean for being our stars). Please keep spreading the good word.

Thank you to all of my brilliant team: Alex, Beth, Dani, Holly, Ian, James, Jane, Jayne, Susan, Susana and Tony. To Jenny, I could not have juggled writing two books with a very busy day job without you, thank you for always being the best support, your cheerfulness is a blessing. To my sister Victoria, and Dave, and the wonderful staff at Cooksons. Manufacturing in the UK is tough, you all work so hard, I know there are so many easier ways to make a living, but this is important. A massive thank you. Thanks to all our other amazing manufacturing and other partners and their brilliant staff. You are a pleasure to work with and the clothes and textiles you make are a joy to wear. Thanks to everyone who has worked at CC during our first eight years, especially Alastair, Emma, Frances, Iain, Laura, Lucy, Lucy, Mark, Matt, Milly and Olivia. Thank you to the many individuals and agencies who also help to make it what it is: to Emma, Harriet and Laura at Whitehair,

Acknowledgements

Vanessa Podmore, Will Broome, Chris and Tammy Kane, all at Queen St Mill and Quarry Bank Mill, Stuart Clapp (and the Leigh-on-Sea skate community), Aaron Dunleavy, Jack Bolton, Chris Mason, Chris Floyd, Josh Laurence, Ian Denyer, Daniel Benson and Arthur Comely, Steph Wilson, Josh John, Mat Heinl, Tom Bunning, Ella Thomson, Claire Benson, Mike Maddams, Oli Machin, Ed at Limelite, Tom Mills, Morgan at Teddy's in Cardiff, Nathan at Vue Studio, Tom Wilson, and to Peter, Nick and the team at Show, JK&K, everyone at Milk, Industry, Select, Supa, Nevs and Colours. Thanks to all of our wonderful models and contributors, both amateur and professional, the machinists, weavers dyers and knitters, the rugby players, the crown green bowlers, the amazing stall holders at Darwen Market, the *Sewing Bee* camera crew and the many others who have brought our clothes to life.

Thank you to my long-suffering shareholders, Andrew, Dave and Jo, and Richard and Nikki, for believing in the idea of Community Clothing, and putting their money into a business that puts people and jobs before your financial reward. You will be spiritually rich, if not exactly financially so. Thank you to Jason for seeing our potential, and to Alex, Hilmar, Joan, Oscar, Zoheb, and especially Nial, for keeping the wheels turning. Thank you to Kate, your support has been invaluable. Thanks to eBay who helped fund us in the beginning, and to Unltd who helped fund us a little later on (and for helping us to focus more clearly on our impact). Thanks to everyone from the press, especially the *Guardian*, the *FT*, *The Times* and *Sunday Times*, the *Evening Standard*, *Paperboy* and the BBC, who has helped propel us forward.

Massive thanks to everyone I work with in Blackburn: Phil Riley, Clare Turner, Julia Simpson, Denise Park, Rebecca Johnson, the Hive team, Ed Matthews-Gentle and all at Creative Lancashire, BBC Radio Lancashire and Source Creative. You all work so hard, with such scant resources, and have such optimism, and such a passion to make things better for everyone living in your town. You and the people doing similar jobs in thousands of towns like Blackburn deserve so much better. Thanks to Wayne Hemmingway, Lauren, Alex, Elena and the team at the wonderful Festival of Making. Thanks to Laurie Peak, Jenny Rutter and the team at the British Textile Biennial. Thanks to Jamie Holman and all the art kids. You're all amazing and if every town had a crew like you they'd all be better places. Thanks to Justine Aldersey-Williams, and all the amazing Homegrown/Homespun volunteers. It was a real treat to get to spend the occasional Friday in a field with you all. Thank to Lucy Guard and Sian Ferguson at the JJ Trust for not hesitating to fund this amazing project, to the Society of Dyers & Colourists, and the National Lottery Climate Action Fund for funding us too. Thanks to Keith Brymer-Jones for being part of the Festival of Making, for indulging my massive rant about pans during our talk in Blackburn Cathedral last year, and for sharing your deeply personal reflections on a career in making. Thanks to everyone I work with at the King's Foundation, especially Jax, Ashleigh, Kelly, Laura, Colin, Costa, Gordon, Emily and John my co-chair.

Big thanks to everyone who has worked on *Sewing Bee*, especially Claudia Winkleman, Joe Lycett, Sara Pascoe, Kiell Smith-Bynoe, May Martin and the amazing Esme Young for listening to me bang on and on about this stuff ad infinitum. And for the current crew for putting up with me writing a book (and doing my day job) whilst you are working your socks off to make our wonderful telly show. Especially thanks to Joe, who not only listened but actually did something about it: for campaigning for British wool farmers, calling out 'PooHoo', and for taking on Shell, you are a hero.

Thanks to all the odd places that have made me and my laptop welcome whilst writing this book. Thanks to Northern, Aviva, GWR, LNER, TFL and the operators of all the various trains and station waiting rooms (Settle is the best) and even the odd bench or shelter on a platform. There's something about being on a train that just helps you think clearly. Thanks to the Edward Boyle Library staff (and Chris Carr) for giving me a visiting reader pass, meaning I could write part of this book in the exact desk that I sat at to study for my engineering finals 30 years ago. I'm so happy this beautiful library hasn't changed. Thanks to Fulham Library where I would take myself off to write at weekends in London in their beautiful upstairs reading room. Please, we have to increase funding for libraries.

Thanks to my hillwalking/cycling/wild places buds for making the time I spend outdoors the most fun: James and Ali, my first partners in outdoor crime, Dave, James, and Tom with whom I have covered so many wonderful miles (and a few gruelling ones), Ropey and Matt (and sheep chasing Evie), Rusty, Cara, Dave, Lorna, Isla (and Georgie), Emma, Colin and Jinky (and occasionally Rasper), Geordie, Mairi and all the Mickel/Rahoy clan, and Jimmy and Ta. Thanks to my farming (and cheesemaking) neighbours for being such wonderful custodians of the land and allowing nature to thrive in our corner of North Yorkshire, not everyone gets to see barn owls, curlews, weasels and woodpeckers in their garden, or wake up to a chorus of larks, thrushes and wrens. Plant more trees folks, and stop paving over your gardens.

Thanks and much love to my dear family. To Victoria, Owen, Max and Theo for the tuck-ins, the trompetti pattimaxi and the walks in the woods. To my dear departed granny who taught me to scrape the mould off cheese and jam, and to reuse everything. To my dad who taught me to care for my things, to polish shoes and hang clothes, and who revealed to me the simple joy of hot tomato soup in a stone bothy on a wet day, and of growing veg, which he did with such aplomb. And all my love and thanks to my wonderful mum with whom I have so often shared the simple pleasures of life, a walk up a hill, a sit on a bench on a sunny day, a crossword, a potter in her beautifully tended garden. Thank you for being so kind, for keeping me straight, making me work hard, teaching me the value of everything, and being proud of (most of) the things I do. If I avoid saying 'umm' on the audio version of this book all credit will be yours.

And finally thank you to Rachael who put up with me 'doing book' at almost every waking moment for what seems like forever: the 5am's before work, the midnight stretches, the weekends in the library, the improvised offices in hotel rooms. Thank you for always understanding how important it was to me. Thanks for the flowers in the little vase on my desk, the cups of tea, the snacks, the thousand other small kindnesses, and for your love. I love you. There is no one I would rather share my flask and my *sangwidges* with.